Trade and the environment

CAMBRIDGE STUDIES IN INTERNATIONAL AND COMPARATIVE LAW

This series (established in 1946 by Professors Gutteridge, Hersch Lauterpacht and McNair) is a forum for studies of high quality in the fields of public and private international law and comparative law. Although these are distinct legal sub-disciplines, developments since 1946 confirm their interrelationship. Comparative law is increasingly used as a tool in the making of law at national, regional and international levels. Private international law is increasingly affected by international conventions, and the issues faced by classical conflicts rules are increasingly dealt with by substantive harmonisation of law under international auspices. Mixed international arbitrations, especially those involving state economic activity, raise mixed questions of public and private international law. In many fields (such as the protection of human rights and democratic standards, investment guarantees and international criminal law) international and national systems interact. National constitutional arrangements relating to 'foreign affairs', and to the implementation of international norms, are a focus of attention.

Professor Sir Robert Jennings edited the series from 1981. Following his retirement as General Editor, an editorial board has been created and Cambridge University Press has recommitted itself to the series, affirming its broad scope.

The Board welcomes works of a theoretical or interdisciplinary character, and those focusing on new approaches to international or comparative law or conflicts of law. Studies of particular institutions or problems are equally welcome, as are translations of the best work published in other languages.

General Editors	James Crawford
	Whewell Professor of International Law, University of Cambridge
	David Johnston
	Regius Professor of Civil Law, University of Cambridge
Editorial Board	Professor Hilary Charlesworth *University of Adelaide*
	Mr John Collier *Trinity Hall, Cambridge*
	Professor Lori Damrosch *Columbia University Law School*
	Professor John Dugard *Director, Research Centre for International Law, University of Cambridge*
	Professor Mary-Ann Glendon *Harvard Law School*
	Professor Christopher Greenwood *London School of Economics*
	Professor Hein Kötz *Max-Planck-Institut, Hamburg*
	Dr Vaughan Lowe *Corpus Christi College, Cambridge*
	Professor D. M. McRae *University of Ottawa*
	Professor Onuma Yasuaki *University of Tokyo*
Advisory Committee	Professor D. W. Bowett QC
	Judge Rosalyn Higgins QC
	Professor Sir Robert Jennings QC
	Professor J. A. Jolowicz QC
	Professor Eli Lauterpacht QC
	Professor Kurt Lipstein
	Judge Stephen Schwebel

A list of books in the series can be found at the end of this volume

Trade and the environment

A comparative study of EC and US law

Damien Geradin
University of Liège

CAMBRIDGE
UNIVERSITY PRESS

PUBLISHED BY THE PRESS SYNDICATE OF THE UNIVERSITY OF CAMBRIDGE
The Pitt Building, Trumpington Street, Cambridge CB2 1RP, United Kingdom

CAMBRIDGE UNIVERSITY PRESS
The Edinburgh Building, Cambridge, CB2 2RU, United Kingdom
40 West 20th Street, New York, NY 10011-4211, USA
10 Stamford Road, Oakleigh, Melbourne 3166, Australia

First published 1997

Printed in the United Kingdom at the University Press, Cambridge

Typeset in 9.75/13pt Swift regular [CE]

A catalogue record for this book is available from the British Library

Library of Congress Cataloguing in Publication data

Geradin, Damien.
Trade and the environment: a comparative study of EC and US law /
Damien Geradin.
      p.   cm. – (Cambridge studies in international and comparative law.
New series)
ISBN 0 521 59012 4 (hardbound)
1. Foreign trade regulation – Environmental aspects.
2. Environmental law, International – Economic aspects.
3. Foreign trade regulation – United States.
4. Environmental law – United States.
5. Foreign trade regulation – European Economic Community countries.
6. Environmental law – European Economic Community countries.
I. Title.   II. Series.
K3943.G47   1997
341.7′54 – dc21   96–53037   CIP

ISBN 0 521 59012 4 hardback

Contents

Preface

This book discusses and compares the relationship between trade and environmental-protection policies in the European Community and the United States. The central thesis of this book is that the various tensions that may arise between trade and environmental protection in federal-type systems can generally be solved through two complementary institutional means. First, using the free-trade provisions of the EC Treaty and the United States Constitution, the European Court of Justice and the US Supreme Court can place limits on the ability of states to enact legislation restricting trade ('negative harmonization'). Second, the Community and US federal legislatures can set common environmental standards for all states ('positive harmonization'). In this context, a central objective of this book is to discuss the respective contributions of the judiciary and the legislature to the solution of the tensions arising between trade and environmental policies, as well as to show the interactions existing between such policies. As argued in this book, such interactions shape the balance between trade and environmental objectives in the Community and the United States. More generally, they define the progress of environmental protection in these systems.

The most pleasant duty that falls when writing a preface is to recall the names of those who have acted as an inspiration and helped in the completion of the work. Two persons deserve particular mention. Professor James Crawford supervised my doctoral thesis on which this study is based and I have greatly benefited from his wise advice and suggestions. I also express my gratitude to Professor Paul Demaret who first introduced me to European Community and United States federal law. He encouraged me to write a doctoral thesis and helped me to draft the initial project. He also helped me to gather the funding that was necessary to carry out this project.

Most of my research work was carried out at the Squire law library at Cambridge University. My work was, however, considerably facilitated by two research trips in the United States. The first of these trips, which took place at Columbia University during the summer of 1992, was made possible by Jacques Buhart and Professor Richard Gardner. The first introduced me to the second who, in turn, introduced me to his colleagues in the law school and did everything within his power to maximize my time in New York. The second trip, which took place at the University of California at Berkeley during the spring term of 1993, was considerably facilitated by Raoul Stewardson. Raoul helped me to obtain the status of visiting scholar in the law school and offered me his warm hospitality during my stay at Berkeley. Part of my research was also conducted in the Institute for Advanced Legal Studies of the University of London, the Institute for European Legal Studies of the University of Liège and the library of Coudert Brothers in Brussels. I would like to express my gratitude to the staff of these institutions for their assistance.

This study could not have been undertaken without a Paul-Henri Spaak Fellowship in European Community law from the Belgian National Fund for Scientific Research as well as a generous grant from the Pôles d'Attraction Interuniversitaires, a research programme initiated by the Science Policy Programme of the Belgian Prime Minister's Office. Financial aid was also provided by the British Council which awarded me a Foreign and Commonwealth Office Scholarship and the Faculty of Law of the University of Cambridge which awarded me a Humanitarian Trust studentship in public international law respectively. I would like also to express my gratitude to the President and the Fellows of Wolfson College, Cambridge for electing me to a junior research fellowship during the last year of my doctoral thesis.

My final thanks go to my family. My parents have always done their utmost to enable me to fulfil my wish to become an academic lawyer. Without them, it would not have been possible. I am also grateful to my wife, Mercedes, for her patience and unquestioning support. I dedicate this book to her.

Table of cases

Community law

United States law

International law

Table of legislation

European Community

Regulations

Regulation 1734/88 of 16 June 1988 concerning export from and import to the Community of certain dangerous chemicals, OJ 1988, L 155/2

Regulation 259/93 of 1 February 1993 on the supervision and control of shipments of waste within, into and out of the Community, OJ 1993, L 30/1

Directives

Directive 67/548 of 27 June 1967 on the approximation of the laws, regulations and administrative provisions relating to the classification, packaging and labelling of dangerous substances, OJ 1967, L 196/1

Directive 70/220 of 20 March 1970 on the approximation of the laws of the member states relating to measures to be taken against pollution by gases from positive-ignition engines from motor vehicles, OJ 1970, L 76/1

Directive 73/173 of 4 June 1973 on the approximation of member state laws relating to the classification, packaging and labelling of dangerous preparations, OJ 1973, L 189/7

Directive 75/439 of 16 June 1975 on the disposal of waste oils, OJ 1975, L 194/23

Directive 75/442 of 15 July 1975 on waste, OJ 1975, L 194/39

Directive 75/716 of 24 November 1975 on the approximation of the laws of the member states relating to the sulphur content of certain liquid fuels, OJ 1975, L 307/22

Directive 76/403 of 6 April 1976 on the disposal of polychlorinated biphenyls and polychlorinated terphenyls, OJ 1976, L 108/41

Decisions

United States

Administrative Procedure Act, 5 USC paras. 551–703 (1978 and Supp. 1995)

Clean Air Act, 42 USC paras. 7,401–61(q) (1983 and Supp. 1995)

Clean Water Act, 33 USC paras. 1,251–387 (1995)

Comprehensive Environmental Response, Compensation and Liability Act (CERCLA), 42 USC paras. 9,601–75 (1983 and Supp. 1995)

Endangered Species Act, 16 USC paras. 1,531–44 (1985 and Supp. 1995)

Federal Insecticide, Fungicide and Rodenticide (FIFRA), 7 USC paras. 136–136(y) (1995)

Marine Mammal Protection Act, 16 USC paras. 1,361–407 (1985 and Supp. 1995)

National Environmental Policy Act (NEPA), 42 USC paras. 4,321–70 (1978 and Supp. 1994)

Noise Control Act, 42 USC paras. 4,901–18 (1984 and Supp. 1995)

Resource Conservation and Recovery Act (RCRA), 42 USC paras. 6,901–92(k) (1983 and Supp. 1995)

Superfund Amendments and Reauthorization Act of 1986 (SARA), 42 USC (1983 and Supp. 1995).

Toxic Substances Control Act (TSCA), 15 USC paras. 2,601–92 (1982 and Supp. 1995)

International treaties and conventions

Fourth ACP–EEC Convention, reprinted in ILM 29 (1990) 788

Basle Convention on the Control of the Transboundary Movement of Hazardous Wastes and their Disposal, reprinted in ILM 28 (1989) 567

General Agreement on Tariffs and Trade, 30 October 1947, 51 Stat. A11, 55 UNTS 187

Agreement on Technical Barriers to Trade, GATT Doc. MTN/FA II-A1A-6 (15 December 1993) in Final Act Embodying the Results of the Uruguay Round of Multilateral Trade Negotiations, reprinted in ILM 33 (1994) 9

Agreement on the Application of Sanitary and Phytosanitary Measures, GATT Doc. MTN/FA II-A1A-4 (15 December 1993) in Final Act Embodying the Results of the Uruguay Round of Multilateral Trade Negotiations, reprinted in ILM 33 (1994) 9

Abbreviations

BADT	Best Adequately Demonstrated Technology
BAT	Best Available Techniques
CERCLA	Comprehensive Environmental Response, Compensation, and Liability Act (US) (also known as the 'Superfund')
CFR	*Code of Federal Regulations*
CMLR	*Common Market Law Reports*
ECR	*European Court of Justice Reports*
EPA	Environmental Protection Agency (US)
FIFRA	Federal Insecticide, Fungicide and Rodenticide Act (US)
FLSA	Fair Labor Standards Act (US)
GATT	General Agreement on Tariffs and Trade
NAPE	National Agency for the Protection of the Environment (US)
NEPA	National Environmental Policy Act (US)
NIMBY	Not In My Backyard
NO_x	Nitrogen Oxides
NSPS	New Source Preference Standards (US)
PCP	Pentachlorophenol
PSD	Prevention of Significant Deterioration programme (US)
RCRA	Resource Conservation and Recovery Act (US)
SARA	Superfund Amendments and Reauthorization Act (US)
SEA	Single European Act
SO_2	Sulphur Dioxide
SPS	Sanitary and Phytosanitary Agreement
Superfund	Comprehensive Environmental Response, Compensation, and Liability Act (US) (also known as CERCLA)
TBT	Technical Barriers to Trade Agreement
TEU	Treaty on European Union
TSCA	Toxic Substances Control Act (US)
WTO	World Trade Organization

Introduction

Despite important contextual and institutional differences, one problem shared by the European Community and the United States systems relates to the tension that may arise between free trade and environmental protection. In both systems, free trade is a value of central importance that has been promoted through constitutional principles designed to bring about the creation of a common market based on the free movement of goods and services and the absence of distortions of competition between their component entities (the European Community member states and the states of the United States federation, both hereafter referred to as 'the states').[1] Yet, the environmental policies developed by the states may conflict with the free-trade principles on which these systems are based. The objective of the present study is to evaluate in a comparative manner how the competing Community or federal interest in free trade and the state interest in preserving their domestic environmental policies can be reconciled in Community and United States law.

It is important to note at the outset that the tension between trade and environmental protection may take different forms depending on the

---

[1] The benefits from a common market and the perceived detriments of commercial warfare between states during the period of the Articles of Confederation were the primary catalyst for the Convention of 1787 which led to the adoption of the United States Constitution. Similar considerations induced the creation one-and-a-half centuries later of the European Community. See P. Kapteyn and P. Verloren van Themaat, *Introduction to the Law of the European Communities* (Deventer, Boston: Kluwer, 2nd edn, by Gormley, 1990) at 13. For a general discussion on the benefits brought about by the creation of the United States and European Community common markets, see T. Heller and J. Pelkmans, 'The Federal Economy: Law and Economic Integration and the Positive State – The USA and Europe Compared in an Economic Perspective' in Cappelletti, Seccombe and Weiler (eds.), *Integration through Law* (Walter de Gruyter, 1985) vol. I, at 245*ff*.

area of environmental regulation involved.[2] In this regard, it is useful to distinguish between three areas of environmental regulation: waste, product standards and process standards.[3] As will be seen throughout this study, these areas of regulation generally raise different trade issues and require separate treatment.

First, a tension between trade and environmental protection may arise in the area of waste. Although it is sometimes considered as having a negative commercial value,[4] waste constitutes a good whose free movement is protected under the free-trade provisions of the EC Treaty and the US Constitution.[5] There may be circumstances, however, where states attempt to restrict imports or exports of waste. For example, states may restrict imports of waste in order to protect their environment against the environmental damage created by the disposal of such waste and/or to retain their waste-disposal resources for local use.[6] States may also restrict exports of waste in order to protect their waste-treatment undertakings against out-of-state competitors.[7] There is therefore a tension between the free interstate movement of waste and the ability of states to control such movement.

Trade and environmental protection may also conflict in the area of product standards. Product standards regulate the (environmental) char-

---

[2] For a good discussion on the different forms of tension that may arise between trade and environmental policies, see R. Stewart, 'International Trade and Environment: Lessons from the Federal Experience', *Washington and Lee Law Review* 49 (1992), 1,329.

[3] A tension between trade and environmental protection may also arise in the context of wildlife protection. For example, states may restrict exports of wildlife in order to protect endangered species located within their territory. Conversely, they may restrict imports of wildlife in order to protect endangered species located within the territory of other states. Although the movement of wildlife raises important questions, it has not been the object of specific cases (the exception being Case C-169/89, *van den Burg* [1990] ECR I-2,143) or legislation (a regulation on the movement of wildlife is currently in preparation, but it is unclear whether it will be adopted) in Community law. No meaningful comparison is therefore possible between Community and United States law, which is far more developed on this aspect. The trade aspects of wildlife protection are accordingly outside the scope of this study.

[4] See Second Opinion of Advocate-General Jacobs in Case C-2/90, *Commission* v. *Belgium* [1992] ECR I-4,431.

[5] See Case C-2/90, *Commission* v. *Belgium* [1992] ECR I-4,431, at para. 28 and *City of Philadelphia* v. *State of New Jersey*, 437 US 617, 626 (1978) (holding that waste constitutes goods the free movement of which should be protected).

[6] See, e.g., Case C-2/90, *Commission* v. *Belgium* [1992] ECR I-4,431 and *Fort Gratiot Sanitary Landfill Inc.* v. *Michigan Department of Natural Resources*, 112 S. Ct 2,019 (1992) (cases involving restrictions on the imports of out-of-state waste).

[7] See, e.g., Case 172/82, *Interhuiles* [1983] ECR 555 and *C&A Carbone Inc.* v. *Town of Clarckstown*, 114 S. Ct 1,677 (1994) (cases involving restrictions on the exports of waste).

acteristics of products offered for sale on a given state market.[8] Although they do not directly regulate interstate trade, such standards may be used as an instrument of protectionism when their effect is to discriminate between domestic and out-of-state products. In addition, in the absence of a discriminatory effect, inconsistent product standards impede interstate trade since they deny manufacturers the ability to realize economies of scale in production and distribution and generally create market fragmentation.[9]

Finally, a tension between trade and environmental protection may arise in the area of process standards. Contrary to product standards, process standards do not regulate the characteristics of the products themselves, but the production methods used in the manufacture of products.[10] Although inconsistent process standards do not generally impede interstate trade, they may distort it.[11] Because the costs of production will differ from one state to another, inconsistent process standards may create unequal conditions of competition and, hence, give incentives for producers operating in states enforcing strict process standards to relocate in states where such standards are less stringent.

In this study, I will suggest that the various kinds of tension that may arise between trade and environmental protection can be adequately dealt with through two complementary institutional responses offered in the Community and United States systems. First, in the absence of harmonized legislation, the European Court of Justice (the 'Court of Justice') and the United States Supreme Court (the 'Supreme Court') can place limits on the ability of states to adopt environmental legislation impeding trade. The Court of Justice and the Supreme Court have

[8] Product standards 'prescribe the physical or chemical properties of a product (e.g., lead additives in gasoline), the maximum permissible polluting emissions from a product during its use (e.g., automobile emissions, detergent biodegradability) and the rules for making up, packaging or presenting a product (e.g., prescribed conditions for the elimination of packaging material, product labelling)': C. Thomas and G. Tereposky, 'The Evolving Relationship between Trade and Environmental Regulation', *Journal of World Trade* 27 (1993), 35, 37.

[9] See, e.g., Case 302/86, *Commission* v. *Denmark* [1988] ECR 4,607 and *American Can Co.* v. *Oregon Liquor Control Commission*, 517 P. 2d 691 (1973) (cases involving regulations on containers for drinks that have a restrictive effect on trade).

[10] Process standards 'include emission and effluent standards and other standards governing the production process': Thomas and Tereposky, 'The Evolving Relationship' at 37.

[11] See, e.g., Case C-300/89, *Commission* v. *Council* [1991] ECR I-2,867, 2,901 ('provisions which are made necessary by considerations relating to the environment and health may be a burden upon the undertakings to which they apply and, if there is no harmonization of national provisions on the matter, competition may be appreciably distorted').

respectively used Articles 30*ff* of the EC Treaty and the dormant Commerce Clause doctrine to invalidate state environmental measures impeding trade in an unacceptable manner (a process of 'negative' harmonization of state environmental standards). Alternatively, the Community and US federal legislatures can set common environmental standards for all states in order to avoid the trade distortions that may be generated by inconsistent state regulations (a process of 'positive' harmonization of state environmental standards).[12] In this context, a central objective in this study will be to discuss the respective contributions of the judiciary and the legislature to the solution of the various kinds of tension that may arise between trade and environmental protection, as well as to show the interactions existing between such judicial and legislative contributions. Another important objective will be to observe the tension that may arise between the Community or federal interest in uniformity and the national or state interest in (environmental) diversity. In this regard, the techniques that have been developed by the Court of Justice and the Supreme Court, on the one hand, and the Community and US federal legislatures, on the other hand, to deal with these competing interests will be discussed.

Two important remarks should be made regarding the scope and the orientation of this study. First, I will concentrate exclusively on the relationship between free trade and state *regulatory* environmental policies. Although state environmental taxes and subsidies may have some impact on interstate trade,[13] they are excluded from the scope of this

---

[12] The terms 'negative' and 'positive' harmonization or integration were developed in Pinder, 'Positive Integration and Negative Integration: Some Problems of Economic Union in the EEC', *World Today* 24 (1968), 88. They are now frequently used in the legal literature to describe the respective contributions of the judiciary and the legislature to free trade. The contribution of the judiciary takes a 'negative' form since free trade is achieved through the abolition of trade-restrictive state rules. On the other hand, the contribution of the legislature takes a 'positive' form since free trade is achieved through the adoption of a common regulatory regime. In the European Community context see, e.g., S. Weatherill and P. Beaumont, *EC Law* (London: Penguin, 1993) at 419; M. van Empel, 'The 1992 Programme: Interaction Between the Legislator and the Judiciary', *Legal Issues of European Integration* (1992/1), 1, 2. In the United States context see, e.g., R. Stewart, 'Interstate Commerce, Environmental Protection and US Federal Law' in Cameron, Demaret and Geradin (eds.), *Trade and the Environment – The Search for Balance* (London: Cameron & May, 1994) at 342.

[13] Taxes may restrict interstate trade when they discriminate on their face or in their effects between domestic and out-of-state products. Although they do not generally restrict interstate trade, subsidies may nevertheless distort such a trade by giving an advantage to domestic producers in relation to out-of-state ones.

study.[14] Second, I will proceed on the assumption that both trade and environmental policies are valuable means to promote human welfare, as understood in a broad sense.[15] This assumption has the consequence that I reject the position defended by some environmentalists according to whom environmental values are absolute, i.e., they may not be sacrificed at any price even if they impose disproportionately large costs on society.[16] Since both trade and environmental policies are useful tools to further human welfare, I will attempt to develop mechanisms to reconcile these policies in the best way possible rather than to establish any absolute priority between them.

A word should also be said about the method of comparative analysis that will be used throughout this work. By its very nature, comparative analysis contains a 'dialectical tension'.[17] On the one hand, the objects of comparison must have a point of identity or similarity in order to render analysis meaningful. On the other hand, comparative analysis is meaningless in conditions of total identity or similarity. In the light of this observation, it seems that, with regard to the matter at hand, the Community and United States systems offer excellent objects of comparison. On the one hand, these systems face the same problem (i.e., how to

---

[14] On the use of taxes and subsidies by Community member states and their impact on intra-Community trade see, however, E. Rehbinder, 'Environmental Regulation Through Fiscal and Economic Incentives in a Federalist System', *Ecology Law Quarterly* 20 (1993), 57; E. Grabitz and C. Zacker, 'Scope for Action by the EC member states under EEC Law: The Example of Environmental Taxes and Subsidies', *Common Market Law Review* 26 (1989), 423. Little has been written on the impact of state environmental taxes and subsidies on the US common market. For some analysis of the fiscal aspects, see Stewart, 'Interstate Commerce'. See also S. Levmore, 'Interstate Exploitation and Judicial Intervention', *Virginia Law Review* 69 (1983), 563.

[15] For a more elaborated treatment of this position, see Stewart, 'International Trade'. In his article, Professor Stewart makes reference to the conception of human welfare similar to that proposed by John Stuart Mill, 'which goes beyond the maximization of existing preferences to include qualities of diversity, education, aspiration, reflection and solidarity'. He also claims that this conception 'rejects the position that environmental protection is an autonomous moral duty – an independent absolute': *ibid.* at 1,332. Professor Stewart's position has been strongly criticized by environmentalists such as R. Housman for whom 'Mill's approach generally fails to take into account the widely held belief that certain values are so central to humanity that they must be protected even at a cost to the larger society'. According to the same author those values can be best understood by the concept of categorical imperative used by Emmanuel Kant in his philosophical works. See R. Housman, 'A Kantian Approach to Trade and the Environment', *Washington and Lee Law Review* 49 (1993), 1,373, 1,374.

[16] See, e.g., Housman, 'A Kantian Approach'.

[17] See M. Cappelletti, M. Seccombe and J. Weiler, 'Integration through Law: Europe and the American Federal Experience: A General Introduction' in Cappelletti *et al.* (eds.), *Integration through Law* (Walter de Gruyter, 1985), vol. I, at 9.

reconcile trade and environmental policies) and, as will be seen, generally attempt to solve this problem through a comparable mix of negative (i.e., judicial) and positive (i.e., legislative) harmonization. On the other hand, because of important contextual and institutional differences,[18] the nature of the judicial and legislative solutions adopted in each system will often differ, thereby providing a fertile ground for comparison. In this context, the use of the comparative method in this study will have two main objectives. The first, and perhaps the more important of these, will be to understand better the various aspects of the tension between free trade and environmental protection, transcending the specific manifestation of this problem in the Community and United States systems. The second objective will be of a policy nature, i.e., to see to what extent the solutions found to this tension in one system are suitable for adoption by the other.

In Part 1, I analyse and compare the case law of the Court of Justice and the Supreme Court dealing with state environmental measures affecting trade. I also argue that, with regard to the tension that may arise between trade and environmental protection, these courts have an important although limited role to play. In a number of circumstances, some form of legislative action is needed. In the light of this observation, in Part 2, I first discuss the respective powers of the Community and United States federal legislatures to regulate environmental matters, as well as the potential limits that may be placed on such powers. Then, I evaluate how, through or in the context of their legislative action, the Community and the US federal legislatures have attempted to balance trade and environmental objectives in the areas of product standards, process standards and waste. I also deal with the question of pre-emption, i.e., to what extent states may apply stricter standards than Community or US federal environmental standards, as well as the impact of this question on the relationship between trade and environmental protection. Finally, I draw some general conclusions.

---

[18] The contextual and institutional differences between the Community and the United States systems have been described at length elsewhere and will not be the object of systematic attention here. For good discussions on these differences see, e.g., F. Jacobs and K. Karst, 'The "Federal" Legal Order: The USA and Europe Compared – A Juridical Perspective' in Cappelletti *et al.* (eds.), *Integration through Law* (Walter de Gruyter, 1985), vol. I, at 169–72; E. Stein and T. Sandalow, 'On the Two Systems: An Overview' in Stein and Sandalow (eds.), *Courts and Free Markets* (Oxford University Press, 1982) at 3. For a discussion on the impact of these differences on the development of Community and United States federal environmental policies, see L. Kramer, 'The European Economic Community' in Smith and Kromarek (eds.), *Understanding US and European Environmental Law* (London: Graham & Trotman, 1989) at 4*ff.*

PART 1

Negative harmonization

As we have seen, various kinds of tension may arise between trade and environmental protection in the Community and United States legal orders. The objective of Part 1 is to discuss and compare how, through their power to review state (environmental) measures interfering with trade, the Court of Justice and the Supreme Court have attempted to reconcile these tensions.

Part 1 is divided into four chapters. Chapter 1 first discusses the principle of free intra-Community trade as it is established and protected by the EC Treaty and interpreted by the Court of Justice in its case law. It then discusses the case law of the Court of Justice dealing with trade-restrictive member state environmental measures. Chapter 2, which is devoted to United States law, follows the same structure as chapter 1. First, it discusses the development by the Supreme Court of a principle of free trade between states. It then discusses the Supreme Court cases dealing specifically with trade-restrictive state environmental measures. Chapter 3 consists of a comparative analysis of the findings made in chapters 1 and 2. First, it draws a parallel between the case law of the Court of Justice and of the Supreme Court in so far as they establish and protect a principle of free interstate trade. It then compares the case law of these courts specifically dealing with trade-restrictive state environmental measures. Finally, chapter 4 discusses to what extent judicial intervention through selective judicial invalidation of trade-restrictive state environmental measures offers an adequate response to the various kinds of tension that may arise between trade and environmental protection in the European Community and United States systems. It concludes that, in a number of circumstances, such tensions can only be properly solved through the adoption of positive rules of harmonization.

1   The case law of the Court of Justice

The principle of free trade

Article 3 of the EC Treaty states that, in order to achieve the general objectives of the Community expressed in Article 2 of the Treaty, the activities of the Community include, *inter alia*:

the elimination, as between Member States, of customs duties and quantitative restrictions on the import and export of goods, and all measures having equivalent effect.

As far as quantitative restrictions on the import and export of goods and measures having equivalent effect are concerned, their elimination is to be achieved through the application to member states' laws of the prohibitions contained in Articles 30 and 34 of the Treaty respectively.[1]

Article 30 of the Treaty provides that all quantitative restrictions on imports and measures having equivalent effect shall be prohibited between member states.[2] The concept of quantitative restrictions is relatively straightforward. Quantitative restrictions were defined by the Court of Justice as 'measures which amount to a total or partial restraint of, according to the circumstances, imports, exports or goods in transit'.[3] The definition of the concept of 'measure having equivalent effect' has created more difficulty.[4] After an initial attempt at definition by the

---

[1] Articles 95–8 of the Treaty also prohibit member states from restricting the free movement of goods by adopting discriminatory fiscal measures. As already noted, fiscal measures will not be examined here.

[2] On the Article 30 case law, see generally P. Oliver, *Free Movements of Goods in the EEC* (London: European Law Centre, 2nd edn, 1988); L. Gormley, *Prohibiting Restrictions on Trade within the EEC* (Amsterdam, New York, Oxford: North-Holland, 1985).

[3] See Case 2/73, *Geddo* v. *Ente Nazionale Risi* [1973] ECR 881; and Case 34/79, *Henn and Darby* [1979] ECR 3,795.

[4] From the very early life of the Treaty, the concept of measures having equivalent effect

9

Commission,[5] this concept has been interpreted by the Court of Justice in its leading judgment in *Procureur du Roi* v. *Dassonville et al.* as covering:

all trading rules enacted by Member States which are capable of hindering, actually or potentially, directly or indirectly, intra-Community trade.[6]

It is clear from this formula that one must look to the effects of a measure and not to its nature or purpose in deciding whether it falls under Article 30. As defined in *Dassonville*, Article 30 appears to cover three kinds of measure depending on their effects.[7] First, it clearly covers national measures which discriminate on their face against imports (formal discrimination). Article 30 also covers national measures which, although applying to both domestic and imported products, have a discriminatory effect against the latter (material discrimination).[8] Finally, the scope of Article 30 is sufficiently broad to cover national measures which, although they do not discriminate on their face or in their effects against imported products, make such imports more difficult.[9]

---

has generated a considerable amount of academic writing. For a survey of different views see, Gormley, *Prohibiting Restrictions*, at 13.

[5] Directive 70/50 on the abolition of measures which have an effect equivalent to quantitative restrictions on imports and are not covered by other provisions adopted in pursuance of the EEC Treaty (1970) OJ (Special Edition) (I), at 17.

[6] Case 8/74, *Procureur du Roi* v. *Dassonville et al.* [1974] ECR 837, 852. The *Dassonville* formula has been criticized as being too broad and a number of authors have advised the court to reduce the scope of application of Article 30. See, e.g., W. Wils, 'The Search for the Rule in Article 30 EEC: Much Ado About Nothing?' *European Law Review* 19 (1993), 475; D. Chalmers, 'Free Movement of Goods within the European Community: An Unhealthy Addiction to Scotch Whisky?' *International and Comparative Law Quarterly* 42 (1993), 269; J. Steiner, 'Drawing Lines: Uses and Abuses of Article 30 EEC', *Common Market Law Review* 29 (1992), 749; E. White, 'In Search of the Limits to Article 30 of the EEC Treaty', *Common Market Law Review* 26 (1989), 235. It should be noted that in Joined Cases C-267 and C-268/91, *Keck and Mithouard* [1993] ECR I-6,097, the Court of Justice held that non-discriminatory measures relating to marketing arrangements for products (such as a prohibition on resale at a loss) would fall outside the scope of Article 30. Although this decision has generated some uncertainty as to the scope of Article 30, it is likely to have little impact on the way the Court of Justice deals with member state environmental measures. As will be seen, such measures typically apply to the product themselves (e.g., product standards) rather than to marketing arrangements. On *Keck and Mithouard*, see generally A. Mattera, 'De l'Arrêt "Dassonville" à l'Arrêt "Keck": L'Obscure Clarté d'une Jurisprudence Riche en Principes Novateurs et en Contradictions' ,*Revue du Marché Unique Européen* (1994/1), 117; D. Chalmers, 'Repackaging the Internal Market – The Ramifications of the Keck Judgment', *European Law Review* 19 (1994), 585.

[7] For a survey of the type of measure capable of falling within Article 30, see A. Mattera, 'Protectionism inside the EC', *Journal of World Trade Law* 18 (1984), 283.

[8] On the distinction between formal and material discrimination, see F. Burrows, *Free Movement in European Community Law* (Oxford: Clarendon Press, 1987) at 50.

[9] In its interpretation of Article 30, the Court of Justice goes therefore beyond the

Article 34(1) of the Treaty provides that quantitative restrictions on exports and all measures having equivalent effect shall be prohibited by the member states. As in the case of quantitative restrictions on imports, the interdiction of quantitative restrictions on exports prohibits all partial and total restraints on the exports of goods to one or more member states.[10] On the other hand, contrary to what we have seen in the context of import restrictions, the notion of a 'measure having equivalent effect' on exports has been interpreted by the Court of Justice as only covering measures that on their face or in their effects discriminate against exports. Non-discriminatory measures would therefore fall automatically outside the scope of Article 34. This approach can be clearly perceived in *Groenveld* where the court stated that Article 34 of the Treaty concerns:

national measures which have as their specific object or effect the restriction of pattern of exports and thereby the establishment of a difference in treatment between the domestic trade of a Member State and its export trade in such a way as to provide a particular advantage for national production or for the domestic market in question at the expense of the production or of the trade of other Member States. This is not so in the case of a prohibition of goods of a certain kind without drawing a distinction depending on whether such goods are intended for the national market or export.[11]

The court's different treatment of the concept of a 'measure having equivalent effect' under Articles 30 and 34 has been regretted by a number of authors. According to Gormley, the discrimination criterion adopted by the Court of Justice in *Groenveld* pays insufficient attention to the central position in the Treaty of the prohibition of measures capable of hindering trade between member states.[12] In his view, it would have been preferable

'national treatment' principle traditionally applied in international economic law. See E. U. Petersmann, 'Trade and Environmental Protection: The Practice of GATT and the European Community Compared' in Cameron, Demaret and Geradin (eds.), *Trade and the Environment – The Search for Balance* (London: Cameron & May, 1994) at 147. But see G. Marenco, 'Pour une Interprétation Traditionelle de la Notion de Mesure d'Effet Equivalent à une Restriction Quantitative', *Cahiers de Droit Européen* (1984), 291, who attempts to demonstrate that discrimination is the foundation of the Court of Justice's Article 30 case law. This view is, however, isolated and unconvincing.

[10] Case 2/73, *Geddo v. Este Nazionale Risi* [1973] ECR 881.
[11] Case 15/79 [1979] ECR 3,409, 3,415. See also Case C-80/92, *Commission v. Belgium* [1994] ECR I-1,019, 1,035; Case C-47/90, *Delhaize* [1993] ECR I-3,369; Case 15/83, *Denkavit* [1984] ECR 2,171, 2,184; Case 251/83, *Haug-Adrion* [1984] ECR 4,277, 4,289; Case 238/82, *Duphar* [1984] ECR 523, 543; Case 237/82, *Jongeneel Kaas BV* [1984] ECR 483, 504; Case 172/82, *Interhuiles* [1983] ECR 555, 566; Case 286/81, *Oosthoek's* [1982] ECR 4,575, 4,587; Joined Cases 141 to 143/81, *Holdijck* [1982] ECR 1,299, 1,313; Case 155/80, *Oebel* [1981] ECR 1,993, 2,009.
[12] See Gormley, *Prohibiting Restrictions*, at 108.

to interpret Article 34 in the same way as Article 30 given that the primary aim of these provisions is to promote integration through trade and that this involves prohibiting all restrictions or disincentives to trade between member states save those permitted by Community law itself (Article 36 and the rule of reason).[13] In *Oebel*, Advocate-General Capotorti also argued that keeping a broad and uniform interpretation of Article 34 would be 'clear and functional', making it possible to block all measures whose effect is to restrict the free movement of goods.[14]

Despite these criticisms, it seems that the criterion of discrimination adopted by the court in Article 34 has the advantage of flexibility. On the one hand, as will be seen in a number of cases discussed below, this criterion is wide enough to catch 'local grab' measures designed to favour domestic producers at the expense of non-domestic ones.[15] On the other hand, it is narrow enough to avoid a number of national measures having only incidental effects on exports falling under the prohibition of Article 34.[16] This is, for example, the case with measures regulating the conditions of production of goods (process standards).[17] If, as in the case of imports, the concept of a measure having equivalent effect to quantitative restrictions on exports was interpreted as covering equally applicable measures having an actual or potential effect on exports, such measures, which may have a restrictive effect on production and, hence, on exports, would be prohibited under Article 34 unless justified by a legitimate objective and found proportionate. This would in turn oblige the Court of Justice to review national measures which have only a remote effect on intra-Community trade.[18]

---

[13] *Ibid.* at 109.   [14] See Case 155/80 [1981] ECR 1,993, 2,019.

[15] See, e.g., Case C-37/92, *Vanacker and Lesage* [1993] ECR I-4,947; Case 118/86, *Nertsvoederfabriek Nederland* [1987] ECR 3,883; Case 173/83, *Commission v. France* [1985] ECR 491; Case 295/82, *Rhône-Alpes Huiles* [1984] ECR 575; Case 172/82, *Interhuiles* [1983] ECR 555 (Court of Justice finding that restrictions on exports designed to favour domestic producers were incompatible with Article 34).

[16] See Joined Cases 141 to 143/81, *Holdijck* [1982] ECR 1,299 (holding that a Danish regulation laying down minimum standards for enclosures of fatting calves, without any distinction as to whether the animal or the meat were intended for the national market or export, did not fall within the prohibition of Article 34).

[17] See D. Kommers and M. Waelbroeck, 'Legal Integration and the Free Movement of Goods: The American and the European Experience' in Cappelletti *et al.* (eds.), *Integration through Law* (Walter de Gruyter, 1985), vol. I, at 199.

[18] See, *mutatis mutandis*, the difficulties created by the application of the *Dassonville* formula in the Sunday-trading cases (e.g., Case C-332/89, *Marchandise* [1991] ECR I-1,027; Case C-312/89, *Conforama* [1991] ECR I-997; Case 145/88, *Torfaen* [1989] ECR 3,851) and the reaction of the Court of Justice in Cases C-267 and 268/91, *Keck and Mittouard* [1993] ECR I-6,097 (discussed at note 6 above).

The exceptions to the principle

Article 36

Assuming that certain conditions are met, Article 36 allows member states to adopt measures which are *prima facie* incompatible with Articles 30 to 34 for the purpose of protecting a series of non-economic values such as public policy or public security and the protection of human health or life, animals or plants. In a consistent line of case law, the Court of Justice has made clear that Article 36 must be strictly interpreted and that it does not extend to justifications not mentioned in the article.[19] Environmental protection does not in itself figure in Article 36. However, environmental measures may be designed to protect some of the values listed in Article 36.[20] For example, it is clear that a member state can justify under Article 36 an environmental-protection measure which primarily aims at protecting the health or life of humans. Article 36 could therefore be used as a basis to legitimize measures which aim at controlling the imports of dangerous waste.[21] This provision could also be used to justify legislation regulating the sale of products containing substances that may impose serious risks on human health or life.[22] Moreover, environmental-protection objectives can sometimes be related to the protection of the health and life of animals and plants. Article 36 could thus justify regulations prohibiting trade in certain animal or vegetal species[23] or in substances that may endanger such species.[24]

---

[19] See, e.g., Case 229/83, *Leclerq* [1985] ECR 1, 35; Case 95/81, *Commission v. Italy* [1982] ECR 2,187, 2,204; Case 113/80, *Commission v. Ireland* [1981] ECR 1,625, 1,638; Case 13/68, *Salgoil* [1968] ECR 453, 463; Case 7/68, *Commission v. Italy* [1968] ECR 423, 431.

[20] See B. Jadot, 'Observations – Mesures Nationales de Police de l'Environnement, Libre Circulation des Marchandises et Proportionalité', *Cahiers de Droit Européen* (1990), 408, 411.

[21] See, *a contrario*, the first opinion (10 January 1991) of Advocate-General Jacobs in Case C-2/90, *Commission v. Belgium* [1992] ECR I-4,431, at para. 20.

[22] See, e.g., Case C-293/94, *Brandsma*, judgment of 27 June 1996, unreported; Case 54/85, *Mirepoix* [1986] ECR 1,067, 1,078; Case 94/83, *Heijn* [1984] ECR 3,263, 3,280; Case 174/82, *Sandoz* [1983] ECR 2,445, 2,463; Case 272/80, *Biologische Producten* [1981] ECR 3,277, 3,291.

[23] See Opinion of Advocate-General van Gerven in Case C-169/89, *van den Burg* [1990] ECR I-2,143, 2,145.

[24] See Case C-131/93, *Commission v. Germany* [1994] ECR I-3,303, 3,321 (holding that a national ban on the imports of live freshwater crayfish for commercial purposes in order to protect the health and life of domestic crayfish was covered by the exception contained in Article 36).

The rule of reason

In the famous *Cassis de Dijon* case the Court of Justice phrased the rule of reason in the following words:

Obstacles to movement within the Community resulting in disparities between the national laws relating to the marketing of the products in question must be accepted in so far as those provisions may be recognized as being necessary in order to satisfy mandatory requirements relating in particular to the effectiveness of fiscal supervision, the protection of health, the fairness of commercial transactions and the defence of the consumer.[25]

From this statement, it appears that the Court of Justice recognizes that, in the absence of Community measures of harmonization, member states may, when adopting measures which apply equally to domestic and imported products,[26] restrict intra-Community trade for motives other than those specifically recognized by Article 36.[27] Since non-discriminatory measures fall automatically outside the scope of Article 34, the rule of reason is of no practical use in the context of national measures restricting exports. On the other hand, the rule of reason is very useful as a potential justification for national measures which, although they are of a non-discriminatory nature, have the effect of impeding imports.

An important question in this context is whether environmental protection may fall within the mandatory requirements enunciated by the Court of Justice in *Cassis de Dijon*. In 1980, the EC Commission underlined the importance of environmental protection as a potential limitation on the prohibition contained in Article 30.[28] Such an interpretation was also accepted by the Court of Justice in *Procureur de la République* v. *Association de Défense des Brûleurs d'Huiles Usagées* (the 'Waste Oils' case).[29] In *Waste Oils*, the

[25] Case 120/78 *Rewe-Zentral AG* v. *Bundesmonopolverwaltung für Branntwei* [1979] ECR 649, 662. This holding has since been confirmed in a large number of cases. See, e.g., the references cited in Gormley, *Prohibiting Restrictions*, at 51ff.

[26] Contrary to the exceptions contained in Article 36, mandatory requirements only apply to indistinctly applicable measures. See, e.g., Case 207/83, *Commission* v. *United Kingdom* [1985] ECR 1,202, 1,212; Case 16/83, *Prantl* [1984] ECR 1,299, 1,327; Case 788/79, *Gilli and Andres* [1980] ECR 2,071, 2,078.

[27] *Prima facie*, this approach seems to be inconsistent with the Court of Justice's repeated statements that Article 36 is exhaustive. The explanation generally advanced is that, contrary to Article 36, the rule of reason does not operate as an exception to the prohibition of Article 30 but rather as a limitation to its scope. See D. Wyatt and A. Dashwood, *European Community Law* (London: Sweet & Maxwell, 3rd edn, 1993) at 230; S. Weatherill and P. Beaumont, *EC Law* (London: Penguin, 1993) at 439.

[28] Communication from the Commission concerning the consequences of the judgment given by the Court of Justice on 20 February 1979 in Case 120/78 ('Cassis de Dijon'), 1980 OJ (C 256), 2.

[29] Case 240/83 [1984] ECR 531.

court was not asked to evaluate the validity of a member state environmental measure but to determine whether Council Directive 75/439 on the disposal of waste oils was in conformity with the principles of freedom of trade, the free movement of goods and free competition. Particularly at issue were the provisions of the directive which envisaged the possibility of exclusive zones being assigned to waste-oil collectors, the prior approval of undertakings responsible for the disposal and the possibility of indemnities being granted to undertakings. The court began by recalling that '[t]he principles of free movement of goods and freedom of competition, together with freedom of trade as a fundamental right, are general principles of Community law'.[30] However, the court insisted that:

[t]he principle of freedom of trade is not to be viewed in absolute terms but is subject to certain limits justified by the objectives of general interest pursued by the Community provided that the rights in question are not substantially impaired . . . There is no reason to conclude that the Directive has exceeded these limits. The Directive must be seen in the perspective of *environmental-protection*, which is *one of the Community's essential objectives*.[31]

The *Waste Oils* decision may be considered a landmark, for it may be inferred from it that national measures taken for environmental-protection reasons are capable of constituting 'mandatory requirements' recognized by *Cassis de Dijon* as limiting the application of Article 30 of the Treaty in the absence of Community rules.[32] As will be seen below, this has since been confirmed in subsequent cases and is now a well-established aspect of Community law.[33]

The principle of proportionality

According to the case law of the Court of Justice, measures justifiable under Article 36 of the Treaty or the rule of reason must be subject to a so-called test of 'proportionality': (i) they must be pertinent, i.e., there must be a causal relationship between the measure adopted and the attainment

---

[30] *Ibid.* at 548.

[31] *Ibid.* at 549 (emphasis added).

[32] It has been argued, however, that the court had already implicitly applied the rule of reason to environmental issues in Cases 3, 4 and 6/76, *Kramer et al.* [1976] ECR 1,279. See, e.g., P. Kapteyn and P. Verloren van Themaat, *Introduction to the Law of the European Communities* (Deventer, Boston: Kluwer, 2nd edn, by Gormley, 1990) at 389.

[33] See Case C-2/90, *Commission v. Belgium* [1992] ECR I-4,431; Case 302/86, *Commission v. Denmark* [1988] ECR 4,607. See also the environmental provisions introduced in the EC Treaty by the Single European Act (Article 100(A)3, 130R) and the Treaty on European Union (Article 2 and 3(K)), which considerably increased the status of environmental protection in the Community legal order.

of the objective pursued; and (ii) the measures must be the least restrictive method of attaining that purpose.[34] The *Gilli and Andres* case[35] illustrates the first of these requirements. There, the court found that the prohibitions enacted by Italy on the sale of vinegar other than wine vinegar were not justified, since other kinds of vinegar were not damaging to human health. The court indicated that 'there is no factor justifying any restriction on the importation of the product in question from the point of view either of the protection of public health and the fairness of commercial transactions or of the defence of the consumer'.[36] The Italian measure was declared incompatible with the Treaty because the court could not find a causal connection between this measure (the ban on vinegar other than wine vinegar) and the objectives it attempted to promote (the protection of public health and the fairness of commercial transactions).

The *de Peiper* case[37] provides an illustration of the criterion of least restrictive alternative. In that case, a Dutch legal provision required parallel importers of pharmaceutical products to submit to the national health authorities certain documents which could be obtained only from the manufacturers of the products or their appointed distributor. The effect of this provision was to make all parallel imports of pharmaceutical products dependent on the goodwill of the manufacturer or of the official distributor. The court considered that such a regulation did not fall within the exception provided in Article 36, since public health could be protected as effectively by a less restrictive measure, such as a collaboration between the Dutch authorities and the member states in which the pharmaceutical products in question were produced.[38] Also in the *Rau* case,[39] the Court of Justice had to decide whether the application of a Belgian regulation, which did not allow margarine imported from another member state to be sold unless packaged in cube-shaped blocks, constituted a measure of equivalent effect within the meaning of Article 30. The Belgian government contended that the measure was necessary to prevent confusion between butter and margarine. However, the court rejected this argument since it found that 'consumers may in fact be protected just as effectively by other measures, for example by rules on labelling, which hinder the free movement less'.[40]

---

[34] For a good discussion on the principle of proportionality in European Community law, see G. de Burca, 'The Principle of Proportionality and its Application in EC Law', *Yearbook of European Law* 13 (1994), 105.

[35] Case 788/79 [1980] ECR 2,071.   [36] *Ibid.* at 2,078.

[37] Case 104/75 [1976] ECR 613.   [38] *Ibid.* at 637.

[39] Case 261/81 [1982] ECR 3,961.   [40] *Ibid.* at 3,973.

The application of the principle

Since these cases generally deal with different problems and issues, I will distinguish here between the Court of Justice cases dealing with trade-restrictive environmental measures depending on whether they apply to waste, products standards, or process standards.

Waste

In the area of waste, two important issues deserve particular attention: (i) to what extent member states are free to ban or adopt restrictions on the imports of non-domestic waste into their territory; and, conversely, (ii) to what extent member states should be entitled to ban or impose restrictions on the exports of their own waste to other member states.[41]

The first issue was expressly addressed by the Court of Justice in Case C-2/90, *Commission* v. *Belgium* (the *Belgian Waste* case).[42] In that case, the Commission challenged a Decree of the Walloon Regional Executive whose effect was to impose a global ban on the imports of all waste products into Wallonia, subject only to the exceptions contained in the Decree and to the possibility of further derogations. The Commission argued that the prohibitions of the Walloon Decree were contrary to the schemes and objectives of Directives 75/442 on waste and 84/361 on the supervision and control within the European Community on the trans-frontier shipment of hazardous waste, but also to Articles 30 to 36 of the Treaty since they discriminated between imported and domestic waste.

In its judgment, the Court of Justice rejected the Commission's argument that Directive 75/442 did not authorize Wallonia to impose a full ban on imports of waste. As the court observed, none of the provisions of this directive specifically aim at waste exchanges between member states. By contrast, the court concluded that Directive 84/361 set up a complete system for the control of dangerous waste based on prior compulsory and

---

[41] Generally on these issues, see N. de Sadeleer, *Le Droit Communautaire et les Déchets* (Paris; Brussels: LGDJ/Bruylant, 1995) at 95ff.

[42] [1992] ECR I-4,431. Noted by D. Geradin, *European Law Review* 18 (1993), 145; L. Hancher and A. Sevenster, *Common Market Law Review* 30 (1993), 351; M. Wheeler, *Journal of Environmental Law* 5 (1993), 133. See also J. Stuyck, 'Le Traitement des Déchets dans la (Non-)Réalisation du Marché Intérieur', *Journal des Tribunaux Européen* (1994), 10; N. de Sadeleer, 'La Reconnaissance du Principe de Proximité comme Autorisant les Etats Membres à Interdire l'Importation des Déchets dont les Transfers n'ont pas Eté Harmonisés par une Règle de Droit Communautaire Dérivé: Une Victoire à la Pyrrhus?' *Aménagement – Environnement* (1993/2), 166; J. Jans, 'Waste Policy and European Community Law: Does the EEC Treaty Provide a Suitable Framework for Regulating Waste?' *Ecology Law Quarterly* 20 (1993), 165, 171.

detailed notification on the part of the waste producer. This system did not therefore leave any possibility for the member states to ban movements of dangerous waste globally.[43] Dangerous waste being covered by Directive 84/361, the court only examined the compatibility of the Belgian measures to Article 30 of the Treaty in the case of non-dangerous waste.[44] The Court of Justice first considered whether or not such waste constitutes goods, the free movement of which must be ensured throughout the Community. The Belgian government had argued for a distinction between recyclable and non-recyclable waste. Waste which cannot be used again, it stated, has no intrinsic commercial value. It cannot be sold. It does not therefore come under the provisions of the Treaty on the free movement of goods.[45] The court rejected that distinction. It reasoned that, from a practical standpoint, serious difficulties would arise, especially with respect to border control, if a distinction between recyclable and non-recyclable waste were made.[46] Such a distinction would also be based upon uncertain factors which, depending on technical developments, could change in time.[47] Because of these factors, the court found that all waste should be treated as goods the free movement of which should not in principle be impeded.[48]

On the other hand, the court accepted the argument put forward by the Belgian government that its restrictions on the imports of waste were a temporary measure to safeguard Wallonia from an influx of waste from neighbouring countries and that they should therefore be legitimized under the rule of reason.[49] The court rejected the Commission argument

---

[43] As will be seen below, it is a principle of Community law that when a matter has been fully regulated by a Community measure, further national measures are not permissible, even in cases where they are adopted to safeguard important values such as those listed in Article 36 of the Treaty.

[44] Judgment of the court at para. 28.

[45] The Belgian government based its argument on the traditional definition of 'goods' provided in Case 7/68, *Commission* v. *Italy* [1968] ECR 423. In that case, the court defined 'goods' as 'products which can be valued in money and which are capable, as such, of forming the subject of commercial transactions'. Generally on the definition of waste, see Joined Cases C-206/88 and C-207/88, *Vessoso and Zanetti* [1990] ECR 1,461, 1,476 and the second opinion (19 September 1991) of Advocate-General Jacobs, at paras. 5–24. See also P. de Bruycker and P. Morrens, 'Qu'est ce qu'un Déchet dans l'Union Européenne?' *Aménagement – Environnement* (1993/3), 154.

[46] Judgment of the court at para. 27.

[47] *Ibid.*   [48] *Ibid.* at para. 28.

[49] In this regard, the court noted that '[s]o far as the environment is concerned . . . waste has a special characteristic. The accumulation of waste, even before it becomes a hazard, constitutes a threat to the environment because of the limited capacity of each region or locality for receiving it': *ibid.* at para. 30.

that the rule of reason could not be used here because the Belgian restrictions discriminated against waste from other member states which were no more harmful than waste produced in Wallonia.[50] The court held that to appreciate whether the Belgian restrictions were discriminatory or not, the special character of waste had to be taken into account.[51] In this regard, the court considered the principle of correction of environmental harm at source enunciated in Article 130R(2) of the Treaty which implies that it is incumbent on each region and other local government to take appropriate measures to ensure the treatment and elimination of its own waste.[52] Such a principle was also in accordance with the principles of self-sufficiency and proximity contained in the 1989 Basle Convention on the Control of the Transboundary Movement of Hazardous Waste and their Disposal.[53] As a result, given the difference between waste produced in one area or another, and their connection with the place they were produced, the Walloon restrictions were not to be seen as discriminatory.[54]

The reasoning sustained by the Court of Justice in its decision presents a number of troubling elements. First, this was the first time the court used the rule of reason to uphold trade restrictions which appeared as discriminatory on their face. To achieve this result, the Court of Justice chose as its point of departure the characteristic of the product as opposed to the nature of the measure concerned. The Walloon restrictions did not discriminate because imported and domestic waste were different.[55] From an ecological point of view, the correctness of this assertion

---

[50] The Court of Justice here also contradicted Advocate-General Jacobs for whom the Belgian measure 'which favours waste produced in one region of a member state is plainly not indistinctly applicable to domestic or imported products'. First opinion (10 January 1991) at para. 20.

[51] *Ibid.* at para. 30. [52] *Ibid.* at para. 34.

[53] *Ibid.* at para. 35. The Basle Convention is reprinted in ILM 28 (1989) 567.

[54] Judgment of the court at para. 36.

[55] From the point of view of the coherence of its case law, it would have been better if the court had found the Walloon restrictions discriminatory and then attempted to justify them under one of the exceptions contained in Article 36 of the Treaty. The court was, however, probably discouraged to adopt this approach by Advocate-General Jacobs who, in his first opinion, indicated that Article 36 must be interpreted restrictively and that it is therefore not possible to adopt a wide interpretation of the 'human health' exception contained in that provision in order to permit restrictions on substances (in the present case non-hazardous waste) which do not threaten health or life but at most the quality of life. See his first opinion (10 January 1991) at para. 20. This interpretation seems, however, to underestimate the danger for health or life created by non-hazardous waste. For example, research conducted by the US Environmental Protection Agency indicated that, presently, the risks related to solid-

is questionable. Although some kinds of waste may be more dangerous than others, the degree of dangerousness of waste does not appear to be linked with its origin.[56] From a legal point of view, the Court of Justice also created a dangerous precedent. The possibilities for arguing that differences could be attributed to the intrinsic qualities of a product and the connection with its place of production are virtually limitless.[57] This may stimulate the adoption of trade-restrictive measures and, hence, threaten the accomplishment of the internal market. Second, the Court of Justice evaded the question of proportionality. This question was essential since we have seen that trade-restrictive national measures can only be justified under the rule of reason provided that they are pertinent and represent the least restrictive means of attaining a legitimate objective.

Despite the weaknesses of the reasoning, this Court of Justice decision remains a landmark case with important implications on the relationship between trade and environmental policies, as well as on the evolution of Community waste policy. The reference to the principles of proximity and self-sufficiency contained in the Basle Convention in support of the Walloon restrictions is particularly significant. Prior to the *Belgian Waste* case, a number of authors had argued that the principles of proximity and self-sufficiency contained in the Basle Convention were not compatible with the free-trade provisions of the Treaty.[58] As a result, these principles should only apply between the Community and third states, but not between member states.[59] By expressly referring to proximity and self-

waste disposal are no less serious than the risks associated with hazardous-waste disposal. See Solid Waste Disposal Facility Criteria, codified at 40 CFR, Parts 257–8.

[56] See P. von Wilmowsky 'Waste Disposal in the Internal Market: The State of Play After the ECJ's Ruling on the Walloon Import Ban', *Common Market Law Review* 30 (1993), 541, 547. ('As foreign wastes cause no different dangers for the environment than waste of domestic provenance, the origin of the wastes seems to have no effect on the pollution caused by their disposal'). Von Wilmowsky also insists that the court's reasoning in this case may be difficult to reconcile with Case 172/82, *Interhuiles* [1983] ECR 555 where the court emphasized that 'it makes no difference from an ecological point of view whether wastes are disposed of in an [authorized] plant in the country of origin or in an [authorized] plant in another member state'.

[57] See Hancher and Sevenster, *Common Market Law Review* 30 (1993), 351 at 364.

[58] See A. Schmidt, 'Transboundary Movements of Waste under EC Law: The Emerging Regulatory Framework', *Journal of Environmental Law* 4 (1992), 57, 67; C. de Villeneuve, 'Les Mouvements Transfrontières des Déchets Dangereux (Convention de Bâle et Droit Communautaire)', *Revue du Marché Commun* (1990), 568, 576. See also D. Vandermeersch, 'Het Vrije Verkeer van Alfvalstoffen binen de Europese Gemeenschap', *Tijdschrift Voor Milieurecht* (1992), 84.

[59] See also para. 26 of the first opinion of Advocate-General Jacobs (10 January 1991) in which he indicated that the principles of proximity and self-sufficiency are in

sufficiency in support of restrictions on imports of non-domestic waste, the Court of Justice seems to contradict this position. By the same token, it also implicitly confirms the compatibility with the Treaty of the provisions of Community secondary law, such as Articles 5 and 7 of Directive 91/156 on waste,[60] which are expressly based on these principles.[61] Finally, as will be seen below, the *Belgian Waste* case has had a substantial impact on the negotiations of the Regulation on the transfrontier movements of waste which, as adopted, authorizes member states to 'object systematically' to transfrontier movements of waste in order to implement the principles of proximity and self-sufficiency.[62]

In a number of cases, the Court of Justice has also examined the compatibility with the Treaty of national measures restricting the exports of waste. For example, in *Interhuiles*,[63] the court found that French legislation for the recovery of waste oils, which provided that collectors had to deliver their waste oils to approved undertakings for disposal and that the latter had to treat the waste oils in their own facilities on pain of having their approval withdrawn, effectively prohibited the exports of waste oils and, thus, came within with the scope of the prohibition by Article 34. The court also felt that the French legislation could not be justified on environmental grounds since the need to protect the environment would be as adequately met through sale to authorized disposal undertakings in other member states as much as through sale to authorized domestic undertakings.[64] Similarly, in *Nertsvoederfabriek Nederland*,[65] the Court of Justice found that an obligation on producers to deliver poultry offal to their local authorities involved by implication a prohibi-

---

conformity with the Treaty only provided they are applied in a Community as opposed to a national framework.

[60] OJ 1991, L 78/32.

[61] See N. de Sadeleer, 'Observations – Les Limites Posées à la Libre Circulation des Déchets et Exigences de Protection de l'Environnement', *Cahiers de Droit Européen* (1993), 693.

[62] See pp. 123–5 below.

[63] Case 172/82 [1983] ECR 555, 556. This decision has since been confirmed in a number of judgments. See Case C-37/92, *Vanacker and Lesage* [1993] ECR I-4,947; Case 173/83, *Commission v. France* [1985] ECR 491; Case 295/82, *Rhône-Alpes Huiles* [1984] ECR 575, 583. For a discussion on this case law, see N. de Sadeleer, 'L'Agrément des Collectes de Déchets au Regard des Règles du Droit Communautaire', *Aménagement – Environnement* (1993/4), 238. See also S. Soumastre, 'Les Leçons d'une Expérience pour une Politique de Gestion des Déchets Industriels en France: La Récupération des Huiles Usagées' in *Les Déchets Industriels et l'Environnement* (Paris: PUF, 1984), 29.

[64] Directive 75/439 of 16 June 1975 on waste oils, OJ 1975 (L 194), 23, harmonizes the conditions for disposal of waste oils in the European Community. In this regard, it provides for a procedure of authorization of undertakings disposing waste oils.

[65] Case 118/86 [1987] ECR 3,883, 3,907.

tion on exports and, hence, was within the scope of the prohibition contained in Article 34. The court also found that, in so far as it implied a prohibition on exports, the Dutch measure could not be justified under Article 36 since a prohibition of exports was not necessary to safeguard public health.[66]

Contrary to the *Belgian Waste* case, the court decisions in *Interhuiles* and *Nertsvoederfabriek Nederland* were hardly surprising. In both cases, the court determined that the main motivation for restricting exports of waste was to ensure the profitability of local waste-disposal facilities by providing them with a sufficient quantity of waste at a low price. By contrast, the exports of waste oils and poultry offal did not create any serious threat to the environment of other member states.[67] On the other hand, it is not entirely clear how the Court of Justice would react if, independently of any protectionist objective, a member state was able to demonstrate that restrictions on the exports of certain categories of waste are necessary to protect the environment of other member states which do not possess adequate disposal facilities to deal with these wastes.[68] So far, the Court of Justice has not addressed the question of whether Article 36 or the rule of reason can be used by a member state in order to justify trade-restrictive measures designed to protect the environment of another member state.[69]

---

[66] See para. 16 of the judgment.

[67] See J. Jans, 'Self-Sufficiency in European Waste Law', *European Environmental Law Review* (1994), 223, 224 (discussing the profitability justification for restrictions on the exports of waste).

[68] This issue is of central importance since some member states appear to be prepared to restrict exports of certain categories of waste for environmental reasons. For example, the Netherlands prohibits the exports of waste when the standards of the recipient state do not meet the Dutch standards. See Decision of the 'Voorzitter van de Afdeling Geschillen van de Raad van de State' (Chairman of the Public Disputes Division of the Council of State), 23 March 1989, *Sociale-Economische Wetgeuing* (1989): cited by Jans, 'Waste Policy and European Community Law' at 174.

[69] Two Advocates-General have, however, expressed some reluctance to interpret Article 36 as allowing member states to justify trade restrictions designed to protect environmental resources located in other member states. In Case C-169/89, *van den Burg* [1990] ECR I-2,143, Advocate-General van Gerven took the view that although Article 36 'does not expressly state that the interests which it protects must be located in the legislating Member State', it would appear to be 'still less appropriate to regard that article as an encouragement to adopt legislation for the protection of interests located in other Member States': *ibid.* at 2,155. Advocate-General Trabucchi took a similar view in his opinion in Case 8/74, *Dassonville* [1974] ECR 837 where he noted that 'on the basis of [Article 36], States can derogate (to the prohibition on quantitative restrictions and measures having equivalent effect) only for the purpose of the protection of their own interests and not for the protection of the interests in other States . . . Article 36 allows

Product standards

Contrary to restrictions imposed on imports or exports of waste, environmental product standards (i.e., legal dispositions regulating the environmental characteristics of products) do not usually discriminate on their face against intra-Community trade. They may nevertheless have important effects on that trade. In this regard, two situations must be distinguished. First, there may be circumstances where, although they formally apply to both domestic and imported products, product standards discriminate in their effects against the latter. An example of this kind of discrimination would be a member state regulation prohibiting the sale of a toxic substance that is largely imported from other member states while allowing a substance of similar toxicity which is mainly manufactured by domestic producers.[70] Another example would be a member state measure prohibiting the use of cars which are not equipped with catalytic converters in order to favour domestic car producers manufacturing models equipped with such a system.[71] Second, even when they do not discriminate on their face or in their effects against imported products, product standards may nevertheless have the effect of making such imports more difficult. This may be for example the case when member states require the use of certain types of labelling or packaging.[72] Such regulations impose an extra burden on manufacturers located in other member states since they will have to meet both the standards of their own member state and those of the member state of sale, or perhaps those of several member states of sale.[73] This will increase the costs of

every State the right to protect exclusively its national interests.' For a good discussion on this question, see L. Kramer, 'Environmental Protection and Article 30 of the Treaty', *Common Market Law Review* 30 (1993), 111, 119.

[70] See, *mutatis mutandis*, Case 152/78, *Commission v. France* [1980] ECR 2,299 (French rules on the advertising of alcoholic beverages found to be discriminatory in practice against imports by subjecting imported products to control when competing national products escaped any restriction by virtue of their different categorization).

[71] See, *mutatis mutandis*, Case 433/85, *Feldain* [1987] ECR 3,521; and Case 112/84, *Humblot* [1985] ECR 1,367 (French road tax found discriminatory because, in practice, it penalized non-French powerful cars (over 16 CV) in order to favour the domestic production of small and medium-sized cars).

[72] See, e.g., the German Waste Packaging Ordinance ('Verordnung unter die Vermeidung von Verpackungsabfällen'), *Bundesgestzblatt* (*Federal Gazette*), I, 20 June 1991, 1,234, which has been strongly criticized by companies exporting to Germany as making their exports to this country extremely difficult. On 6 July 1994, the Commission decided to start legal action against the German Ordinance on the ground that it would be incompatible with Article 30 of the Treaty. See *Environment Watch*, 15 July 1994, at 1.

[73] This problem is clearly expressed by Advocate-General van Gerven in his opinion in

their products to the point where they may become uncompetitive. From the point of view of the Treaty, both discriminatory product measures and non-discriminatory measures that have restrictive effects on trade fall under the prohibition of Article 30. Provided that they pursue a legitimate environmental objective and they fulfil the test of proportionality, these measures may, however, be justified under Article 36 or the rule of reason.

The question of the compatibility with the Treaty of member state environmental product standards affecting trade arose in Case C-302/86, *Commission* v. *Denmark* (the '*Danish Bottles*' case).[74] In that case, the Commission challenged a Danish law of 2 July 1981 whose main feature was that manufacturers had to market beer and soft drinks in 'returnable containers'. According to the definition given in the implementing order, this meant that there had to be a system for collection and refill under which a large proportion of the containers sold would be refilled. In addition, the containers had to be approved by the National Agency for the Protection of the Environment ('NAPE'), which was entitled to refuse approval of a new container if it considered that the planned system of collection did not ensure that a sufficient proportion of the containers would be re-used or if a container of equal capacity, already approved and suitable for the same use, was available. Following protests from producers of beverages and containers in other member states, the Commission urged the Danish government to change the law. As a consequence of the Commission intervention, in 1984 the Danish government amended the 1981 law so as to allow the use of non-approved containers, either within well-defined limits (3,000 hl per producer per annum) or to test the market, provided that in both cases a deposit-and-return system was

Joined Cases C-401/92 and C-402/92, *Boermans* [1994] ECR I-2,199, 2,215 ('Product requirements by nature impede the access to the market of the member state which laid them down, because they mean that a product lawfully manufactured and marketed in the member state of origin must be adapted where it is imported into another member state in order to suit the product requirements in force there, and therefore have the effect of requiring the product to satisfy the requirements of two differents sets of legislation . . . In view of the costs entailed by this where the product is imported, the producer has an additional burden imposed upon him, which almost certainly has the effect of impeding the imported product's access to the market or even, when these costs are prohibitive, of making access impossible.')

[74] [1988] ECR 4,602. Noted by L. Kramer, in *European Environmental Law Casebook* (London: Sweet & Maxwell, 1994) at 91; P. Kromarek, *Journal of Environmental Law* 2 (1990), 89. See also T. Sexton, 'Enacting National Environmental Laws More Stringent than Other States' Laws in the European Community: *Re Disposal Beer Cans: Commission* v. *Denmark*', *Cornell International Law Journal* 24 (1991), 563.

established for the non-approved containers. The Commission was not satisfied with the 1984 amendment and in 1986 brought Article 169 proceedings against Denmark to have both the compulsory deposit-and-return system and the NAPE approval system declared incompatible with Article 30 of the Treaty.

In his opinion, Advocate-General Slynn supported the Commission's case and argued that both the compulsory deposit-and-return system and the NAPE approval system were in breach of the Treaty.[75] In the first place, Advocate-General Slynn found that the Danish measures were contrary to Article 30 of the Treaty and did not fall within any of the exceptions listed in Article 36.[76] Moreover, he found that the Danish measures had a discriminatory effect in that, even though on the surface indiscriminately applicable to Danish and non-Danish manufacturers, the rules bore more heavily on the latter.[77] As a result, it was not possible for Denmark to rely on the rule of reason, even if environmental protection could be considered as a mandatory requirement.[78] In addition, even if the Danish measures could be considered as indistinctly applicable, they were not proportionate to achieve the legitimate environmental aim. Although the Advocate-General admitted that the Danish legislation achieves the highest standard of environmental protection and that it may be difficult by other methods to achieve the same high standards, he considered that:

[t]here has to be a *balancing of interests* between the free movement of goods and environmental protection, even if in achieving the balance the high standard of the protection sought had to be reduced. The level of protection sought must be a *reasonable* level.[79]

Applying this formula to the Danish measures, Advocate-General Slynn stated that he was not satisfied that alternative methods, such as a voluntary deposit system or penalties for litter were 'incapable of achieving a *reasonable* standard which impinges less on the provisions of Article 30'.[80]

The court did not agree with the Advocate-General in respect of the deposit-and-return system. Applying the rule of reason, it found that the deposit-and-return system was:

---

[75] [1988] ECR 4,602 at 4,626.   [76] *Ibid.* at 4,621.
[77] For a discussion on the implications of the Danish legislation for non-Danish manufacturers, see J. Clarck and M. Arnold, 'The Danish Bottles Case' in *The Greening of World Trade* (US Environmental Protection Agency, 1993) at 161.
[78] [1988] ECR 4,602 at 4,622.   [79] *Ibid.* at 4,626 (emphasis added).
[80] *Ibid.* (emphasis added).

an indispensable element of a system intended to ensure the re-use of containers and therefore . . . *necessary* to achieve the aims pursued by the contested rules. That being so, the restrictions which it imposes on the free movement of goods cannot be regarded as disproportionate.[81]

However, as regards the NAPE approval system, the court found that by restricting the quantity of beer and soft drinks which could be marketed by a single producer in non-approved containers to 3,000 hl a year Denmark had failed to fulfil its obligations under Article 30 of the Treaty. According to the court, even though the existing system of approved containers offered a better degree of environmental protection than a system of non-approved containers:[82]

[t]he system for returning non-approved containers is capable of protecting the environment and, as far as imports are concerned, affects only limited quantities of beverage compared with the quantity of beverages consumed in Denmark owing to the restrictive effect which the requirement has on imports. In these circumstances, a restriction of the quantity of products which may be marketed by importers is *disproportionate* to the objective pursued.[83]

The court's reasoning contains some troubling elements. First, the court applied the rule of reason without raising anywhere in its decision the issue of discrimination. The court focused exclusively on the principle of proportionality. This is surprising especially since, as pointed out by Advocate-General Slynn, even though they were on their face indiscriminately applicable to Danish and non-Danish manufacturers, the Danish measures arguably placed a heavier burden on the latter.[84] The court should have at least questioned the applicability of the rule of reason.[85]

Second, the analysis by the court of the proportionality of the Danish measures is ambiguous.[86] When the court analysed the proportionality of the deposit-and-return system it did so against the background of Denmark's very high rate of reutilization of empty bottles. This implies

---

[81] *Ibid.* at 4,630 (emphasis added).

[82] Empty approved containers can be returned to any retailer of beverages whereas non-approved containers can be returned only to the retailer who sold the beverage.

[83] [1988] ECR 4,602 at 4,632 (emphasis added).

[84] *Ibid.* at 4,625.

[85] Compare the attitude of the court in Case 207/83, *Commission* v. *United Kingdom* [1985] ECR 1,202; Case 177/83, *Kohl* [1984] ECR 3,651; Case 113/80, *Commission* v. *Ireland* [1981] ECR 1,625 (court refusing to apply the rule of reason to national measures discriminating against imported products). But see the approach taken by the court in Case C-2/90, *Commission* v. *Belgium* [1992] ECR I-4,431 (applying the rule of reason to national measures which appeared to be discriminatory on their face).

[86] On the principle of proportionality and its lack of clarity in the court's case law, see J. Jans, 'Envenredigheid: Ja, Maar Wartussen?' *Sociale-Economische Wetgeving* (1992), 751.

that the court will take for granted the level of protection chosen by a member state (even if that level is very high) and thus will assess only whether the restrictions resulting from the measure in question are effective and essential to achieve the aims adopted by the member state. By contrast when the court examined the NAPE approval system and the 3,000 hl limit, it considered them in the context of the more general objective of environmental protection. The court then estimated that this general objective could be sufficiently satisfied by the deposit-and-return system and, hence, that the extra burden the NAPE approval system imposed on intra-Community trade was disproportionate in relation to the marginal increase in environmental protection (compared with the level of protection already ensured by a deposit-and-return system) such a system guaranteed. Although this part of the judgment is not entirely clear, it seems that the court in effect balanced the level of environmental protection sought by the member state against the harm to intra-Community trade, and reduced the level of environmental protection that the member state could choose.[87] This suggests that the court in practice follows a position very similar to Advocate-General Slynn who argued that the level of environmental protection chosen by the member state should not be unreasonable.

It is not easy to assess the potential impact of *Danish Bottles* on the relationship between trade and environmental protection in the Community market. On the one hand, some perceived that, by upholding the Danish deposit-and-return system, the Court of Justice gave a green light to pro-environment member states to develop their own schemes of environmental protection even if at the expense of the unity of the internal market. This would in turn lead to a proliferation of inconsistent product standards the with resulting risks of market fragmentation.[88] On

---

[87] Elsewhere, Raoul Stewardson and I have argued that in the *Danish Bottles* case, the court moved from a traditional necessity test (assessing the pertinence of national measures and the availability of less restrictive alternatives) to a new more intrusive proportionality (in the strict sense) test (assessing whether or not the burden national measures impose on intra-Community trade is worth the objective they seek to protect). We also warned that one of the implications of the development of this new test may be an increased control by the Court of Justice over certain subject areas traditionally within the control of the member states. See D. Geradin and R. Stewardson, 'Trade and Environment: Some Lessons from Castlemaine Tooheys (Australia) and Danish Bottles (European Community)', *International and Comparative Law Quarterly* 44 (1995), 41.

[88] See, e.g., 'The Freedom to be Cleaner than the Rest', *The Economist*, 14 October 1989, at 21. See also L. Gormley, 'Recent Case Law on the Free Movement of Goods: Some Hot Potatoes', *Common Market Law Review* 27 (1990), 825, 846.

the other hand, the second part of the judgment, which deals with the NAPE approval system and the 3,000 hl limit, suggests that the degree of scrutiny that the Court of Justice is prepared to apply to trade-restrictive environmental measures is important. In particular, the court seems prepared to control whether the level of protection chosen by a member state is reasonable (when balanced against the Community interest in the free movement of goods) and, when this level is perceived as unreasonable, to reduce it. This approach, however, appears to be in contradiction with the previous case law of the court, pursuant to which, provided that the measures adopted pursue a legitimate objective and are necessary (i.e., are pertinent and are the least restrictive method available) to attain that objective, it is the responsibility of the member states to choose the level of health, safety or environmental protection they wish.[89] Although suggested in several cases by Advocate-General van Gerven,[90] the more intrusive balancing approach developed by the court in *Danish Bottles* has not been confirmed in its more recent case law.[91]

The implications of the *Danish Bottles* case are therefore rather unclear. Although the Court of Justice made clear that environmental protection qualifies as a mandatory requirement and may therefore in certain circumstances take precedence over the free movement of goods it is not entirely clear how far the member states can go.[92] In this context, it will

---

[89] This is particularly clear in Case 174/82, *Sandoz* [1983] ECR 2,445, 2,463 ('in so far as there are uncertainties at the present state of scientific research it is for the Member States, in the absence of harmonization, to decide what degree of protection of health and life of humans they intend to assure'). See also Case 125/88, *Nijman* [1989] ECR 3,533, 3,549; Case 272/80, *Biologische Producten* [1981] ECR 3,277, 3,291; Case 93/80, *Eyssen* [1981] ECR 409, 422.

[90] See, e.g., his opinion in Case C-169/89, *van den Burg* [1990] ECR I-2,143, 2,164 ('[T]he restriction of intra-Community trade resulting from an absolute prohibition of imports in the Netherlands is *out of proportion* . . . to the small contribution such a prohibition is capable in concreto . . . to the achievement of the objective pursued, namely the improvement of stocks of bird species which is not endangered and whose protection is not a priority under Community law') (emphasis added); and Case C-169/91, *Stoke-on-Trent* v. *B&Q* [1992] ECR I-6,335 ('even if the national measure is effective and essential with regard to the objective pursued, it must be determined whether the restriction caused thereby to intra-Community trade is in relation, that is to say *proportionate* to that objective') (emphasis added). A summary of Advocate-General van Gerven's views on this issue can be found in 'Principle de Proportionalité, Abus de Droit et Droits Fondamentaux', *Journal des Tribunaux* (1992), 305–9.

[91] In Cases C-2/90, *Commission* v. *Belgium* [1992] ECR I-4,431 (discussed at pp. 17–21 above) and C-169/89, *van den Burg* [1990] ECR I-2,143, the court failed to take a position on this issue.

[92] See D. Demiray, 'The Movement of Goods in a Green Market', *Legal Issues of European Integration* (1994/1), 73, 91.

be the task of the court in subsequent cases to define better the boundaries of Article 30 of the Treaty when this provision applies to environmental product standards.

Process standards

As we have seen in the preceding subsection, member states may decide to regulate the environmental characteristics of the products sold on their market (product standards). Such standards will generally be applied to both domestic and imported products and the imported products which do not comply with such standards will not have market access.[93] It is not clear, however, what would happen if a member state decided to deny market access to certain products not because they do not conform to their product standards but because they have been produced according to production methods that do not conform to their environmental process standards.[94] It should be noted at the outset that so far member states have refrained from using such restrictions (hereafter 'process-related trade restrictions') and there is no relevant case law. Some states have, however, adopted such restrictions at the international level and process-related trade restrictions have become an issue of central importance in the context of GATT.[95] In this context, it is interesting to

---

[93] Although they may be extended to imported products, product standards may nevertheless be found incompatible with the Treaty when their effect is to discriminate against these products or when they are found to impose a disproportionate burden on intra-Community trade.

[94] Generally on the distinction between product and process standards, see pp. 2–3 above.

[95] In *US – Restrictions on Imports of Tuna*, Basic Documents and Selected Documents BISD 39S/155, reprinted in ILM 30 (1991), 1,594, a panel found that a US ban on imports of tuna caught on the high seas by fishing boats that failed to comply with US restrictions on the incidental take of dolphins were not compatible with GATT. The ban was designed both to protect the environment and to eliminate the competitive disadvantage suffered by US fishing fleets that complied with such restrictions. This panel decision generated an enormous controversy since environmentalists perceived it as exaggeratedly interfering with domestic environmental policies. For a discussion on this case, see R. Housman and D. Zaelke, 'The Collision of Environment and Trade: The GATT/Dolphin Decision', *Environmental Law Reporter* 22 (1992), 10,268. The US ban on tuna imports was again found incompatible with GATT by a second panel. See *US – Restrictions on the Imports of Tuna*, reprinted in ILM 33 (1994), 839. For a discussion on this second panel decision, see S. Charnovitz, 'Dolphins and Tuna: An Analysis of the Second Panel Report', *Environmental Law Reporter* 24 (1994), 10,567. Generally on the problems created by the application of domestic process standards to imported products, see E. U. Petersmann, 'International Trade and International Environmental Law', *Journal of World Trade* 16 (1993), 43, 68; J. Jackson, 'World Trade and Environmental Policies: Congruence or Conflict?' *Washington and Lee Law Review* 49 (1992), 1,227, 1,242.

speculate on how the Court of Justice would react if a member state decided to adopt such restrictions.

Before examining the compatibility with the Treaty of process-related trade restrictions, the question must be asked in what circumstances member states might be tempted to resort to such restrictions. In this regard, it is important to recall that, although process standards do not in themselves create barriers to trade, variations in the level of stringency of process standards enforced by the member states may create distortions of competition and incentives for industrial relocation. Because their costs of production will be lower, producers located in member states enforcing lax process standards gain a competitive advantage over producers located in member states enforcing stricter standards. When this competitive advantage becomes important, producers located in member states enforcing stricter standards may also be tempted to relocate in member states enforcing laxer standards.[96] Although the adoption by a member state of lax process standards may be a genuine reflection of a lower domestic preference for environmental quality or of a higher local pollution assimilation capacity,[97] it may also be part of a strategy of competitive deregulation whereby the member state attempts to give a competitive advantage to its industry and to attract new investment opportunities by relaxing the regulatory burden applicable to the producers operating on its territory.[98] The difficulty in this context is that the

---

[96] Industrial relocation occurs 'whenever the reduction in the expected costs of complying with the environmental standards is lower than the transactions costs involved in moving': R. Revesz, 'Rehabilitating Interstate Competition: Rethinking the "Race-To-The-Bottom" Rationale for Federal Environmental Regulation', New York University Law Review 67 (1992), 1,210, 1,215. By reducing the transaction costs met by producers when they move from one member state to another, the increased economic integration brought about by the 1992 internal market process should generally facilitate and stimulate industrial relocation.

[97] It might also be the reflection of a member state's ability to externalize the costs of environmental degradation to other member states. For example, for many years, Britain failed to control sulphur emissions from its power plants because the adverse effects were mainly felt abroad. See R. Stewart, 'Environmental Regulation and International Competitiveness', Yale Law Journal 102 (1993), 2,039, 2,054.

[98] See J. Trachtman, 'International Regulatory Competition, Externalization and Jurisdiction', Harvard International Law Journal 34 (1992), 48, 56 ('By absorbing the environmental costs of production, in a context where the environmental costs of production might otherwise be charged to the producer, a particular society can assist its producers by lowering their costs of competing on either domestic or foreign markets'). It should be noted that regulatory competition is not unique to environmental control but has been observed in a variety of areas of regulation. For example, the so-called 'Delaware Effect' has been extensively discussed in the area of company law. See, e.g., D. Charny, 'Competition Among Jurisdictions in Formulating

traditional free-movement-of-goods case law of the Court of Justice offers little protection to member states affected by the fact that other member states adopt lax process standards. Although the adoption of lax process standards may create distortions of competition, it does not create the kinds of barriers to trade susceptible of falling within the scope of Article 30 of the Treaty. Moreover, even if lax process standards could be challenged under this provision, it would be extremely difficult for the court to determine to what extent these standards are excessively lax and, thus, distort commerce.[99] It is therefore not possible for a member state to base a claim on Article 30 to compel other member states to increase their level of pollution controls.[100]

In this context, a possible answer for a member state which is economically affected by other member states' lax process standards would be to attempt to apply its own process standards to products imported from member states applying lax standards. For example, that member state could decide to ban or submit to various restrictions imports of cars which, although they respect its own motor-vehicle-exhaust-emission standards, have been produced in factories that do not enforce environmental process standards as stringent as its own process standards.[101] Car-producing member states applying lax process standards would therefore have to raise their process standards in order to be able to export to the member state applying these restrictions.

Corporate Rules: An American Perspective on the "Race to the Bottom" in the European Communities', *Harvard International Law Journal* 32 (1991), 423. In the area of fiscal competition, see C. Tiebout, 'A Pure Theory of Local Expenditures', *Journal of Political Economy* 64 (1956), 416.

[99] See R. Stewart, 'International Trade and the Environment: Lessons from the Federal Experience', *Washington and Lee Law Review* 49 (1992), 1,329, 1,342.

[100] One may of course argue that process-related trade restrictions should not be examined under Article 30 but under Article 92 of the Treaty which deals with state aids. As observed at note 98, p. 30 above, by reducing the regulatory burden applicable to its producers, a member state effectively assists them. Although the concept of 'state aid' contained in Article 92 is relatively elastic, it does not go as far as to include regulatory subsidies. See, e.g., Case C-72 and 73/91, *Sloman Neptun* [1993] ECR I-887; (holding that state aid under Article 92 necessarily represents a budgetary expenditure or a loss of public revenue). See also M. Slotboom, 'State Aid in Community Law: A Broad or Narrow Definition?' *European Law Review* 20 (1995), 289. Article 92 offers therefore no additional support to a member state economically affected by another member state's lax process standards.

[101] For the sake of the analysis, I start here with the assumption that such process standards have not been harmonized at Community level. As will be seen below, Community harmonization is the only valid option to deal with the distortions of competition created by inconsistent process standards and the Community has extensively harmonized such standards.

As already noted, member states have never attempted to use such restrictions and there is no relevant case law. It is unlikely, however, that process-related trade restrictions of the kind described above would be upheld by the Court of Justice.[102] As they have an impact on intra-Community trade, such restrictions would fall under the scope of Article 30 of the Treaty. The question would therefore become whether they would be justified under Article 36 of the Treaty or the rule of reason.[103] In this context, a first difficulty would come from the fact that these exceptions only provide justification for trade-restrictive measures that further non-economic objectives. The equalization of production costs, that would be sought by member states whose industrial competitiveness is affected by other member states' lax process standards, cannot therefore be considered as an objective to be protected under these exceptions. A member state adopting process-related trade restrictions could perhaps invoke the fact that such restrictions are necessary to protect the environment against the detrimental effects that may be generated by other member states' lax environmental practices.[104] If this justification was admitted, the member state invoking such restrictions would then have to demonstrate that they are proportionate and, in particular, that they represent the least restrictive way of attaining the objective sought. It is likely, however, that, in most cases, approaches that are less restrictive on trade, such as consultations with the member states concerned or the use

[102] Even if these restrictions were to be admitted, they would not be very effective since the export industries of the member states imposing the restrictions would still be penalized in all other member states where their products must compete with those of the member state imposing lax standards. See E. Rehbinder and R. Stewart, 'Environmental Protection Policy' in Cappelletti *et al.* (eds.), *Integration through Law* (Walter de Gruyter, 1985), vol. I, at 287.

[103] It is doubtful, however, whether the Court of Justice would accept that a member state could justify process-related trade restrictions under the rule of reason. Such restrictions seem indeed to present an element of discrimination on their face. Although they have the same physical characteristics as freely marketed domestic products, some non-domestic products will nevertheless be banned because they have been produced in an environmentally harmful fashion. It is only if the Court of Justice accepted that products manufactured following clean processes and products manufactured following environmentally harmful processes are different that such an element of discrimination would be absent.

[104] A difficulty would, however, appear concerning the location of the environmental resources to be protected. Although the Court of Justice has recognized that a member state may, in certain circumstances, adopt trade restrictions in order to protect its environment, it is not certain that trade restrictions would be admitted in order to protect environmental resources that are part of the global commons or that are located within the territory of other member states.

of labelling provisions indicating the methods of production following which the products offered for sale have been produced,[105] could be found. In this context, it is unlikely that process-related trade restrictions could be justified under Article 36 or the rule of reason.[106]

---

[105] An example of labelling provisions designed to inform the consumers about the methods of production following which products offered for sale have been produced is the indication on tuna cans of whether the tuna contained in the can has been fished in a dolphin-friendly manner.

[106] Although it goes beyond the scope of this study, it is interesting to note that a member state could perhaps achieve a similar result through the imposition of process-related environmental taxes. In a number of cases, the Court of Justice has admitted that member states could adopt differential treatment on the basis of the production methods by which goods are manufactured. See, e.g., Case 243/84, *John Walker* [1986] ECR 875, 881; Case 140/79, *Chemial Pharmaceutici* [1981] ECR 1, 7. One way of removing the competitive advantage enjoyed by products manufactured under lax process standards would be therefore for a member state to tax domestic companies depending on the impact of their activities on the environment and then apply a border tax adjustment on imported products. For reasons discussed at note 102 above, such adjustments would not, however, be entirely effective to ensure a level playing field. See P. Demaret and R. Stewardson, 'Border Tax Adjustments under GATT and EC Law and General Implications for Environmental Taxes', *Journal of World Trade* 28 (1994), 5, 52.

2 The case law of the Supreme Court

The principle of free trade

The textual source of the Supreme Court's authority to review the constitutionality of state measures interfering with trade is to be found in Article I, section 8 of the Constitution (the 'Commerce Clause'), which in its relevant part reads: 'The Congress shall have the power . . . to regulate commerce with foreign Nations, and among the several states.' On its face, the Commerce Clause appears to be a grant of authority to Congress to regulate commerce rather than a limitation on state activity when Congress has not acted. However, acknowledging the framers' intention to create a common market and to avoid economic balkanization of the Union, the Supreme Court has long recognized that the Commerce Clause also contains a 'dormant' dimension that operates as a prohibition on interferences with commerce by the states.[1] 'The very purpose of the Commerce Clause,' the court has written, 'was to create an area of free trade among the several states.'[2] Yet, the objective of ensuring free

---

[1] This prohibition was first recognized in *Gibbons* v. *Ogden*, 22 US 1 (1824), 1, 209–11 (1824). On the dormant commerce clause, see generally M. Redish and S. Nugent, 'The Dormant Commerce Clause and the Constitutional Balance of Federalism', *Duke Law Journal* (1987), 569; D. Regan, 'The Supreme Court and State Protectionism: Making Sense of the Dormant Commerce Clause', *Michigan Law Review* 84 (1986), 1,091; D. Farber, 'State Regulation and the Dormant Commerce Clause', *Constitutional Commentary* 3 (1986), 395; M. Smith, 'State Discrimination Against Interstate Commerce', *California Law Review* 74 (1986), 1,203; J. Eule, 'Laying the Dormant Commerce Clause to Rest', *Yale Law Journal* 91 (1982), 425; E. Maltz, 'How Much Regulation is Too Much – An Examination of Commerce Clause Jurisprudence', *George Washington Law Review* 50 (1981), 47; M. Tushnet, 'Rethinking the Dormant Commerce Clause', *Wisconsin Law Review* (1979), 125.

[2] *McLeod* v. *J. E. Dilworth Co.*, 322 US 327, 330 (1944). See also *H. P. Hood & Sons Inc.* v. *Du Mond*, 336 US 525, 537–8 (1949) ('This principle that our economic unit is the Nation, which alone has the gamut of powers necessary to control of the economy, has as its corollary that the states are not separable units . . . What is ultimate is the principle

interstate trade has not been construed as an absolute prohibition on state measures interfering with commerce.[3] In this context, an important task for the court has been to develop devices for distinguishing between permissible and impermissible state interferences with commerce.

Since its first recognition of a dormant dimension in the Commerce Clause more than one and a half centuries ago, the Supreme Court has experimented with a variety of formulations for the Commerce Clause limitation upon the states.[4] In the first century of its Commerce Clause case law, the Supreme Court usually resorted to legal tests based on formalistic criteria such as the nature or the purpose of the measure challenged. In its more recent case law, the Supreme Court has rather focused on the burden imposed on interstate trade by state measures, such a burden being generally weighed against the local benefits the measures aim to promote. A constant element in the Supreme Court's case law, however, has been the difference of treatment between discriminatory and non-discriminatory measures, the former being subject to a higher level of scrutiny than the latter.

Discriminatory measures

The level of scrutiny applied by the Supreme Court to discriminatory state measures has been traditionally very high. The existence of a discrimina-

---

that one state in its dealings with another may not place itself in a position of economic isolation.')

[3] See, e.g., *American Can Co.* v. *Oregon Liquor Control Commission*, 517 P. 2d 691 (1973) ('The purpose of the Commerce Clause . . . was to assure the commercial enterprises in every state substantial equality of access to a free national market. It was not meant to usurp the police power of the states which was reserved under the Tenth Amendment. Therefore, although most exercises of the police power affect interstate commerce to some degree, not every such exercise is invalid under the Commerce Clause').

[4] See, e.g., *Southern Pacific Co.* v. *Arizona*, 325 US 761, 781–2 (1945) (balancing state and national interests). In a prior era, the Supreme Court relied on more formalistic approaches to distinguish between valid and invalid state laws. See, e.g., *Real Silk Mills* v. *Portland*, 268 US 325 (1925) (disallowing 'direct' state regulation against commerce); *Welton* v. *Missouri*, 91 US 275 (1875) (establishing the so-called anti-discrimination principle); *Cooley* v. *Board of Wardens*, 53 US 229, 319 (1851) (holding the that state may regulate matters which are local and susceptible to diverse treatment but may not regulate matters which require uniform 'national' legislation); *Gibbons* v. *Ogden*, 22 US 1 (1824) 1, 209–11 (1824) (denying the right of states to regulate interstate commerce as such). For a historical perspective on these different approaches, see K. Lenaerts, *Le Juge et la Constitution aux Etats-Unis d'Amérique et dans l'Ordre Juridique Européen* (Brussels: Bruylant, 1988), 142–76; L. Tribe, *American Constitutional Law* (Minolea, NY: Foundation Press, 2nd edn, 1988), 403*ff*; V. Blasi, 'Constitutional Limitations on the Power of States to Regulate the Movement of Goods in Interstate Commerce' in Sandalow and Stein (eds.), *Courts and Free Markets* (Oxford University Press, 1982), 174, 176–87.

tory treatment in a state action is indeed generally a strong indication that the state is trying to protect local interests at the expense of out-of-state ones, no matter what justification the state relies upon as a basis for its action. The test applied by the Supreme Court to discriminatory state measures is to be found in *Dean Milk* v. *City of Madison*.[5] In that case, the court examined the validity of an ordinance of the city of Madison, Wisconsin, that made it unlawful to sell any milk as pasteurized unless it had been processed and bottled at an approved pasteurization plant within a radius of five miles from the central square of Madison. Although it formally applied to all milk produced in Madison or elsewhere, the ordinance discriminated against interstate commerce since it rendered considerably more difficult the marketing of milk produced outside Madison.[6] The test applied by the Supreme Court to the Madison ordinance can be found in the following passage:

In thus erecting an economic barrier protecting a major local industry against competition from without the state, Madison plainly discriminates against interstate commerce. This it cannot do, even in the exercise of the unquestioned power to protect the health and safety of its people, if reasonable *non-discriminatory alternatives*, adequate to conserve *legitimate local interests*, are available.[7]

Pursuant to this test, a state measure which discriminates against interstate commerce on its face or in its effects is to be examined under a rebuttable presumption of invalidity: the measure will only be upheld if it furthers a legitimate state goal and there are no reasonable non-discriminatory alternatives.[8]

In a number of cases, the Supreme Court has admitted that environmental protection, including the protection of the life and health of humans and animals, was among the legitimate local interests mentioned in the *Dean Milk* test.[9] For example, in *Hughes* v. *Oklahoma*, the Supreme

---

[5] 340 US 349 (1951). See also, *Healy* v. *The Beer Institute Inc.*, 491 US 324 (1989); *New Energy Company of Indiana* v. *Limbach*, 486 US 269 (1988); *Sporhase* v. *Nebraska*, 458 US 941 (1982); *Lewis* v. *B. T. Investment Managers Inc.*, 447 US 27 (1980).

[6] 340 US 349 (1951) at 354.   [7] *Ibid.*

[8] For a clear illustration of this presumption, see *Hunt* v. *Washington State Apple Advertising Commission*, 432 US 333 (1977) ('[w]hen discrimination against interstate commerce . . . is demonstrated, the *burden falls on the state* to justify it both in terms of the local benefits flowing from the statute and the unavailability of non-discriminatory alternatives adequate to preserve the local interests at stake') (emphasis added).

[9] See, e.g., *C&A Carbone Inc.* v. *Town of Clarckstown*, 114 S. Ct 1,677 (1994); *Oregon Waste Systems Inc.* v. *Department of Environmental Quality*, 114 S. Ct 1,345 (1994); *Fort Gratiot Sanitary Landfill Inc.* v. *Michigan Department of Natural Resources*, 112 S. Ct 2,019 (1992); *Chemical Waste Management Inc.* v. *Hunt*, 112 S. Ct 2,009 (1992); *Maine* v. *Taylor*, 477 US 131 (1986).

Court examined the compatibility with the Commerce Clause of an Oklahoma law prohibiting out-of-state shipments of minnows.[10] The court first recognized that this law discriminated on its face against interstate commerce. Applying *Dean Milk*, it then indicated that '[a]t a minimum such facial discrimination invokes the strictest scrutiny of any purported *legitimate local purpose* and of *absence of non-discriminatory alternatives*'.[11] The court considered 'the states' interests in conservation and protection of wild animals as legitimate local purposes similar to the states' interests in protecting the health and safety of their citizens'.[12] The Oklahoma ban on exports on minnows was, however, struck down as the court felt that Oklahoma had chosen 'to "conserve" its minnows in the way that most overtly discriminated against interstate commerce'.[13]

Non-discriminatory measures

Although they may not hide any protectionist motives, non-discriminatory state measures may nevertheless subvert the scheme of an integrated national market by rendering interstate trade more difficult or even, in some circumstances, impossible. Rather than automatically upholding such measures, the Supreme Court has usually attempted to balance the burden they impose on interstate commerce against the local benefits they aim to achieve. The standard balancing test applied to non-discriminatory measures affecting interstate trade is set forth in *Pike* v. *Bruce Church*:

[W]here the statute regulates *even-handedly* to effectuate a *legitimate level public interest*, and its effects on interstate commerce are only incidental, it will be *upheld unless the burden imposed on such commerce is clearly excessive* in relation to the putative local benefits ... If a legitimate local interest is found, then the question becomes one of degree and the extent of the burden that will be tolerated will of course depend on the nature of the local interests involved, and

---

[10] 441 US 322 (1979).

[11] *Ibid.* at 337 (emphasis added).

[12] *Ibid.*

[13] In this regard, the court explained that Oklahoma 'places no limits on the number of minnows that can be taken by licensed minnow dealers; nor does it limit in any way how these minnows may be disposed of within the state. Yet it forbids the transportation of any commercially significant number of natural minnows out of the state for sale. [The ban] is certainly not a "last ditch" attempt at conservation after non-discriminatory alternatives have proved unfeasible. It is rather a choice of the most discriminatory means even though non-discriminatory alternatives would seem likely to fulfil the state's purported legitimate local purpose more effectively.': *ibid.* at 338.

on whether it could be promoted as well with lesser impact on interstate activities.[14]

Under the *Pike* test a non-discriminatory measure pursuing a legitimate objective (including health, safety and environmental protection) and affecting interstate trade in an incidental manner is examined under a rebuttable presumption of validity: the measure will be upheld unless it is demonstrated that the burden imposed by such a measure on trade is disproportionate in relation to the putative local benefits.[15]

Raymond Motor Transportation Inc. v. *Rice*[16] illustrates this test. In *Raymond*, the Supreme Court examined the compatibility with the Commerce Clause of Wisconsin regulations which generally prevented the operation on state highways of trucks longer than fifty-five feet and of double-trailer trucks. Since other states authorized the operation of such trucks, common carriers were subject to inconsistent requirements. The court started its reasoning by recalling that the test applicable to this case involved 'a sensitive consideration of the weight and nature of the state regulatory concern in light of the extent of the burden imposed on the course of interstate commerce'.[17] The court then stated that, in its previous case law, it had been traditionally deferential to state highway-safety regulations and that those who would challenge such regulations must overcome 'a strong presumption of [their] validity'.[18] In light of the evidence submitted by the parties, the court nevertheless found that the Wisconsin regulations violated the Commerce Clause because 'they place a substantial burden on interstate commerce and they cannot be said to make more than the most speculative contribution to highway safety'.[19] *Raymond* was confirmed a few years later in *Kassel* v. *Consolidated Freightways*[20] where the Supreme Court invalidated an Iowa statute prohibiting the use of sixty-five-foot double-trailer trucks within its borders because

---

[14] 397 US 137, 142 (1970) (emphasis added). The first cases to use a balancing approach to assess non-discriminatory statutes were *Southern Pacific Co.* v. *Arizona*, 325 US 761 (1945) and *Parker* v. *Brown*, 317 US 341 (1942). Justice Stone urged the adoption of a balancing approach earlier in *Disanto* v. *Pennsylvania*, 273 US 34, 44 (1927). An influential article was N. Dowling, 'Interstate Commerce and State Power', *Virginia Law Review* 27 (1940), 1.

[15] Compare *Dean Milk* v. *City of Madison*, 340 US 349 (1951) (discussed at p. 36 above) which establishes a rebuttable presumption of invalidity with regard to discriminatory state measures.

[16] 434 US 429 (1978).   [17] *Ibid.* at 441.   [18] *Ibid.* at 444.   [19] *Ibid.* at 447.

[20] 450 US 662 (1981). For further applications of the *Pike* test, see *Northwest Central Pipeline Corporation* v. *State Corporation Commission of Kansas*, 489 US 493 (1989); *CTS Corp.* v. *Dynamics Corp.*, 107 S. Ct 1,637 (1987); *Minnesota* v. *Clover Leaf Creamery Company*, 449 US 456 (1981); *Bibb* v. *Navajo Freight Lines Inc.*, 359 US 520 (1959).

safety interests promoted by the statute were illusory and it significantly impaired the federal interest in efficient interstate transportation.

The application of the principle

In this section, I will discuss the Supreme Court cases specifically dealing with state environmental-protection measures affecting interstate trade.[21] As in the context of European Community law, I will distinguish between these cases depending on whether they apply to waste, product standards or process standards.[22]

Waste

In a number of cases, the Supreme Court has examined the compatibility with the Commerce Clause of state legislation restricting the imports or the exports of waste.

First, in *City of Philadelphia* v. *New Jersey*,[23] the Supreme Court held to be unconstitutional a New Jersey statute prohibiting the import of most

---

[21] Generally on the impact of the dormant Commerce Clause on trade-restrictive state environmental measures, see R. Stewart, 'Interstate Commerce, Environmental Protection and US Federal Law' in Cameron, Demaret and Geradin (eds.), *Trade and the Environment – The Search for Balance* (London: Cameron & May, 1994) at 342; I. Lefton, 'Constitutional Law – Commerce Clause: Local Discrimination in Environmental Protection Regulation', *North Carolina Law Review* 55 (1977), 461; Note, 'State Environmental Protection Legislation and the Commerce Clause', *Harvard Law Review* 87 (1974), 1,762.

[22] For a recent and excellent review of these cases, see M. Gold, 'Solid Waste Management and the Constitution's Commerce Clause', *Urban Lawyer* 25 (1993), 21. See also J. Pancoast and L. Payne, 'Hazardous Waste in Interstate Commerce: The Triumph of Law over Logic', *Ecology Law Quarterly* 20 (1993), 817; J. Henshaw, 'The Dormant Commerce Clause After *Garcia*: An Application to Interstate Commerce of Sanitary Landfill Space', *Indiana Law Journal* 67 (1992), 511, 534–7; A. Ziebarth, 'Environmental Law: Solid Waste Transport and Disposal Across State Lines – The Commerce Clause versus Garbage Crisis', *Annual Survey of American Law* (1990), 365.

[23] *City of Philadelphia* v. *State of New Jersey*, 437 US 617 (1978). Generally on *Philadelphia* and its consequences, see S. Johnson, 'Beyond *City of Philadelphia* v. *New Jersey*', *Dickinson Law Review* 95 (1990), 131; D. Pomper, 'Recycling *Philadelphia* v. *New Jersey*: The Dormant Commerce Clause, Postindustrial Natural Resources, and the Solid Waste Crisis', *University of Pennsylvania Law Review* 137 (1989), 1,309; S. Brietzke, 'Hazardous Waste in Interstate Commerce: Minimizing the Problem After *City of Philadelphia* v. *New Jersey*', *Valparaiso University Law Review* 24 (1989), 77; A. Danzig, 'The Commerce Clause and Interstate Waste Disposal: New Jersey's Options after the *Philadelphia* Decision', *Rutgers–Camden Law Journal* 11 (1979), 31; Note, 'Waste Embargoes Held a Violation of Commerce Clause: *Philadelphia* v. *New Jersey*', *Connecticut Law Review* 11 (1979), 292; R. Dister and J. Schlesinger, 'State Waste Embargoes Violate the Commerce Clause: *City of Philadelphia* v. *New Jersey*', *Ecology Law Quarterly* 8 (1979), 371.

solid or liquid waste which originated or was collected outside the
territorial limit of the state. In considering the Commerce Clause implications of the New Jersey statute, the court first rejected the notion that
waste is not an item of commerce. As the court stated: '[a]ll objects of
interstate trade merit Commerce Clause protection; none is excluded at
the outset.'[24] The court also refused to resolve the disagreement between
the parties as to the true purpose of the legislation. New Jersey argued
that the purpose was to protect the state's environment and the health,
safety and general welfare of its citizens by slowing the flow of waste into
New Jersey landfill sites. The applicants, on the other hand, contended
that the real purpose was economic in that the law was intended to
stabilize the cost of waste disposal for New Jersey residents. The Supreme
Court conceded that either argued purpose would legitimately support
the statute.[25] However, in the court's view, the goals of the legislation
were irrelevant to the analysis of the legislation's constitutionality
because 'the evil of protectionism can reside in legislative means as well
as legislative ends'.[26] The court assumed that New Jersey could accomplish
this goal 'by slowing the flow of all waste into the scarce landfills, even
though interstate commerce would incidentally be affected'.[27] But the
state could not accomplish its objectives, however worthy, by means
which discriminated against 'articles of commerce coming from outside
the state unless there is some reason, *apart from their origin*, to treat them
differently'.[28] There was neither argument nor evidence that out-of-state
waste was more noxious that the domestic variety, and thus New Jersey's
law was treated as typical protectionist legislation, subject to a 'virtually
per se rule of invalidity'.[29]

The issue of restrictions on the imports of waste was again examined by

---

[24] 437 US at 622.   [25] *Ibid.* at 626.   [26] *Ibid.*   [27] *Ibid.*

[28] *Ibid.* (emphasis added).

[29] *Ibid.* at 624. It is important to note that, in *Philadelphia*, the Supreme Court suggested
that its ruling might not apply in cases in which the state or local governments act as
a market participant rather than a regulator (the 'market-participant doctrine'). See
437 US at 618, note 6. As a result, since *Philadelphia*, federal and state court decisions
have held that state, county or municipal landfills may discriminate against or even
prohibit out-of-state waste without violating the dormant Commerce Clause. See e.g.,
Swin Resource Sys. v. *Lycoming County*, 883 F. 2d 245 (3rd Cir. 1989), cert. denied, 493 US
1,077 (1990); *Lefrancois* v. *Rhode Island*, 669 F. Supp. 1,204 (RI 1987); *Evergreen Waste Sys.* v.
Metropolitan Service District, 643 F. Supp. 127 (Or. 1986), affirmed on other grounds, 820
F. 2d 1,482 (9th Cir. 1987); *Shayne Bros. Inc.* v. *District of Columbia*, 592 F. Supp. 1,128 (DC
1984); *County Commissioners of Charles County* v. *Stevens*, 299 Md 203, 473 A. 2d 12 (Md
App. 1984). On the market-participant doctrine, see D. Coenen, 'Untangling the Market-
Participant Exemption in the Dormant Commerce Clause', *Michigan Law Review* 88
(1989), 395. Given state and local governments own or operate approximately 80 per

the Supreme Court in *Fort Gratiot Sanitary Landfill Inc.* v. *Michigan Department of Natural Resources.*[30] At question in the *Fort Gratiot* case was the compatibility with the Commerce Clause of the waste-import restrictions of Michigan's Solid Waste Management Act ('SWMA') which provided that solid waste generated in another county, state or country was not to be accepted for disposal unless explicitly authorized in the receiving county's plan. The court started its reasoning by saying that *Philadelphia* v. *New Jersey* provided the framework for analysis.[31] For the court, a state statute clearly discriminating against interstate commerce was unconstitutional 'unless the discrimination [was] demonstrably justified by a valid factor unrelated to economic protectionism'.[32] The waste restrictions enacted by Michigan could not satisfy this test. Indeed, Michigan had not identified 'any reason, *apart from its origin*, why solid waste coming from outside the county should be treated differently from solid waste within the county'.[33] The Michigan restrictions therefore authorized each of the eighty-three Michigan counties to 'isolate itself from the national economy'.[34]

The State of Michigan attempted to distinguish the case from *Philadelphia* v. *New Jersey* in that waste-import restrictions contained in the SWMA did not discriminate against interstate commerce on their face or in effect because they treated waste from other Michigan counties no differently than waste from other states. Applying the more lenient *Pike* test, Michigan claimed that its statute regulated even-handedly in order to pursue legitimate local interests and should be upheld because the burden on interstate commerce was not clearly excessive in relation to the local benefits. The court, however, disagreed, stating that 'a State may not avoid the strictures of the Commerce Clause by curtailing the movement of articles of commerce through subdivisions of the State, rather than through the State itself'.[35] As a consequence, 'neither the fact that

---

cent of the nation's landfills, *Philadelphia* has lost some of its practical importance as a barrier against discrimination of out-of-state waste.

[30] 112 S. Ct 2,019 (1992). For applications of *Fort Gratiot* see, e.g., *Government Suppliers Consolidating Services Inc.* v. *Bayh*, 975 F. 2d 1,267 (7th Cir. 1992), cert. denied, 113 S. Ct 977 (1993); *Southeast Arkansas Landfill Inc.* v. *State of Arkansas*, 981 F. 2d 372 (8th Cir. 1992). Generally on the *Fort Gratiot* case and its implications, see E. Fitzgerald, 'The Waste War: *Fort Gratiot Landfill Inc.* v. *Michigan Department of Natural Resources* and *Chemical Waste Management Inc.* v. *Hunt*', *Stanford Environmental Law Journal* 13 (1994), 78; M. Healy, 'The Pre-emption of State Hazardous and Solid Waste Regulations: The Dormant Commerce Clause Awakens Once More', *Washington Journal of Urban and Contemporary Law* 43 (1993), 177.

[31] 112 S. Ct 2,019 at 2,023.   [32] *Ibid.* at 2,024.   [33] *Ibid.* (emphasis added).

[34] *Ibid.*   [35] *Ibid.* at 2,025.

the Michigan statute purports to regulate intercounty commerce in waste nor the fact that some Michigan counties accept out-of-state waste provided an adequate basis for distinguishing this case from *Philadelphia* v. *New Jersey*'.[36]

The court also rejected Michigan's argument that this case was different from *Philadelphia* v. *New Jersey* because the SWMA constituted a comprehensive health and safety regulation rather than 'economic protectionism' of the state's limited landfill capacity. The court found that even assuming that the other provisions of the SWMA could fairly be so characterized, the same assumption could not be made with respect to the waste-import restrictions themselves. Referring to the *Dean Milk* test traditionally applied to discriminatory measures, the court estimated that, because the provisions unambiguously discriminated against interstate commerce, the state bore the burden of proving that they furthered health and safety concerns that could not adequately be served by non-discriminatory alternatives. Michigan did not meet this burden, since it provided no valid health or safety reason for limiting the amount of waste that a landfill operator could accept from outside the state, but not the amount the operator could accept from inside the state.[37] Moreover, Michigan could have attained its objective without discriminating between in and out-of-state waste. For example, it could have limited the amount of waste that landfill operators may accept every year.[38]

In a dissenting opinion, Chief Justice Rehnquist continued to assert the

---

[36] *Ibid*. Compare *Evergreen Waste Systems Inc.* v. *Metropolitan Service District*, 820 F. 2d 1,482 (9th Cir.) (holding that a waste ban that applied to all other districts in the state, as well as to other states was not discriminatory and should therefore be examined under the *Pike* test).

[37] *Ibid*. at 2,027.

[38] *Ibid*. The same day as the *Fort Gratiot* case was decided, the court considered in *Chemical Waste Management Inc.* v. *Hunt*, 112 S. Ct 2,009 (1992), the constitutionality of an Alabama statute which imposed, *inter alia*, a fee on hazardous waste disposed of in in-state commercial facilities, and an additional fee on hazardous waste generated outside, but disposed of inside, the state. As in the *Fort Gratiot* case, the Alabama statute was struck down after failing the *Dean Milk* test. Generally on this case, see Note, 'Hunt v. *Waste Management Inc.*: Alabama Attempts to Spread the Nation's Hazardous Waste Disposal Burden by Imposing a Higher Tax on Out-of-State Hazardous Waste', *Notre Dame Law Review* 67 (1992), 1,215. For a recent decision confirming the approach taken in *Hunt*, see *Oregon Waste Systems Inc.* v. *Department of Environmental Quality*, 114 S. Ct 1,345 (1994) (striking down a regulation of the Oregon Environmental Quality Commission that imposed a greater surcharge on the disposal of waste generated out-of-state than on the disposal of waste generated in-state). On this case, see E. Fitzgerald, 'The Waste War: *Oregon Waste Systems Inc.* v. *Department of Environmental Quality*', *Boston College Environmental Affairs Law Review* 23 (1995), 43.

position, first outlined in *Philadelphia* v. *New Jersey*,[39] that 'the substantial, aesthetic, health and safety problems' associated with waste obviate the need for strict Commerce Clause scrutiny. According to the Chief Justice, the SWMA was unrelated to protectionism.[40] If anything, he noted, it would work to Michigan's economic disadvantage: by limiting the potential disposal volumes for any particular sites, various fixed costs would have to be recovered across smaller volumes, hence increasing the costs of waste disposal for waste consumers.[41] Rather than being protectionist, the Michigan legislation simply incorporated 'the common sense notion that those responsible for a problem should be responsible for its solution *to the degree they are responsible for the problem but not further*'.[42] In this regard, Chief Justice Rehnquist saw no reason why some states, and in particular the poorer and less populated states, should be forced to become dumping grounds for the rest of the nation.[43] I will return to this point below.

In a recent decision, the Supreme Court also examined the constitutionality of a state measure having the effect of restricting the *exports* of waste.[44] In the case of *C&A Carbone Inc.* v. *Town of*

---

[39] In *Philadelphia* v. *New Jersey*, 437 US 617 (1978), Justice Rehnquist strongly opposed the majority decision (arguing that the New Jersey restrictions on imports of out-of-state waste should have been considered as quarantine laws which have traditionally been upheld by the court even when they were directed against interstate commerce). Justice Rehnquist also dissented in *Chemical Waste Management Inc.* v. *Hunt*, 112 S. Ct 2,009, at 2,017–18 (1992) (arguing that the two-tier Alabama tax was an effective but less restrictive means than a ban for protecting environmental resources and that the environment, not waste, was the relevant commodity restricted).

[40] 112 S. Ct 2,019, 2,028 (1992).

[41] *Ibid.* at 2,029. In this regard, Chief Justice Rehnquist noted that 'Commerce Clause cases are at their nadir when a state act works in this fashion – raising prices for all the state's consumers, and working to the substantial disadvantage of other segments of the state's population – because in these circumstances "a state's own political processes will serve as a check against unduly burdensome regulations"'.

[42] *Ibid.*

[43] *Ibid.*

[44] In the period prior to *Carbone* v. *Town of Clarckstown*, 114 S. Ct 1,677 (1994), federal courts had taken inconsistent positions on this issue. See *Waste Systems Corp.* v. *County of Martin, Minnesota*, 985 F. 2d 1,381 (8th Cir. 1993) (holding that a county ordinance providing that all compostable solid waste could not be transported out of the county but had to be delivered to a local solid-waste-composting facility was invalid under the Commerce Clause in that it operated as economic protectionism); and *Stephen D. Devito, Jr. Trucking Inc.* v. *Rhode Island Solid Waste Management Corp.*, 770 F. Supp. 775 (DRJ 1991) (holding that a resolution adopted by Rhode Island Solid Waste Management Corporation (RISWMC) directing that all solid waste originating or collected in Rhode Island be disposed of at facilities licensed by the Rhode Island Department of Environmental Management benefited RISWMC at the expense of out-of-state haulers

Clarckstown,[45] the Supreme Court had to consider the compatibility with the Commerce Clause of a waste flow-control ordinance of the Town of Clarckstown, New York, requiring all non-hazardous solid waste within the town to be deposited at a designated transfer station located in the municipality (the 'Route 303 station'). The avowed purpose of the ordinance was to retain the processing fees charged at the transfer station in order to amortize the cost of the facility. This ordinance clearly discriminated against exports of waste since, pursuant to its provisions, no solid waste could leave the municipality before being processed at the Route 303 station. For the Supreme Court, however, the article of commerce in the case was 'not so much the solid waste itself, but rather the *service* of processing and disposing it'.[46] In other words, the court felt that the essential vice of the ordinance was not so much the fact that it prevented the export of a good (i.e., solid waste) but rather that it prevented the import of a service (i.e., the processing of waste).[47]

Applying the *Dean Milk* test, the court admitted that the discrimination contained in the ordinance against out-of-town processing facilities could

and effectively eliminated interstate commerce). But see *Filiberto Sanitation Inc.* v. *Department of Environmental Protection*, 857 F. 2d 913 (3rd Cir. 1988) (holding that New Jersey legislation requiring deposit of waste collected in county at a designated station for transfer and subsequent disposal did not discriminate against interstate commerce and did not impose an excessive burden on interstate trade); *Harvey and Harvey* v. *Delaware Solid Waste Authority*, 600 F. Supp. 1,369 (D. Del. 1985) (holding that a Delaware regulation which required that all waste generated within Delaware be disposed at an authorized Delaware facility did not violate the Commerce Clause because there was 'no discrimination against out-of-state solid waste'). For a good discussion on these cases, see A. Mesnikoff, 'Disposing of the Dormant Commerce Clause Barrier: Keeping Waste at Home', *Minnesota Law Review* 76 (1992), 1,219.

[45] 114 S. Ct 1,677 (1994), 1994 US Lexis 3,477. For discussions on this case, see E. Petersen and D. Abramovitz, 'Municipal Solid Waste Flow Control in the Post-*Carbone* World', *Fordham Urban Law Journal* 22 (1995), 363; R. Baker, '*C&A Carbone* v. *Clarckstown*: A Wake-Up Call for the Dormant Commerce Clause', *Duke Environmental Law and Policy Forum* 5 (1995), 67; J. Vago, 'The Uncertain Future of Flow Control Ordinances: The Last Trash of *Clarckstown?*' *Northern Kentucky Law Review* 22 (1995), 1,481; H. Shapiro, '*C&A Carbone Inc.* v. *Clarckstown*: Supreme Court Uses the Commerce Clause to Nix a Local Trash Flow-Control Ordinance', *Natural Resources and Environment Journal* (1994), 20.

[46] 1994 US Lexis 3,477, at *12 (emphasis added).

[47] The Supreme Court supported this view by referring to previous decisions striking down processing requirements imposed by states in order to favour local businesses. See, e.g., *South-Central Timber Development Inc.* v. *Wunnicke*, 467 US 82 (1984) (striking down an Alaska regulation requiring all timber to be processed within the state before export); *Toomer* v. *Witsell*, 334 US 385 (1948) (striking down a South Carolina statute that required shrimp fishermen to unload, pack and stamp their catch before shipping it to another state); *Foster-Fountain Packing Co.* v. *Haydel*, 278 US 1 (1928) (striking down a Louisiana statute that forbade shrimp to be exported unless the heads and shells had been first removed within the state).

be justified if the 'municipality can demonstrate that there is no other means to advance a legitimate state interest'.[48] In this regard, the court did not agree with Clarckstown that ensuring the profitability of the Route 303 station was a local interest that could justify discrimination against interstate commerce.[49] The court also rejected Clarckstown's argument that its flow-control ordinance was a way to 'steer solid waste away from out-of-state disposal sites that it might deem harmful to the environment'.[50] For the court, '[t]o do so would extend the town's police power beyond its jurisdictional bounds' and 'states and localities may not attach restrictions to exports or imports in order to control commerce in other states'.[51] Finally, the court felt that Clarckstown had a number of non-discriminatory alternatives at its disposal in order to address the health and environmental problems the ordinance allegedly aimed to promote, the most obvious of these alternatives being the enactment of uniform safety regulations. Such regulations would indeed ensure that competitors like Carbone 'do not underprice the market by cutting corners on environmental safety'.[52]

The foregoing cases reveal that the Supreme Court has taken a very strict approach with regard to state and local measures discriminating against interstate trade in waste. Discriminatory measures will only be justified when the states which have adopted them can demonstrate that they are designed to further a legitimate purpose which cannot be achieved by less discriminatory alternatives. Although the court has admitted that protecting their environment and the general welfare of their citizens is a legitimate purpose, it has not admitted that states restrict transfers in order to protect the environment and the health and safety of the citizens of other states.[53] In addition, the court has not

[48] 1994 US Lexis 3,477, at *16.
[49] Ibid. at *19.   [50] Ibid. at *17.   [51] Ibid. at *18.
[52] Ibid. at *17. The Supreme Court's judgment in Carbone has been applied in a large number of federal court decisions. See, e.g., SSC Corp. v. Town of Smithtown, 66 F. 2d 502 (2nd 1995); Poor Richard's Inc. v. Ramsey County, Minnesota, 992 F. Supp. 1,387 (D. Minn. 1996); National Solid Waste Management Associations, Sanifill Inc. v. Charles W. Williams, 887 F. Supp. 1,367 (D. Minn. 1995) (striking down flow-control legislation). It should be noted, however, that in a number cases, federal courts have admitted the validity of flow-control legislation on the ground of the market-participant exception. See, e.g., USA Recycling Inc. v. Town of Babylon, NY, 66 F. 3d 1,272 (4th Cir. 1995); Barken Brothers Waste Inc. v. William Cloar et al., 993 F. Supp. 1,042 (WD Tenn. 1996).
[53] By contrast, in a number of cases, courts have authorized states to adopt restrictions on interstate commerce in order to protect species of wildlife located in other states. See Cresenzi Bird Importers Inc. v. State of New York, 658 F. Supp. 1,441 (SDNY 1987); Palladio Inc. v. Diamond, 321 F. Supp. 630 (SDNY 1970), affirmed, 440 F. 2d 1,319 (2nd Cir.), cert. denied, 404 US 983 (1971); A. E. Nettleton v. Diamond, 264 NE 2d 118, appeal

agreed that trade restrictions represented the least discriminatory means at the disposal of the states to protect the environment. Rather, the court has consistently argued that the states could attain their environmental objectives in a non-discriminatory manner by raising the level of stringency of their waste-disposal standards. As will be discussed below, it remains to be seen, however, whether uncoordinated state actions can bring about any solution to the difficult issue of interstate transfers of waste.

Product standards

As we have seen, although they do not usually discriminate on their face against interstate trade, environmental product standards may nevertheless have substantial effects on that trade. First, even where product standards are formally applied equally to both domestic and imported products, they may discriminate in their effects against interstate trade. Second, even in the absence of discriminatory intent or effects, product standards may impose a burden on interstate trade. In this context, in reviewing environmental product standards, courts usually attempt to determine (i) whether such standards discriminate in their intent or effects against interstate trade or whether they are even-handed; and, in the absence of discriminatory intent or effects, (ii) whether the burden they impose on interstate trade is proportionate in relation to the environmental objective they aim to promote.

In *Minnesota* v. *Clover Leaf Creamery Co*,[54] the Supreme Court was asked to examine the compatibility with the Commerce Clause of a Minnesota statute banning the retail sale of milk in plastic non-returnable, non-refillable containers, but allowing such sale in other non-returnable, non-refillable containers, such as cardboard milk cartons. The businesses challenging the statute contended that its actual purpose was to protect Minnesota's local pulpwood industry, whose containers would fill the void left by the excluded plastic containers, all of which were made of resins produced outside Minnesota. The court disagreed with this view: the statute did not discriminate against interstate commerce since it regulated even-handedly 'by prohibiting all milk retailers from selling their products in plastic, non-returnable containers, without regard to whether the milk, the containers, the sellers are from outside the

dismissed *sub nom. Reptile Products Association* v. *Diamond*, 401 US 969 (1970). These cases appear to reflect the growing recognition that wildlife, wherever located, is part of a collective heritage that all states should be free to protect.

[54] 449 US 456 (1981).

state'.[55] Referring to the *Pike* balancing test traditionally applied to non-discriminatory statutes, the court then indicated that even if a statute regulates even-handedly and has only an incidental effect on interstate commerce, it must nevertheless be struck down if 'the burden imposed on such commerce is clearly excessive in relation to the putative local benefits'.[56] The court found that this was not the case here. It noted that:

> Even granting that the out-of-state plastic industry is burdened relatively more heavily than the Minnesota pulpwood industry . . . this burden is not 'clearly excessive' in light of the substantial state interest in promoting energy conservation and other natural resources and in easing waste-disposal problems.[57]

The Minnesota statute was not therefore incompatible with the Commerce Clause.

It should be noted that in a number of cases, lower courts have refused to apply the *Pike* balancing test to non-discriminatory environmental product standards having an effect on interstate trade. For example, in *Procter and Gamble Company* v. *City of Chicago*,[58] the Court of Appeals of the Seventh Circuit examined whether an ordinance of the City of Chicago banning the use of detergents containing phosphates in order to prevent the eutrophication of rivers and lakes resulted in an impermissible interference with interstate commerce.[59] Having found that the Chicago ordinance did not discriminate between domestic and out-of-state interests, the Court of Appeals recalled that, pursuant to *Pike*, the predominant test used by the Supreme Court to deal with non-discriminatory measures imposing a burden on interstate trade was to examine whether this burden was not clearly excessive in relation to the putative local

---

[55] On this aspect, the analysis of the court is particularly formalistic. The businesses challenging the statute did not deny that the Minnesota statute was non-discriminatory on its face. They argued, however, that the *effect* of the statute was to protect the local pulpwood industry. The court only addresses this issue later in its judgment when, pursuant to the *Pike* test, it balances the burden imposed on interstate trade by the Minnesota statute against its environmental benefits. But, once again, the court does not really attempt there to quantify the burden placed by the statute on out-of-state interests. Repeating *Pike*, it merely notes that this burden is not 'clearly excessive' in light of the substantial benefits brought about by the statute.

[56] *Ibid.* at 674.   [57] *Ibid.* at 675.

[58] 509 F. 2d 69 (7th Cir. 1975). For other cases involving phosphate bans, see *Soap and Detergent Assn* v. *Clarck*, 330 F. Supp. 1,218 (SD Florida 1971); *Colgate Palmolive Company* v. *Erie County*, 327 NYS 2d 488 (1971). Generally on these cases, see Note, 'Use of the Commerce Clause to Invalidate Anti-Phosphate Legislation: Will it Wash?' *University of Colorado Law Review* 45 (1974), 487.

[59] Eutrophication 'is a process of ageing, whereby a body of water becomes over-nourished in nutrient elements such that there occurs an extensive growth of green plants or nuisance algae': 509 F. 2d 69 (7th Cir. 1975) at 73.

benefits.[60] The court of Appeals, however, found that this test should not be applied in this case. Getting involved in a balancing exercise would be undesirable because it would lead to a 'usurpation of the legislative role'.[61] Rather, the Court of Appeals decided that it should limit its enquiry to verify whether the objective promoted by the state legislation is one of legitimate concern and whether the means chosen to accomplish this end is reasonably effective.[62] Applying this more lenient 'rational relation' test to the Chicago ordinance, the Court of Appeals found that the interest sought to be served by the ordinance (i.e., to prevent the eutrophication of rivers and lakes) was a legitimate local concern and the means chosen to attain this objective (i.e., banning the sale of detergents containing phosphates) was reasonably effective. It then upheld the ordinance without proceeding to any further balancing process.[63]

The same rational relation test was applied in *American Can Co.* v. *Oregon Liquor Control Commission*.[64] In that case, the Supreme Court of Oregon was asked to examine the constitutionality of the Oregon Minimum Deposit Act, a statute requiring the establishment of a deposit-and-return system for all soft drinks and beer bottles and banning the sale of those beverages in pull-top cans.[65] The plaintiffs to the case contented that the Oregon statute discriminated against out-of-state interests. Because of the need to ship back the containers to more distant plants for refill, the deposit-and-return system required by the statute would in effect impose higher handling costs for out-of-state producers, hence raising the costs of their products to the point of making them uncompetitive.[66] As a result, the

---

[60] *Ibid.* at 75.   [61] *Ibid.*

[62] The Court of Appeals found some support for this approach in *Brotherhood of Locomotive Firemen & Enginemen* v. *Chicago, Rock Island & Pacific Railroad Co.*, 393 US 129 (1968), in which the Supreme Court refused to balance the benefits brought about by an Arkansas railroad-safety law with the burden such a law imposed on interstate commerce.

[63] 509 F. 2d 69 (7th Cir. 1975) at 81.

[64] 517 P. 2d 691 (1973). For good discussions on this case, see Note, 'The Oregon Bottle Bill', *Oregon Law Review* 34 (1975), 175; C. Moos, '*American Can*: Judicial Response to Oregon's Non-Returnable Container Legislation', *Ecology Law Quarterly* 4 (1974), 145.

[65] For other cases involving beverage container regulations, see *Bowie Inn Inc.* v. *Bowie*, 274 Md 230, 335 A. 2d 679 (1975); *Anchor Hocking Glass Corp.* v. *Barber*, 118 Vt 206, 105 A. 2d 271 (1954). For a discussion on these cases, see Annotation, 'Validity and Construction of Statute or Ordinance Requiring Return Deposits on Soft Drink or Similar Containers', ALR 3d 73.

[66] For a good discussion on the economic implications of beverage container regulations, see C. Gudger and K. Walters, 'Beverage Container Regulation: Economic Implications and Suggestions for Model Legislation', *Ecology Law Quarterly* 5 (1976), 265. See also E. Slade, D. Wilson and J. Wilson, 'State and Local Regulation of Non-returnable Containers', *Wisconsin Law Review* (1972), 536.

effect of the statute would be a 'balkanization of the beverage industry and a return to the regional markets which existed prior to the one-way system'.[67] The plaintiffs also argued that, even if the Oregon statute was not found to discriminate against interstate commerce, it should nevertheless be struck down because it imposed an 'excessive burden' on that commerce compared to the putative local benefits.

The court rejected these arguments. First, it held that the statute was not discriminatory against interstate commerce and was not intended to operate to give local industry a competitive advantage against outside firms, noting that the cost of adjusting to the requirements of the statute would be spread throughout the beverage industry, and among its suppliers, manufacturers, and distributors, without regard to whether they were state-based firms.[68] The court also noted that, to the extent that some out-of-state firms suffered a competitive disadvantage because of the obligation to use returnable containers, the disadvantage was 'one of distance, not one of state boundaries'.[69] Second, the court also rejected the plaintiffs' argument that the burden imposed by the Oregon statute outweighed the environmental benefits of the statute. The court found that the application of the *Pike* balancing test, on which this argument was based, did not require these benefits to be compared against 'non-comparable' economic losses to the beverage industry:

The blight of the landscape, the appropriation of lands for solid waste disposal, and the injury to children's feet caused by the pull tops discarded in the sands of our ocean shores are concerns not *divisible by the same units of measurement* as is economic loss to elements of the beverage industry and we are unable to weigh them, one against the other.[70]

Applying a less stringent rational relation test similar to the one used in *Procter & Gamble*, the court then found that the interests sought to be served by the statute (i.e., to avoid a blight to the landscape, the appropriation of lands for waste disposal, and the injury to children's feet caused by discarded pull-tops) were legitimate local interests and that the means chosen to achieve these interests (i.e., the establishment of a deposit-and-

---

[67] See Moos, '*American Can*: Judicial Response', at 157 (citing the brief for Intervenors-Appellants at 13–14).

[68] 517 P. 2d 691, 703 (1975).

[69] According to the court, 'a bottler in Southern Oregon, for example, would be at a disadvantage competing to recapture used bottles in the Portland market relative to a competing bottler from Vancouver, Washington': *ibid.*

[70] *Ibid.* at 697 (emphasis added). As the Court of Appeals for the Seventh Circuit in *Procter & Gamble*, the court referred to *Brotherhood of Locomotive Firemen & Enginemen* v. *Chicago, Rock Island & Pacific Railroad Co.*, 393 US 129 (1968).

return system and the ban of beverages in pull-top cans) were reasonably effective.[71] There was therefore no incompatibility between the Commerce Clause and the Oregon statute.

The foregoing cases reveal that when reviewing state environmental product standards having an effect on interstate trade, courts have generally shown deference towards upholding such standards. The fact that such standards impose important economic losses on out-of-state producers will not necessarily mean that they discriminate against interstate commerce.[72] Moreover, the existence of such losses will not be sufficient to demonstrate the presence of an impermissible burden on interstate trade. As indicated by the Supreme Court in *Clover Leaf Creamery*, the burden imposed by a non-discriminatory state measure on interstate trade will only be found impermissible when it is 'clearly excessive' compared to the environmental benefits brought about by these measures. An even greater degree of deference towards state environmental measures can be observed in *Procter & Gamble* and *American Can* where lower courts ruled that it is only when the means used by a state measure are not reasonably effective to attain its environmental objective (i.e., when the measure is not pertinent) that the measure will be considered as an impermissible burden on interstate trade.

Process standards

As we have seen, states may regulate the characteristics of products and exclude from their markets the products that they judge deficient from an environmental standpoint. We have also seen that, although they may have restrictive effects on interstate trade, courts have traditionally been deferent to such product regulations. As we have seen in the context of European Community law, a more delicate question, however, is to what extent states are entitled to restrict imports of products not because they do not correspond to the environmental characteristics contained in their domestic product standards, but because they have been manufactured according to production methods that do not conform to their environmental process standards (process-related trade restrictions).

Although there is no relevant case law,[73] this question has been

---

[71] 517 P. 2d 691 (1975) at 700.

[72] This is especially the case when part of such losses are suffered by domestic producers.

[73] The closest precedent is perhaps *Baldwin* v. *G. A. F. Seelig Inc.*, 294 US 511 (1935) (striking down a New York law that prohibited the sale of milk unless the price paid to the original milk producer equalled the minimum price required by New York). Other relevant precedents are *National Solid Waste Association* v. *Georges Meyer*, 63 F. 3rd 652

discussed in the literature and authors have generally reached the conclusion that process-related trade restrictions of the kind described above would not be compatible with the dormant Commerce Clause.[74] Since such restrictions would probably be found discriminatory,[75] they would be presumed invalid unless justified by a legitimate local purpose and the unavailability of less discriminatory alternatives (*Dean Milk* test). It is unlikely, however, that such restrictions would be upheld under such a test. First, it is doubtful whether the principal purpose behind process-related trade restrictions, which, as we have seen, is generally to ensure a level playing field between domestic and out-of-state producers, would qualify as a legitimate local purpose.[76] The state adopting such restrictions could perhaps invoke the fact that such measures are necessary to protect the environment against the detrimental effects that may be generated by other states' lax environmental practices.[77] A difficulty would, however, appear concerning the location of the environmental

(7th Cir. 1995) (ruling that a Wisconsin statute prohibiting waste generators to dump waste in Wisconsin landfills unless they reside in a community that has adopted an effective recycling programme was unconstitutional); and *Hardage* v. *Hatkins*, 619 F. 2d 871 (10th Cir. 1980) (ruling that an Oklahoma law that prohibited out-of-state waste generators from shipping their waste to Oklahoma disposal facilities unless their home state had adopted substantially similar standards for controlled industrial waste disposal as those which Oklahoma had enacted was unconstitutional). None of these cases, however, squarely addressed the question of whether a state could restrict imports of products on the ground that they have been produced according to lax environmental process standards.

[74] See, e.g., T. Heller, 'Legal Theory and Political Economy of American Federalism' in Cappelletti *et al.* (eds.), *Integration through Law* (Walter de Gruyter, 1985), vol. I, 255, 299 ('State regulation which might attempt to impose quantitative restrictions or increase the production costs of goods produced out of the state under relaxed environmental . . . regulation would contravene the Commerce Clause doctrine even though its intended and actual effect was the preservation of the competitive position of in-state production operating in locally efficiency increasing regulated market.'). For similar arguments made in the context of labour standards, see P. Freund, 'Umpiring the Federal System', *Columbia Law Review* 54 (1954), 561, 568.

[75] As already noted, process-related trade restrictions present an element of discrimination on their face: although they have the same physical characteristics as freely marketed domestic products, some out-of-state products will nevertheless be banned because they have been produced under lax environmental process standards. It is therefore unlikely that courts would apply the *Pike* balancing test traditionally applied to non-discriminatory measures to such restrictions.

[76] The Supreme Court has indeed traditionally considered as legitimate local purposes non-economic objectives, such as protection of health, safety or the environment. See *C&A Carbone* v. *Town of Clarckstown*, 114 S. Ct 1,677 (1994) (court rejecting the argument that ensuring the profitability of a local waste-processing facility was a local interest that could justify discrimination against interstate commerce).

[77] See, *mutatis mutandis*, p. 32 above.

resources to be protected. Although the Supreme Court has recognized that states may, in certain circumstances, adopt trade restrictions to protect their environment, it has made clear in *C&A Carbone* v. *Town of Clarckstown* that states could not adopt trade restrictions to protect the environment of other states.[78] Even if the state adopting the restrictions could demonstrate that they are aimed at protecting its own environment, it would still have to show that such restrictions represent the least discriminatory way to attain that objective. As already noted in the context of European Community law, it is likely, however, that in most cases, non-discriminatory (and perhaps more effective) alternatives, such as consultations between the states concerned or the use of labelling provisions informing consumers about the methods of production following which products offered for sale have been manufactured, could be found. For the foregoing reasons, it seems highly unlikely that process-related restrictions would be found to be compatible with the dormant Commerce Clause doctrine.

[78] See p. 45 above. See also *Healy* v. *Beer Institute*, 491 US 324 (1989) ('a state law that has the "practical effect" of regulating commerce occurring wholly outside that state's borders is invalid under the Commerce Clause'); *Edgard* v. *MITE Corp.*, 457 US 624 (1982) ('any attempt "directly" to assert extraterritorial jurisdiction over persons or property would offend sister states and exceed the inherent limits of the state's power').

3 Comparative analysis

The principle of free trade

With regard to the free movement of goods, the US Constitution and the EC Treaty present similarities but also differences. In the EC Treaty, there is no grant of power to the Community similar to the general power conferred on the Congress by the Commerce Clause. In fact, the EC Treaty starts the other way round: instead of a grant of power to the Community which would by the same token limit to a certain extent the power of the member states to interfere with intra-Community trade, it provides for express prohibitions for the member states to impose quantitative restrictions on imports or exports or measures having an equivalent effect between member states.[1] Thus, one may question whether the two situations are comparable.[2] At least, the context is similar. In both cases, the major incentive for creating a union was the desire to avoid destructive state protectionist policies, coupled with the ambition of creating a common market stretching over the territories of all the states involved in the unitary process.

As a result of this common object, the jurisprudence of the two courts has developed in very similar ways. There are important similarities in the principles both courts have developed for placing restrictions on state legislation that would impede the free movement of goods. Similarly, there are many parallels in the methods that the courts employ for determining the limits of state power.[3] Both courts have demonstrated a

[1] See K. Lenaerts, 'Constitutionalism and the many Faces of Federalism', *American Journal of Comparative Law* 38 (1990), 206, 261.
[2] See Mackenzie, Lord Stuart, 'Problems of the European Community – Transatlantic Parallels', *International and Comparative Law Quarterly* 36 (1987), 183, 188.
[3] See D. Kommers and M. Waelbroeck, 'Legal Integration and the Free Movement of Goods: The American and European Experience' in Cappelletti *et al.* (eds.), *Integration*

strong antagonism to state measures discriminating on their face or in their effects against interstate trade. They have also imposed limits on the ability of states to adopt measures, which although they do not discriminate against interstate trade, have nevertheless a restrictive effect on that trade. In this context, a common difficulty for the courts has been to reconcile the objective of ensuring free interstate trade with the legitimate regulatory powers of the states. Although the exercise of such powers does not always generate impediments to trade, it may indeed often do so. In order to overcome this difficulty, the prevalent method of analysis used by the courts has been to balance the Community or federal interest in free trade with the interest of the states in correcting market failures through regulatory intervention. This method of analysis has been generally contextual. As we have seen, several questions are relevant. Is the objective pursued by the state measure of legitimate local concern? Does the measure discriminate against interstate trade and, if so, could the objective pursued by that measure be achieved through less discriminatory means? How great is the burden imposed by the measure on interstate trade? Does this burden outweigh the local benefits brought about by the measure? It is the answers to these questions that will generally determine the validity or invalidity of trade-restrictive state measures.

As will be seen in the next section, the tension between the Community or federal interest in free interstate trade and the state interest in correcting market failures through regulatory intervention has been particularly acute in the environmental field. On the one hand, in both European Community and United States systems, fear has been expressed over the development of state and local environmental measures as instruments of economic isolationism. On the other hand, there has also been concern that the free-trade ideology on which these systems are based would have the effect of undermining the ability of states to adopt legitimate environmental policies. In this context, it has been a particularly delicate task for the Court of Justice and the Supreme Court to find a fair balance between the competing interests of free trade and environmental protection.

through Law (Walter de Gruyter, 1985), vol. I, at 165; E. Stein, 'On Divided-Power Systems: Adventures in Comparative Law', *Legal Issues of European Integration* (1983/1), 27, 29.

The application of the principle

Waste

As can be seen from the case law of the Court of Justice and the Supreme Court, two important trade issues arise in the area of waste. A first issue is to what extent states should be authorized to impose restrictions on the imports of waste from other states. The states which have adopted such restrictions have usually attempted to justify them by the need to protect their citizens against the health and environmental hazards that may be generated by the excessive accumulation of waste on their territory. Those in favour of such restrictions have also argued that such restrictions are necessary to give proper incentives to all states to develop adequate waste-disposal facilities within their borders rather than to rely on facilities located in other states for waste disposal.[4] On the other hand, those opposed to such restrictions have generally characterized them as highly inefficient: '[f]ree trade in wastes should promote joint welfare for reasons similar to those that justify free trade in ordinary goods and services: economies of scale in disposal techniques, comparative advantage based on geology and transportation access, and innovation though specialization.'[5] A second important issue is to what extent states should be authorized to impose restrictions on the exports of their own waste to other states. Although the states imposing such restrictions have sometimes claimed that they are necessary to protect the environment of other states, restrictions on the exports of waste are, however, generally motivated by economic considerations, such as ensuring the profitability of local waste-processing facilities.

The validity of restrictions on the imports of out-of-state waste has been

---

[4] See P. von Wilmowsky, 'Waste Disposal in the Internal Market: The State of Play After the ECJ's Ruling on the Walloon Import Ban', *Common Market Law Review* 30 (1993), 541, 551. A related argument is that free shipments of waste across frontiers allow exporting states to 'free-ride' on other states' efforts to deal with waste-disposal problems. In this context, the free movement of waste appears to be unfair since it has the effect that some communities have to support the entire social costs for waste disposal, whereas others can entirely avoid such costs. Generally on this problem of environmental justice, see K. Engel, 'Reconsidering the National Market in Solid Waste: Trade-Offs in Equity, Efficiency, Environmental Protection, and State Autonomy', *North Carolina Law Review* 73 (1995), 1,483, 1,526–45; V. Been, 'What's Fairness Got to Do with It?: Environmental Equity and the Siting of Locally Undesirable Land Uses', *Cornell Law Review* 78 (1993), 1,001.

[5] See R. Stewart, 'International Trade and Environment: Lessons from the Federal Experience', *Washington and Lee Law Review* 49 (1992), 1,329, 1,338.

expressly addressed by the Court of Justice in the *Belgian Waste* case[6] and the Supreme Court in *Philadelphia* v. *State of New Jersey*[7] and *Fort Gratiot Sanitary Landfill Inc.* v. *Michigan Department of Natural Resources*.[8] Of the two Supreme Court cases, the *Fort Gratiot* case is certainly the one raising the issues closest to those of the *Belgian Waste* case. In both cases, the regulations in question did not only bear on the importation of waste from other states, but also from the other administrative entities of the states (other regions in the *Belgian Waste* case and other counties in the *Fort Gratiot* case). If the *Belgian Waste* and the *Fort Gratiot* cases raised similar issues, the decisions were very different. The question of discrimination was at the heart of both. On this point, the language in the *Fort Gratiot* case can be contrasted with the language in the *Belgian Waste* case. In the *Fort Gratiot* case, the Supreme Court felt that: 'In view of the fact that Michigan has not identified any reason, *apart from its origin*, why solid waste coming from outside the county should be treated differently from solid waste within the county, the foregoing reasoning would appear to control the disposition of the case.'[9] In contrast, the Court of Justice held the view that, given the differences between wastes produced in one area and another and their connection with the place where they were produced, the Belgian regional law was not to be seen as discriminatory and could therefore be justified under the rule of reason. One can see here that for the Supreme Court, the restriction was discriminatory because it was supposedly based on no reasons other than origin. The reasoning of the Court of Justice was just the opposite in that the origin of waste was seen as a valid justification in itself. What was a cause of condemnation in the Supreme Court was a cause of justification in the Court of Justice.

The outcome the two cases was of course determined by these different findings.[10] Applying the *Dean Milk* test, the *Fort Gratiot* court estimated that because the waste-import restrictions contained in the Michigan legislation 'unambiguously discriminate against interstate commerce, the

---

[6] Case C-2/90, *Commission* v. *Belgium* [1992] ECR I-4,431.

[7] 437 US 617 (1978).

[8] 112 S. Ct 2,019 (1992). See also *Oregon Waste Management Systems Inc.* v. *Department of Environmental Quality*, 114 S. Ct 1,345 (1994); *Chemical Waste Management Inc.* v. *Hunt*, 112 S. Ct 2,009 (1992).

[9] *Ibid.* at 2,024 (emphasis added).

[10] Indeed, if the US Supreme Court had found that the Michigan restrictions were non-discriminatory, the court would have applied the more lenient *Pike* test, presuming the validity of the state legislation in question. See pp. 37–8 above. Conversely, if the European Court of Justice had found the Walloon Region restrictions discriminatory, it would not have been possible for it to apply the 'mandatory requirements' exception to Article 30. See p. 14 above.

state bears the burden of proving that further health and safety concerns cannot be adequately served by non-discriminatory alternatives'.[11] Michigan was, however, found not to have met this burden since it could have attained that objective without discriminating between in- and out-of-state waste. Michigan could, for example, have limited the amount of waste that landfill operators may accept each year.[12] In contrast, the Court of Justice found that the Walloon Region restrictions could be justified as mandatory requirements, and therefore were compatible with the EC Treaty.

Explaining why the Court of Justice and the Supreme Court adopted such different approaches is not an easy matter.[13] In itself, the judgment of the Supreme Court in the *Fort Gratiot* case is not surprising.[14] The court applied its traditional Commerce Clause case law and struck down the apparently discriminatory Michigan legislation. An important element in the background was also the concept of 'economic nationhood' developed by the Supreme Court in natural-resource cases.[15] Landfilling space was seen by the court as a natural resource that all states were under an obligation to share for the common good.[16] The Court of Justice, on the

---

[11] 112 S. Ct 2,019, 2,027 (1992).   [12] *Ibid.*

[13] See my comments in *European Law Review* 18 (1993), 144. See also J. T. Smith, 'The Challenges of Environmental Sound and Efficient Regulation of Waste – The Need for Enhanced International Understanding', *Journal of Environmental Law* 5 (1993), 91.

[14] It should be recalled, however, that the *Fort Gratiot* case was a majority decision: Chief Justice Rehnquist, joined with Justice Blackmun, filing a strong dissenting opinion. See pp. 42–3 above.

[15] See *Oklahoma* v. *Kansas Natural Gas Co.*, 221 US 229, 255 (1911) ('If States have such power [to retain sources for in-state use] a singular situation might result. Pennsylvania might keep its coal, the Northwest its timber, the mining states their minerals. And why may not the products of the field be brought within this principle? . . . If one State has [the power to retain its resources], all States have it; embargo might be retaliated by embargo, and commerce will be halted at State lines. And yet we have said that in matters of foreign and interstate commerce there are no State lines.') See also *New England Power Co.* v. *New Hampshire*, 455 US 331 (1982); *City of Altus* v. *Carr*, 255 F. Supp. 828 (WD Texas), affirmed *per curiam*, 385 US 35 (1966); *Pennsylvania* v. *West Virginia*, 262 US 553 (1923).

[16] This does not explicitly appear in the *Fort Gratiot* case but was the object of an important *dictum* in *Philadelphia* v. *New Jersey*, the precedent on which the *Fort Gratiot* case is based (437 US 617, 629 (1978)) ('Today, cities in Pennsylvania and New York find it expedient or necessary to send their waste into New Jersey for disposal, and New Jersey claims the right to close its borders to such traffic. Tomorrow, cities in New Jersey may find it expedient or necessary to send their waste into Pennsylvania or New York for disposal, and those States might then claim the right to close their borders. The Commerce Clause will protect New Jersey in the future, just as it protects her neighbours now, from efforts by one State to isolate itself in the stream of interstate commerce from a problem shared by all.')

other hand, appeared to be more preoccupied with the regional imbalances in waste disposal that may be created when waste circulates freely. In the absence of control on the movements of waste, some member states of the Community may become dumping grounds, with a considerable reduction in environmental quality in these states.[17] Political factors were also important. At the time of the *Belgian Waste* decision, the member states had been struggling for more than three years over the proposed Regulation on the supervision and control of shipments of waste within, into and out of the Community.[18] In particular, they strongly disagreed over whether member states should be allowed to restrict transfrontier movements of waste. By upholding the Walloon restrictions on the imports of waste, the Court of Justice may well have attempted to influence the political process in order to ensure that such restrictions were permitted, or at least not expressly ruled out. This aspect will be further discussed below.[19]

The validity of restrictions on the exports of waste has also been addressed by the Court of Justice in *Interhuiles*[20] and *Nertsvoederfabriek Nederland*[21] where the court examined the compatibility with Article 34 of the Treaty of member state regulations requiring certain categories of waste to be sent to domestic waste-processing facilities. This issue was also addressed by the Supreme Court in *C&A Carbone* v. *Town of Clarckstown*[22] where the court examined the compatibility with the Commerce Clause of a local ordinance requiring that all solid waste generated within the municipality be sent to a designated local transfer station. Contrary to the issue of restrictions on the imports of waste where they disagreed, the Court of Justice and the Supreme Court reached a similar result here, finding the restrictions on the exports of waste to be incompatible with the EC Treaty and the US Constitution respectively.[23] As already noted,

---

[17] See, *mutatis mutandis*, Chief Justice Rehnquist's dissenting opinion in *Fort Gratiot Landfill* v. *Michigan Natural Resources Department*, 112 S. Ct 2,019, 2,029 ('I see no reason in the Commerce Clause, however, that requires cheap-land States to become waste repositories for their brethren, thereby suffering the many risks that such sites present').

[18] See my analysis in *European Law Review* 18 (1993), 418, 426.

[19] See pp. 124–5 below.   [20] [1983] ECR 555.

[21] [1987] ECR 3,883.   [22] 114 S. Ct 1,677 (1994).

[23] If the Court of Justice and the Supreme Court reached the same result, they adopted a different reasoning. In *Interhuiles* and *Nertsvoederfabriek Nederland*, the Court of Justice analysed the French and the Dutch regulations at question as restrictions on the free movement of goods. On the other hand, in *Carbone*, the Supreme Court analysed the local regulation in question not as a restriction on the free movement of goods but rather as a restriction on the free movement of services. It should be noted, however,

these decisions were hardly surprising since the restrictions in question had clear protectionist overtones.[24] Their main objective was indeed to ensure the profitability of domestic waste-processing facilities by providing them with a sufficient quantity of waste at low price.

An interesting aspect of the decision of the Supreme Court in *Carbone* is, however, that it made clear that under no circumstances could states or localities justify restrictions on the exports of waste (or, more generally, any form of trade restriction) as a way to protect the environment in other states. For the Supreme Court to allow states to do so would unduly extend their police powers outside their jurisdictions. As we have seen, this issue has not been clearly addressed by the Court of Justice. Although the court indicated in *Interhuiles* that restrictions on the exports of waste oils could not be justified as necessary to protect the environment since such waste could be properly processed in other member states' facilities, the court has not made clear whether such restrictions would be authorized if the member state adopting them could demonstrate that the member states to which such waste is sent do not possess adequate facilities to process them. For the same reasons as those mentioned by the Supreme Court in *Carbone*, it is, however, unlikely that the court will permit member states to adopt such restrictions.

that in a recent case (Case C-37/92, *Vanacker and Lesage* [1993] ECR I-4,947) Advocate-General Lenz analysed a French regulation which in effect created local monopolies for the disposal of waste oils under the light of the Treaty provisions designed to ensure the free movement of services. The court, however, rejected this analysis and, in conformity with its traditional approach, analysed the French regulation as a restriction on the exports of goods.

[24] The protectionist nature of these restrictions has, however, been challenged by a number of commentators, especially in the United States law context. See, e.g., M. Gold, 'Solid Waste Management and the Constitution's Commerce Clause', *Urban Lawyer* 25 (1993), 21, 46–8 ('[courts] have applied the decision in *Philadelphia* v. *New Jersey* [and now *Fort Gratiot*] to any direct or indirect impact on interstate commerce, even when a part of a carefully put-together solid waste-management plan was at stake . . . Such management plans are not at all "protectionist" in the way the Supreme Court intended that word in *Philadelphia* v. *New Jersey* . . . Facilities controlling exportation that are part of a bona fide state and locally authorized Comprehensive Solid Waste Management plans, and which satisfy the requirements of federal laws and regulations, should be given a very high deference.'). See also, E. Petersen and D. Abramovitz, 'Municipal Solid Waste Flow Control in the Post-*Carbone* World', *Fordham Urban Law Journal* 22 (1995), 363; A. Mesnikoff, 'Disposing the Dormant Commerce Clause Barrier: Keeping Waste at Home', *Minnesota Law Review* 76 (1992), 1,219. These authors suggest that Congress should exercise its power to regulate interstate commerce in order expressly to authorize states to impose restrictions on the exports of waste.

Product standards

Although, contrary to restrictions on trade in waste, product standards do not usually formally discriminate against interstate trade, we have seen that they may nevertheless have substantial effects on that trade. First, there may be circumstances where states attempt to design product standards in such a way that, although they formally apply to domestic and imported products, they discriminate in their effects against the latter. Second, even in the absence of discriminatory intent or effects, product standards may nevertheless impose a burden on interstate trade. This is, for example, the case where the imposition of inconsistent product standards by states prevents producers from realizing economies of scale in production and distribution, and generally creates market fragmentation. Because of these trade-restrictive effects, the Court of Justice and the Supreme Court have been asked in a number of cases to examine the compatibility of state environmental product standards with the EC Treaty and the US Constitution respectively.

In *Minnesota* v. *Clover Leaf Creamery Co.*[25] and in the *Danish Bottles* case,[26] the Supreme Court and the Court of Justice examined the validity of state measures regulating containers for drinks. In both cases, an important question was whether the challenged measures discriminated against interstate commerce or were even-handed. In *Clover Leaf Creamery*, the business interests challenging the Minnesota statute argued that the main purpose of the ban imposed by the statute on the retail sale of milk in plastic containers was to protect the state's pulpwood industry at the expense of the out-of-state plastic industry.[27] Similarly, in *Danish Bottles*, the Commission argued that, although it formally applied to domestic and imported products, the Danish legislation, which in its essence required the establishment of a deposit-and-return system for soft drinks and beer containers and the use of containers approved by the National Agency for the Protection of the Environment (NAPE), discriminated in its effects against non-Danish producers.[28] The Danish legislation being discriminatory, it could not therefore be justified under the rule of reason.[29] Despite these arguments, the courts gave little attention to the issue of discrimination. Using a formalistic reasoning, the Supreme Court merely said that the Minnesota ban on the retail sale of milk in plastic containers did not discriminate against interstate commerce since it applied equally to all milk retailers, without regard to whether the milk,

[25] 449 US 456 (1981).   [26] [1986] ECR 4,607.
[27] 449 US 456, 471 (1981).   [28] [1986] ECR 4,610.   [29] *Ibid.*

the containers or the sellers are from outside the state.[30] The Minnesota statute being non-discriminatory, it was the *Pike* balancing test, rather than the more stringent *Dean Milk* test applicable to discriminatory measures, that provided the legal framework for the case. Similarly, in *Danish Bottles*, the Court of Justice applied the rule of reason without discussing anywhere whether the Danish legislation discriminated in its effects against non-Danish producers.[31]

The courts, however, devoted more attention to the question of proportionality which is an essential part of the *Pike* test and the rule of reason. Pursuant to the *Pike* test, even if a measure is non-discriminatory and has only an incidental effect on interstate trade, it must nevertheless be struck down 'if the burden imposed on such commerce is clearly excessive in relation to the putative local benefits'.[32] Applying this test to the Minnesota statute, the Supreme Court found that the burden imposed on interstate commerce by this statute was relatively minor.[33] On the other hand, the environmental benefits brought about by the statute in terms of promoting the conservation of energy and other natural resources and of easing the problems created by the disposal of solid waste were substantial.[34] For the court, the burden imposed on interstate trade by the Minnesota statute was therefore proportionate (i.e., was not 'clearly excessive') to the environmental benefits the statute attempted to achieve.[35]

The Court of Justice also became involved in a proportionality analysis, though of a more ambiguous nature. Applying the rule of reason to the deposit-and-return system (the first aspect of the Danish legislation), the court found that such a system was not disproportionate since it was 'an indispensable element of a system intended to ensure the re-use of containers and therefore . . . necessary to achieve the aims pursued by the contested rules'.[36] In conformity with its previous case law, the court took the level of protection chosen by the member states for granted and limited its analysis of proportionality to check whether the restrictions imposed by the deposit-and-return system were effective and essential to achieve that level of environmental protection. By contrast, when it examined the NAPE approval system (the second aspect of the Danish legislation), it found that the extra burden imposed by that system on intra-Community trade was disproportionate in relation to the marginal increase in environmental protection (compared with the level of protec-

---

[30] 449 US 456, 472 (1981).   [31] [1986] ECR 4,607, 4,630.
[32] *Pike* v. *Bruce Church*, 387 US 137, 142 (1970).   [33] 449 US 472.
[34] *Ibid.* at 473.   [35] *Ibid.*   [36] [1986] ECR 4,630.

tion already guaranteed by the deposit-and-return system) such a system was able to ensure. Contrary to the approach taken with regard to the deposit-and-return system, the Court of Justice did not therefore limit its analysis of proportionality to check whether the restrictions imposed by the NAPE approval system were effective and essential to achieve the level of protection chosen by Denmark. Rather, adopting an approach which clearly evokes the *Pike* test used by the Supreme Court in *Clover Leaf Creamery*, the Court of Justice balanced the burden imposed by the approval system on intra-Community trade and the level of environmental protection such a system promoted, and eventually decided that the former outweighed the latter.

As already noted, the balancing approach adopted by the Court of Justice in *Danish Bottles* appears to be an isolated instance.[37] However, fear has been expressed that such an approach could be used by the court in the future to second guess the level of environmental protection chosen by the member states.[38] Although this balancing approach is better established in United States constitutional law, it has been the object of intense controversy.[39] In this context, although this goes beyond the narrow area of product standards, it is perhaps interesting to discuss briefly here the respective advantages and disadvantages of such a balancing approach. First, from a theoretical standpoint, a balancing approach presents a practical method for reconciling legitimate local interests with free-trade values. If both trade and environmental protection are such important interests that neither can be sacrificed at the outset, it makes sense to introduce a balance between them when they clash in a specific case. Trade and environmental protection are placed on an equal footing: if a state measure creates a great burden on trade and

---

[37] See p. 28 above.

[38] See, e.g., L. Kramer, 'Environmental Protection and Article 30 of the Treaty', *Common Market Law Review* 30 (1993), 111, 126; B. Jadot, 'Observations – Mesures Nationales de Police de l'Environnement, Libre Circulation des Marchandises et Proportionnalité', *Cahiers de Droit Européen* (1990), 408, 427.

[39] It should be noted that to what extent the burden imposed by state measures on interstate trade should be balanced with the environmental objectives such measures aimed to promote has also been a controversial issue in the context of GATT. Compare, e.g., S. Walker, *Environmental Protection and Trade Liberalization: Finding the Balance* (Brussels: Facultés Universitaires St Louis Press, 1993) at 87; S. Charnovitz, 'Trade and the Environment – Examining the Issues', *International Environmental Affairs* (1992), 203, 215 (strongly rejecting the use of a balancing approach in the GATT context) with J. Dunoff, 'Reconciling International Trade with Preservation of the Global Commons: Can We Prosper and Protect?' *Washington and Lee Law Review* 49 (1992), 1,407, 1,447 (suggesting the use of a balancing approach by GATT panels).

generates little environmental benefits, it will be held invalid; conversely, if the environmental benefits brought about by a measure are great, and the burden on trade is slight, the measure will be found valid.[40] Moreover, from a practical standpoint, this approach may also have positive consequences since it gives the courts the opportunity to strike down capricious measures, i.e., measures bringing about minor environmental benefits but at a very high cost to interstate trade.

On the other hand, a balancing approach presents a number of difficulties. First, in practice, such a test may not be easy to operate. For a balancing test to work, the costs (in terms of loss of economic opportunities) and benefits (in terms of increased welfare for domestic citizens) of the environmental measure in question must be properly assessed. In this regard, only sophisticated economic analysis can properly identify the true size and distribution of the burdens and benefits.[41] It is doubtful, however, whether courts are adequately equipped to produce this kind of analysis. For example, the *Danish Bottles* decision contains errors and omissions in the treatment of the facts.[42] This leads one to ask whether the Court of Justice could reach a justifiable decision in a more marginal case.[43] Second, even if it were possible for the courts properly to assess the respective costs and benefits of an environmental measure, it may not be

---

[40] This approach, which is based on the idea that both trade and environmental policies aim at furthering human welfare and that therefore the role of courts is to find a balance between these policies that will promote the greatest good for the greatest number, may not satisfy some environmentalists for whom environmental values are absolute, i.e., they may not be sacrificed at any price even if their preservation imposes disproportionately large costs on society. See R. Housman, 'A Kantian Approach to Trade and the Environment', *Washington and Lee Law Review* 49 (1992), 1,373, 1,374.

[41] For example, in the so-called transportation cases which involved the constitutionality of even-handed state road-safety regulations, parties submitted to federal courts hundreds of pages of evidence regarding the respective costs and benefits of such regulations. This led to what Justice Black called 'extraordinary trials'. See *Southern Pacific Co.* v. *Arizona*, 325 US 761, 787 (1945) (Black J, dissenting).

[42] For some illustrations of these errors and omissions, see D. Geradin and R. Stewardson, 'Trade and Environment: Some Lessons from *Castlemaine Tooheys* (Australia) and *Danish Bottles* (European Community), *International and Comparative Law Quarterly* 44 (1995), 41, 68. See also K. Culp Davis, 'Judicial, Legislative, and Administrative Lawmaking: A Proposed Research Service for the Supreme Court', *Minnesota Law Review* 71 (1986), 1 (criticizing the Supreme Court for its inability to deal with factual matters).

[43] From a technical standpoint, the *Danish Bottles* case did not present any particular difficulties and, although it did not do so, the court could have developed a fairly accurate cost–benefit analysis of the Danish system. A cost–benefit analysis of measures that are precautionary in nature such as regulations prohibiting the sale or use of products containing carcinogenic substances or genetically modified organisms may be far more difficult to make.

easy to compare them. Is a marginal reduction of discarded bottles in the streets worth the actual loss of substantial economic opportunities?[44] As we have seen, it is this problem which induced the Supreme Court of Oregon in *American Can* v. *Oregon Liquor Control Commission*[45] to refuse to balance environmental objectives with the potential burden they impose on trade. Finally, and perhaps more fundamentally, one may wonder if it is the role of courts to decide whether the level of environmental protection chosen by a state is 'unreasonable' or 'disproportionate'.[46] As pointed out by the Court of Appeals of the Seventh Circuit in *Procter & Gamble* v. *Chicago*,[47] a strong argument can be made that this is a legislative rather than judicial choice and, hence, that courts should not transform themselves in 'super-legislatures'.[48]

Although since the beginning of the post-Second World War period, the majority of the Supreme Court has favoured the use of a balancing approach to deal with non-discriminatory statutes, this approach has been strongly criticized and opposed by a number of justices.[49] Their opposition has been echoed by a number of scholars arguing that courts should refrain from second-guessing what they perceive as legitimate exercises of state regulatory powers.[50] In the environmental area, however, the use of a balancing approach has had a limited impact on state measures since, when balancing trade and environmental objectives,

---

[44] See, *mutatis mutandis, Brotherhood of Locomotive Firemen & Enginemen* v. *Chicago, Rock Island & Pacific Railroad Co.*, 393 US 129, 140 (1968) ('It is difficult at best to say that financial losses should be balanced against the loss of lives and limbs of workers and people using the highways').

[45] 517 P. 2d 691, 697 (1973).

[46] See, e.g., *Stoke-on-Trent City Council* v. *B&Q*, English High Court, Chancery Division (Hoffman J) [1990] 3 CMLR 41, 49 ('In my judgment it is not my function to carry out the balancing exercise or to form my own view on whether the legislative objective could be achieved by other means. These questions involve compromises between competing interests which in a democratic society must be resolved by a legislature.'); *Southern Pacific Co.* v. *Arizona*, 325 US 761, 794–5 (1945) (Black J, dissenting) ('Representatives elected by the people to make their laws, rather than judges appointed to interpret these laws, can best determine the policies which govern the people. That at least is the basic principle on which our domestic society rests.').

[47] 509 F. 2d 69, 76 (7th Cir. 1975), cert. denied, 421 US 978 (1975).

[48] *Ibid.*

[49] See, e.g., *CTS Corp.* v. *Dynamics Corp.*, 107 S. Ct 1,637 (1987) (Scalia J, concurring); *Kassel* v. *Consolidated Freightways*, 450 US 662, 687 (1981) (Rehnquist J and Stewart J, dissenting); *Southern Pacific Co.* v. *Arizona*, 325 US 761, 784 and 795 (1945) (Black J and Douglas J, dissenting).

[50] See, e.g., D. Farber, 'State Regulation and the Dormant Commerce Clause', *Constitutional Commentary* 3 (1996), 395; J. Eule, 'Laying the Dormant Commerce Clause to Rest', *Yale Law Journal* 91 (1982), 425, 442.

courts have generally shown a great degree of deference towards environmental objectives.[51] In the European Community context, the debate has
not really started yet. This is certainly due to the fact that the Court of
Justice has generally admitted that, provided that the measures they
adopt pursue a legitimate objective and are 'necessary', it is for the
member states to choose the level of health, safety and environmental
protection they wish. If, however, the Court of Justice were to apply again
the balancing process adopted in *Danish Bottles*, in the area of product
standards or elsewhere, it is suggested that it should defer to member
states' environmental objectives in this process.[52]

Process standards

Contrary to product standards, process standards do not in themselves
impede (i.e., make more difficult or impossible) interstate trade.[53] Process
standards may, however, distort (i.e., make unfair) that trade. Because
their environmental production costs are lower, producers located in
states enforcing lax process standards enjoy a competitive advantage over
producers enforcing strict process standards. When this advantage
becomes important, scenarios of industrial relocation, whereby producers
located in states enforcing strict process standards decide to move to
states enforcing lax standards, may also take place. Against this background, I have speculated on how the Court of Justice and the Supreme
Court would react if states economically affected by other states' lax
process standards decided to apply their own process standards to
products imported from states enforcing lax standards. What would
happen if, for example, some states decided to ban or impose various

---

[51] See D. Geradin, 'Free Trade and Environmental Protection in an Integrated Market: A
Survey of the Case Law of the United States Supreme Court and the European Court of
Justice', *Florida State University Journal of Transnational Law and Policy* 2 (1993), 141, 158.

[52] See Geradin and Stewardson, 'Trade and Environment: Some Lessons' at 71.

[53] It is true, however, that, because they will make production more costly, process
standards may have some restrictive effects on exports. Such effects will nevertheless
be incidental and process standards will generally be upheld under the free-trade
provisions of the EC Treaty and the dormant Commerce Clause doctrine. See, e.g.,
Joined Cases 141 to 143/81, *Holdijck* [1982] ECR 1,299, 1,313 (holding that, although it
could have restrictive effects on the exportation of calves, a Dutch regulation laying
down minimum standards for enclosure of fatting calves, without any distinction as to
whether the animal or meat were intended for the national market or export, did not
fall within the prohibition of Article 34); *Northwest Central Pipeline Corporation v. State
Corporation Commission of Kansas*, 489 US 493 (1989) (holding Kansas regulations
governing the timing of natural-gas production to be compatible with the Commerce
Clause).

restrictions on the imports of cars, videos or other products manufactured under lax process standards in other states?[54]

Although there is no relevant case law, several reasons indicate that it is unlikely that these kinds of process-related trade restrictions would withstand judicial scrutiny. First, in their respective free-movement-of-goods case law, it is only to further non-economic objectives that the Court of Justice and the Supreme Court have allowed states to deviate from the principle of free trade. The imposition of a 'level playing field' of environmental costs that would be sought by the states adopting process-related restrictions would not therefore be seen as a legitimate local purpose justifying restrictions on interstate trade. As has been seen, a state adopting process-related trade restrictions could perhaps invoke the fact that such restrictions are necessary to protect the environment against the harm created by industrial plants operating under lax process standards. Such an argument would probably be accepted if the state could demonstrate a link between the pollution generated by industrial plants located in other states and damage to its own environment. The Court of Justice and the Supreme Court would, however, reject state attempts to justify process-related restrictions by the need to protect the environment of other states. Finally, even if they could be justified under a valid environmental reason, it is unlikely that process-related restrictions could survive an analysis of proportionality. First, it seems that in most cases less restrictive alternatives, such as consultations between states or the use of labelling provisions, would be readily available. Moreover, if the courts decided to apply a balancing approach, such as the one applied in the container cases described above, they would probably find that the burden imposed on interstate trade by process-related restrictions (which is important) is disproportionate in relation to the (hypothetical) benefits brought about by such restrictions.

In conclusion, in the absence of co-operation between states, it seems impossible for the states applying strict process standards to remove the competitive disadvantage suffered by their industry by adopting unilateral restrictions. As will be seen below, this strongly suggests the need for harmonization of environmental process standards at Community or US federal level.

---

[54] For the sake of the analysis I assume here that no harmonization of process standards has taken place. This is for the most part a fiction since, as will be seen below, both Community and US federal legislatures have extensively harmonized environmental process standards.

4 Judicial and legislative intervention

The previous chapters examined how the Court of Justice and the Supreme Court have attempted to deal with the various kinds of tension that may arise between trade and environmental protection through a process of selective invalidation of state environmental measures restricting trade. In order to bridge the two central parts of this study, the objective of this chapter is to discuss to what extent judicial intervention can be complemented by centralized legislative action taking the form of harmonization of state environmental standards.

Of all areas of environmental regulation, it is perhaps in the area of process standards that there is the most obvious need for the adoption of positive rules of harmonization. As we have seen, variations in the level of stringency of state environmental process standards may create distortions of competition between states. However, the traditional free-movement-of-goods case law of the Court of Justice and the Supreme Court appears to offer little protection to states whose industrial competitiveness is harmed by other states' lax process standards. Although the adoption by one state of lax process standards may generate distortions of competition, lax process standards do not in themselves generate the kind of barriers to trade susceptible of falling within the scope of Article 30 of the Treaty or of the dormant Commerce Clause doctrine. On the other hand, although there is no relevant case law, it seems that if a state enforcing strict process standards attempted to equalize the conditions of competition by imposing restrictions on the imports of products manufactured under lax process standards, such restrictions would probably violate Article 30 or the Commerce Clause.

The danger in this situation is that states enforcing strict process standards may be tempted to reduce the level of stringency of these standards in order to re-establish the competitive position of their industries on domestic and foreign markets. This may in turn trigger an environmentally destructive 'race to the bottom',[1] i.e., 'a race from the desirable levels of environmental quality that states would pursue if they did not face competition for industry to the increasingly undesirable levels that they choose in the face of such competition'.[2] In the absence of adequate judicial intervention to remove the distortions of competition created by inconsistent process standards and given the resulting danger of a 'race to the bottom', it appears to be of central importance that the Community and US federal legislatures adopt compulsory minimum environmental process standards applicable to all states.

The area of product standards also seems to require judicial intervention to be completed by legislative action taking the form of harmonization of state environmental standards. As we have seen, product standards may be designed in such a way as to discriminate against out-of-state products. In this context, courts play an important role in reviewing protectionist state laws. In the absence of discrimination, we have also seen that courts can invalidate state standards that impose an excessive burden on interstate trade in relation to the putative environmental benefits. There are, however, clear limitations in relying exclusively on courts to bring about a unified market in products. Court decisions have essentially a negative or corrective effect: they can only remove specific obstacles to interstate trade. They are, however, generally unable to prevent such obstacles from arising.[3] This is a particularly serious

---

[1] This term was apparently first introduced in the corporate law field by William Cary in 'Federalism and Corporate Law: Reflections upon *Delaware*', *Yale Law Journal* 83 (1974), 663, 666. Justice Brandeis had previously referred to the concept of 'race of laxity': see *Ligget Co.* v. *Lee*, 288 US 517, 559 (1933) (Brandeis J, dissenting).

[2] See R. Revesz, 'Rehabilitating Interstate Competition: Rethinking the "Race-To-The-Bottom" Rationale for Federal Environmental Regulation', *New York University Law Review* 67 (1992), 1,210. See also V. Been, '"Exit" as a Constraint on Land Use Exactions: Rethinking the Unconditional Conditions Doctrine', *Columbia Law Review* 91 (1991), 473, 509; R. Stewart, 'Pyramids of Sacrifice? Problems of Federalism in Mandating State Implementation of National Environmental Policy', *Yale Law Journal* 86 (1977), 1,196, 1,212; R. Stewart, 'Quasi-Constitutional Law in Judicial Review of Environmental Decisionmaking: Lessons from the Clean Air Act', *Iowa Law Review* 62 (1977), 713, 747.

[3] In the United States context, see, e.g., C. Sunstein, 'Protectionism, the American Supreme Court, and Integrated Markets' in Bieber *et al* (eds.), *1992: One European Market* (Baden-Baden: Nomos, 1988), 127, 141 ('courts are passive; they do not initiate the lawsuits they decide. By contrast, legislatures can stem a problem before it starts. If interferences with free trade . . . are widespread, this distinction may assume great importance.'). In the European Community context see, e.g., Weatherill and Beaumont, *EC Law* (London: Penguin, 1993) at 419 ('The Court [of Justice] can influence the nature of legitimate national action through its interpretation of the scope of Article 36, yet its activity is typically in response to national practice. It cannot intervene directly to set

handicap in the area of product standards where, because of growing consumer demand for environmental quality, states tend to enact an increasing number of regulations governing the environmental character- istics of products, including the biodegradability or the environmental impact of their components,[4] the size, weight and content of their packaging,[5] etc.[6] In this context, legislative action appears to provide a swifter and surer remedy than selective judicial invalidation of state environmental measures restricting trade. This does not imply that all matters, however trivial, should be regulated at central level.[7] This would not be sensible or feasible.[8] It does, however, suggest that unless a comprehensive and carefully thought-out policy of harmonization of environmental product standards is elaborated, inconsistent state product standards are likely to impede the free movement of goods in the Community and the United States.

common standards in advance. Harmonization is an altogether more positive contribution to the development of the Community and the common regulation of the single economic space').

[4] See, e.g., *Procter & Gamble* v. *City of Chicago*, 509 F. 2d 69 (7th Cir. 1975), cert. denied 421 US 978 (1975) (examining the compatibility with the Commerce Clause of an ordinance of the City of Chicago banning the use of detergents containing phosphates).

[5] See, e.g., Case 302/86, *Commission* v. *Denmark* [1988] ECR 4,607 and *American Can* v. *Oregon Liquor Control Commission*, 517 P. 2d 691 (1973) (examining the compatibility with the EC Treaty and the US Constitution respectively of state legislation regulating containers for drinks).

[6] See the numerous examples of trade-restrictive state product standards given by Ludwig Kramer in *EC Treaty and Environmental Law* (London: Sweet & Maxwell, 1995) at 118*ff.*

[7] In the absence of harmonization, it seems, for example, that an important number of trade restrictions can be avoided through a dialogue between local and central (federal) authorities. In the Community context, Directive 83/189 of 28 March 1983 laying down a procedure for the provision of information in the field of technical standards and regulations is designed to establish such a dialogue, OJ 1983, L 109/8. On Directive 83/ 189 of 28 March 1983, see S. Lecrenier, 'Les Articles 30 et Suivants CEE et les Procédures de Contrôle Prévues par la Directive 83/189/CEE', *Revue du Marché Commun* (1985), 6. However, a similar procedure does not seem to exist in the United States: see J. Choper, 'The Scope of National Power *vis-à-vis* the States: The Dispensability of Judicial Review', *Yale Law Journal* 86 (1977), 1,552, 1,586 ('Congress has never established a machinery for bringing to its attention the myriad of state and local rules that may arguably intrude on the national domain').

[8] See, e.g., Sunstein, 'Protectionism', 127 ('The allocation of authority to the courts is justified in part on the ground that Congressional resources are limited, and it is unrealistic to rely on Congress as a guardian against state interferences with commerce. Such interferences are frequent, and the agenda of Congress is large; the national legislature cannot be expected to invalidate every such interference.'). For a similar view in the European context, see R. Dehousse, 'Completing the Internal Market: Institutional Constraints and Challenges' in Bieber *et al.* (eds.), *1992: One European Market* (Baden-Baden: Nomos, 1988), 311, 312.

Finally, in the area of waste disposal, judicial intervention can also be usefully completed by legislative action. As we have seen, some states have adopted restrictions on the interstate movements of waste and, in particular, on the imports of out-of-state waste.[9] Although protectionist purposes may not always be lacking, such restrictions usually represent last-resort measures used by states to avoid their territory becoming a dumping ground for the rest of the Community/nation. If one wishes to avoid such situations, it is important to understand why waste moves between states and why some states receive disproportionate quantities of waste from other states. One central reason for interstate movements of waste is economic: waste produced in one state tends to be transferred to another state if the cost of disposal in that state plus the transport cost is less than the cost of disposal in the state of origin.[10] Since cost disparities in waste disposal primarily result from the variations in the legal requirements applied by the states to such a disposal, waste will usually be disposed of in the states where waste-disposal standards are the least stringent with a resultant degradation of environmental quality there.[11] This clearly suggests the need for a policy of harmonization of waste-disposal standards at a high level of environmental protection in the Community and the United States. Such a harmonization should indeed reduce cost disparities in waste disposal between states and, hence, interstate movements of waste.

It should be noted, however, that, since the cost of waste disposal partly depends on non-regulatory factors, such as the cost of land and labour, and the type of installations which are compatible with the geographical

[9] See, e.g., Case C-2/90, *Commission* v. *Belgium* [1992] ECR I-4,431 and *Fort Gratiot Sanitary Landfill Inc.* v. *Michigan Department of Natural Resources*, 112 S. Ct 2,019 (1992) (examining the compatibility with the EC Treaty and the US Constitution respectively of state restrictions on the imports of waste).

[10] See A. Schmidt, 'Transboundary Movements of Waste under EC Law: The Emerging Regulatory Framework', *Journal of Environmental Law* 4 (1992), 56, 57.

[11] The movements of waste in the northeastern part of the United States in the 1970s and 1980s seem to confirm this point. Because of its notoriously lax waste policy, New Jersey attracted throughout the 1970s large amounts of waste from neighbouring states, including Pennsylvania. When this waste flow became uncontrollable, New Jersey decided to ban the imports of out-of-state waste. Striking down this ban, the Supreme Court declared in *Philadelphia* v. *New Jersey* (437 US 617 (1978)) that New Jersey could have protected its territory by raising its waste-disposal standards. When New Jersey decided to tighten its waste-disposal standards in the beginning of the 1980s, the immediate effect was, however, to produce a considerable increase in dumping of waste in Pennsylvania, whose disposal standards had then become laxer than New Jersey's. See K. Florini, 'Issues of Federalism in Hazardous Waste Control: Cooperation or Confusion?' *Harvard Environmental Law Review* 6 (1983), 307, 311.

constraints of the states, harmonization of waste-disposal standards will not prevent all transfers of waste between states.[12] Moreover, independently of the cost of waste disposal, there may be circumstances where interstate transfers of waste are rendered necessary by the lack of waste-disposal facilities in a number of states. In this context, in addition to setting up harmonized waste-disposal standards, there is a need for the Community and US federal legislatures to establish some form of control over interstate movements of waste.

[12] See p. 118 below.

PART 2

Positive harmonization

As we have seen in Part 1, a process of negative harmonization of trade-restrictive state environmental standards through judicial intervention may not be sufficient to ease the various kinds of tension that may arise between trade and environmental protection. Against this background, the central objective of Part 2 is to examine how the Community and the US federal government have attempted to reconcile free-trade and environmental-protection objectives by setting common environmental standards for all states through centralized legislative action (a process of positive harmonization).

In Part 2, Community and United States law will be discussed separately (chapters 5 and 6 respectively). A comparative analysis of the various findings made in chapters 5 and 6 will then be made in chapter 7. Chapters 5 and 6 will each be divided in four comparable sections. The first two sections will deal with two important institutional questions. The first section will tackle the question of the existence of a legal or constitutional basis for environmental action in the EC Treaty and the US Constitution. The existence of such a basis is essential since both European Community and United States systems are based on the principle of attributed powers. Pursuant to this principle, the Community and the US federal government may only act within the limits of the powers that are assigned to them by the EC Treaty and the US Constitution respectively. The EC Treaty now contains specific provisions (Articles 100A, 130R, 130S and 130T) allowing Community action in the environmental field. Some uncertainties remain, however, as to the respective scope of these provisions. The US Constitution makes no reference to environmental protection. As will be seen, federal action in the environmental field has nevertheless been authorized on the basis of a broad interpretation of the interstate Commerce Clause. The second section will deal with the

principles of subsidiarity and proportionality. In addition to the requirement of the existence of a legal basis, the EC Treaty contains additional
conditions before authorizing a particular Community action. Although
the Community may be competent to act in a particular field, it must
only do so in conformity with the principles of subsidiarity and proportionality according to which the Community shall act in the areas of
shared competence 'only if and insofar as the objectives of the proposed
action cannot be sufficiently achieved by the Member States' (subsidiarity)
and all Community actions 'shall not go beyond what is necessary to
achieve the objectives of the Treaty' (proportionality). Although such
principles are absent from the US Constitution, I will nevertheless
examine to what extent the federal government is subject to similar
restraints in the areas of shared competence, with particular reference to
environmental protection.

Having discussed the respective powers of the Community and the US
federal government to act in the environmental field as well as the
potential limits that may be placed on the exercise of such powers out of
respect for the regulatory autonomy of the states, the third section will
examine how in the areas of product standards, process standards and
waste, the Community and the US federal government have concretely
attempted to balance trade and environmental protection through or in
the context of their legislative action. In this regard, particular emphasis
will be placed on the various difficulties they may encounter in this
balancing exercise as well as on the various compromises that must be
made between the competing trade and environmental objectives in
order to overcome these difficulties. Finally, the fourth section will deal
with the question of pre-emption. As will be seen, this question is of
central importance since it determines the degree of autonomy that is left
to the states once the Community or the US federal government have
legislated. In particular, it offers a good illustration of the tension
between uniformity and diversity that can be found in divided-power
systems that promote free trade between their component states. On the
one hand, pre-emption of further state intervention can be seen as a
guarantee that the unity of the relevant integrated market will not be
disrupted by inconsistent state regulations. On the other hand, pre-
emption can be seen as a direct attempt against the freedom of states to
choose their own level of environmental protection.

5   Harmonization in European Community law

The principle of attributed powers

The EC Treaty is founded on a system of attributed powers.[1] The essential feature of such a system is that the Community can only act when it has been expressly given the power to do so by a provision of the Treaty. Without the existence of a legal basis establishing its power to act in a particular field, no Community action in that field is possible.

With regard to the specific question of the existence of one or several legal bases for Community action in the environmental field, a distinction can usefully be drawn between two distinct phases. The first phase covers the period prior to the amendments made to the Treaty by the Single European Act (SEA). Although this period was characterized by the absence of a proper legal basis in the Treaty for Community environmental action, a brief examination of this period will provide us with the necessary background for a better understanding of the important modifications brought about successively by the SEA and the Treaty on European Union (TEU). The second phase covers the period, from July 1987 onwards, following the entry into force of the SEA. In this second phase, distinctions will also be drawn between the period following the entry into force of the SEA but preceding the entry into force of the TEU and the period, from November 1993 onwards, following the entry into force of the TEU.

When it was signed in 1957, the Treaty establishing the European Community had no express provisions relating to environmental protection. This omission can be explained by the fact that in the years during which the Treaty of Rome was being drawn up, protection of the environment was not considered to be of great importance. However,

[1]   Article 3B(1) and Article 4 of the Treaty.

against a background of increasing prosperity, it was soon felt that economic expansion should also result in improvements to the quality of life, including a better environment.[2] In the absence of a specific Treaty provision for the implementation of an environmental policy, two provisions originally created for economic purposes, Articles 100 and 235, were employed as the legal basis for initial Community environmental legislation.[3] Article 100 provides for the harmonization of national laws which affect the functioning of the common market. If the view that environmental measures can be based on Article 100 has been implicitly acknowledged by the Court of Justice,[4] this provision, however, only provides an incomplete basis for environmental action. Indeed, a clear economic nexus with the functioning of the common market is necessary for the use of this provision as a legal basis for Community action.[5] Environmental measures in the pre-SEA period were also sometimes based on Article 235 which empowers the Council to take action which 'should prove necessary to attain, in the course of the operation of the common market, one objective of the Community'. If the wording of Article 235 requires that its use is linked with the operation of the common market,

---

[2] In October 1972, the Heads of State of the member states declared that '[e]conomic expansion is not an end in itself. Its aim should be to enable disparities in living conditions to be reduced . . . It should result in an improvement in the quality of life as well as its standard of living. As befits the genius of Europe, particular attention will be given to intangible values and protecting the environment': Commission, *Sixth General Report* (1972) at 8. This declaration was soon followed by the first Programme of Action of the European Communities on the Environment, OJ 1973, C 112/1. For the texts of subsequent programmes, see Second Programme (1977–81), OJ 1977, C 139/1; Third Programme (1982–6), OJ 1983, C 46/1; Fourth Programme (1987–92), OJ 1987, C 328/1; Fifth Programme (1993–9), OJ 1993, C 138/1.

[3] See G. Close, 'Harmonization of Laws: Use and Abuse of Powers under the EC Treaty?' *European Law Review* 6 (1978), 461. See also R. C. Béraud, 'Fondements Juridiques de la Protection de l'Environnement dans le Traité de Rome', *Revue du Marché Commun* (1979), 35; A. Gérard, 'Les Limites et les Moyens Juridiques de l'Intervention des Communautés Européennes en Matière de Protection de l'Environnement', *Cahiers de Droit Européen* (1975), 14; H. Scheuer, 'Aspects Juridiques de la Protection de l'Environnement dans le Marché Commun', *Revue du Marché Commun* (1975), 441.

[4] See Case 91/79, *Commission v. Italy* [1980] ECR 1,099, 1,106 and Case 92/79, *Commission v. Italy* [1980] ECR 1,115, 1,122 (holding that Article 100 was a sufficient legal basis for the directive on the biodegradability of detergents and the sulphur content of liquid fuels respectively).

[5] For some examples of measures based on Article 100, see Directive 79/117 of 21 December 1979 prohibiting the placing on the market and the use of plant protection products containing certain active substances, OJ 1979, L 33/36; Directive 76/769 of 27 July 1976 on the approximation of the laws, regulations and administrative provisions of the member states relating to restrictions on the marketing and use of certain dangerous substances and preparations, OJ 1976, L 262/201.

the link required apparently does not need to be as close as that required by Article 100. A flexible interpretation of Article 235 thus permitted the Community to take environmental action in matters not directly related to the harmonization of national rules having an influence on the common market.[6] In a pragmatic approach, action taken by the Community has often been based on both Articles 100 and 235.[7]

An important difference between Article 100 and Article 235 is that the latter does not limit Community action to the issuance of directives but permits action by any of the legal instruments listed in Article 189 of the Treaty, including regulations directly applicable in all member states. The fundamental characteristic is, however, that in both cases decision-making requires unanimity by the members of the Council, and not a simple or qualified majority. This had the effect of making the decision-making process much more cumbersome since one member state could block the adoption of a measure contrary to its political or economic interests.[8] The fundamental inconvenience created by the rigidity of the decision-making process, combined with the lack of a proper legal basis for environmental action, motivated the amendments to the Treaty by the SEA.

The inadequate legal foundation of Community action in the environmental field was rectified by the SEA which introduced two categories of provisions capable of constituting a legal basis for Community action in this area.[9] First, the environment *per se*, that is independently of its

---

[6] See, e.g., Council Decision 81/462 of 11 June 1981 on the conclusion of the Convention on long-range transboundary air pollution, OJ 1981, L 171/1; Directive 79/409 of 2 April 1979 on the conservation of wild birds, OJ 1979, L 103/1.

[7] See, e.g., Directive 85/337 of 27 June 1985 on the assessment of the effects of certain public and private projects on the environment, OJ 1985, L 175/40; Directive 82/883 of 3 December 1982 on procedures for the surveillance and monitoring of the environments concerned by waste from the titanium dioxide industry, OJ 1982, L 378/1; Directive 82/501 of 24 June 1982 on the major-accident hazards of certain industrial activities, OJ 1982, L 230/1.

[8] A notorious example of this occurred in the context of Directive 76/464 of 4 May 1976 on pollution caused by certain dangerous substances discharged into the aquatic environment, OJ 1976, L 129/23, discussed at pp. 114–15 below.

[9] See generally C. Zacker, 'Environmental Law of the European Economic Community: New Powers Under the SEA', *Boston College International and Comparative Law Review* 14 (1991), 249; F. Roelants du Vivier and J. P. Hannequart, 'Une Nouvelle Stratégie Européenne pour l'Environnement dans le Cadre de L'Acte Unique', *Revue du Marché Commun* (1988), 225; D. Vandermeersch, 'The Single European Act and the Environmental Policy of the European Community', *European Law Review* 12 (1987), 407; L. Kramer, 'The Single European Act and Environment Protection: Reflections on Several New Provisions in Community Law', *Common Market Law Review* 24 (1987), 659.

connection with the internal market, was made the subject of a special Title of the Treaty (Title VII, including Articles 130R, 130S and 130T). Article 130R specified the objectives of Community environmental policy and the principles such a policy must observe. Article 130S(1) provided that environmental action could be taken by the Council unanimously on a proposal from the Commission and after consultation with the European Parliament. Following Article 130S(3), the Council could also unanimously decide to take action by a qualified majority.[10] Finally, Article 130T provided that the environmental-protection measures adopted under Article 130S shall not preclude any member state from maintaining or introducing more stringent measures so long as they are not incompatible with other articles of the Treaty.

Concern for environmental protection was also present in the chapter devoted to the internal market.[11] Article 100A(1) granted the Council, acting by a qualified majority on a proposal from the Commission in cooperation with the European Parliament, the power to adopt measures for the approximation of national laws to achieve the internal market. This undoubtedly included measures related to environmental protection. If it were not the case, Article 100A(3), which provides that in respect of proposals concerning, *inter alia*, environmental protection the Commission shall take 'as a base a high level of environmental protection', would not make sense. Article 100A(4) also allows a member state to derogate from a Community measure that was adopted by a qualified majority vote

---

[10] For some applications of this provision, see Article 9 of Regulation 1734/88 of 16 June 1988 concerning export from and import into the Community of certain dangerous chemicals, OJ 1988, L 155/2; Article 3.5 of Directive 88/609 of 24 November 1988 on the limitation of emissions of certain pollutants into the air from large combustion plants, OJ 1988, L 336/1.

[11] Article 7A of the Treaty defines the 'internal market' as 'an area without internal frontiers in which the free movement of goods, persons, services and capital is ensured in accordance with the provisions of [the EC] Treaty'. In this context, an important question is how the notion of internal market, as defined in Article 7A, relates to the traditional notion of 'common market', to which I referred earlier. The term common market is nowhere defined in the Treaty but its meaning can be gathered from Article 2 of the Treaty. According to Wyatt and Dashwood: '[In Article 2] "common market" is used as a term of art, covering the whole range of Community activities other than those connected with the approximation of economic policies; and legislative practice over the years suggests that a similarly broad meaning has been given to the term in Articles 100 and 235. The internal market should, therefore, be regarded as the more specific notion, introduced to provide a sharper focus for the project that was set in motion by the 1985 White Paper': D. Wyatt and A. Dashwood, *European Community Law* (Sweet & Maxwell, 3rd edn, 1993) at 357–8.

'on grounds of major needs . . . related to the protection of the environment'.

The entry into force of the TEU has introduced important amendments with regard to the competence of the Community and the member states to take environmental action.[12] First, Article 130S(1) of the TEU provides that environmental action is to be taken by the Council acting in accordance with the procedure referred to in Article 189C. Article 189C incorporates the text of Article 149(2) of the Treaty as modified by the SEA, i.e., the co-operation procedure.[13] This constitutes a very important step forward since it means that qualified majority in the Council becomes the norm for environmental matters. However, by way of derogation from Article 130S(1), Article 130S(2) of the TEU provides that a certain number of measures must still be decided unanimously by the Council: (i) provisions primarily of a fiscal nature; (ii) measures concerning town and country planning, land use with the exception of waste management and measures of a general nature, and management of water resources; and (iii) measures significantly affecting a member state's choice between energy sources and the general structure of its energy supply.[14] The second sentence of this second paragraph provides, nevertheless, that the Council may, unanimously, on a proposal from the Commission and after consulting the European Parliament, define those matters referred to in the first sentence on which decisions are to be taken at a qualified majority. In addition to the procedures mentioned in the first two paragraphs of Article 130S, Article 130S(3) states that 'general action programmes setting out priority objectives to be attained' must be adopted following the procedure contained in Article 189B, i.e., the co-decision procedure that is especially applied in the context of Article

[12] See generally L. Kramer, 'Community Environmental Law under the Maastricht Treaty on European Union and the Fifth Environmental Action Programme' in F. Abraham, K. Deketelaere and J. Stuyck (eds.), *Recent Economic and Legal Developments in European Environmental Policy* (Leuven University Press, 1995) at 75; M Hession and R. Macrory, 'Maastricht and the Environmental Policy of the European Community: Legal Issues for a New Environmental Policy' in O'Keeffe and Twomey (eds.), *Legal Issues of the Maastricht Treaty* (London: Wiley, 1993) at 151; D. Wilkinson, 'Maastricht and the Environment: Implications for the EC's Environment Policy of the Treaty on European Union', *Journal of Environmental Law* 4 (1992), 221; P. Renaudière, 'Le Droit Communautaire de l'Environnement après Maastricht', *Aménagement – Environnement* (1992), 70.

[13] The new legislative procedures adopted pursuant to the TEU are not easily described due to their extreme sophistication and complexity. For a detailed analysis of these procedures, see A. Dashwood, 'Community Legislative Procedures in the Era of the European Union', *European Law Review* 19 (1994), 343.

[14] For a good discussion on the scope of this provision, see L. Kramer, *EC Treaty and Environmental Law* (London: Sweet & Maxwell, 1995) at 74ff.

100A. Finally, it should be noted that Article 130T has remained unchanged by the TEU.

Second, Article 100A of the TEU provides that when the Council adopts measures for the approximation of national laws to complete the internal market, it has to act in accordance with the procedure referred to in Article 189B. Article 189B reinforces the powers of the Parliament in the decision-making process. As already noted, it introduces a co-decision procedure which places the Parliament and the Council as equal partners in the legislative process and includes a conciliation procedure aimed at resolving differences between the two institutions.[15] Under the procedure of co-decision, the Parliament also possesses a veto (by an absolute majority of its component members) over the legislative proposals to which it remains opposed.

From a general standpoint, the various amendments made to the Treaty environmental provisions by the TEU are expected to strengthen the Community's commitment to environmental policy and to facilitate the development of such a policy in a number of new substantive areas.

Drawing a line between Articles 100A and 130S

If the SEA resolved once and for all the question of the existence of a Community competence for environmental action, it gave birth to another question, the one of the establishment of a dividing line between Article 100A and Article 130S. The question of the scope of Article 100A and Article 130S is not only of a formal character. It has important practical implications, especially from a procedural point of view. In its SEA version, Article 100A provided for Council decisions to be taken on the basis of a qualified majority and the use of the co-operation procedure. On the other hand, Article 130S required a unanimous decision after consultation with the European Parliament. This question may also have implications on the relationship between trade and environmental policies. As will be seen below, measures adopted under Article 100A seem indeed to provide for more regulatory uniformity than measures adopted under Article 130S. Due to the important interests at stake, it should not

---

[15] For examples of directives adopted under this procedure, see European Parliament and Council Directive 94/63 of 20 December 1994 on the control of volatile organic compound (VOC) emissions resulting from the storage of petrol and its distribution from technical service stations, OJ 1994, L 365/24; European Parliament and Council Directive 94/62 of 20 December 1994 on packaging and packaging waste, OJ 1994, L 365/10. In both cases, the directives were adopted after an intervention of the Conciliation Committee provided for in Article 189B.

therefore be surprising that the question of the adequate legal basis for Community environmental action has generated fierce litigation between Community institutions.[16] The legal-basis case law of the Court of Justice, which deals with the Treaty provisions in their SEA version, will be analysed below. Then, I will briefly discuss whether the amendments to Article 100A and Article 130S brought about by the TEU provide any clarification over the respective scope of these provisions.

First, it should be noted that the delimitation of the respective field of application of Article 100A and Article 130S does not always pose a problem. For example, it seems clear that measures establishing common product standards should be taken under Article 100A.[17] By removing disparities between national standards, such measures help to ensure the free movement of the products in question and, hence, contribute to the establishment of the internal market. Before the coming into force of the SEA, these measures were taken under Article 100.[18] Similarly, there is no doubt regarding the applicability of Article 130S as a legal basis for environmental-protection measures which do not imply the harmonization of rules having an influence on the internal market.[19] In the period prior to the SEA, these measures were adopted under Article 235.[20] However, as will be seen below, the delimitation of the respective field of application of Article 100A and Article 130S presents a difficulty with regard to the Community measures designed to protect the environment against the harmful consequences of industrial processes as well as measures regulating the movement and disposal of waste. Before the coming into force of the SEA, these measures, which usually in some degree attempt to promote both environmental protection and economic

---

[16] For general discussions on the problem of the choice of a legal basis for Community action, see N. Emiliou, 'Opening the Pandora's Box: The Legal Basis of Community Measures Before the Court of Justice', *European Law Review* 19 (1994), 488; R. Barents, 'The Internal Market Unlimited: Some Observations on the Legal Basis of Community Legislation', *Common Market Law Review* 30 (1993), 85; K. Bradley, 'The European Court and the Legal Basis of Community Legislation', *European Law Review* 13 (1988), 379.

[17] See, e.g., Directive 91/441 of 26 June 1991 amending Directive 70/220 of 20 March 1970 on the approximation of the laws of the member states relating to measures to be taken against air pollution by emissions from motor vehicles, OJ 1991, L 242/1.

[18] See, e.g., Directive 70/220 of 20 March 1970 on the approximation of the laws of the member states relating to measures to be taken against air pollution by emissions from motor vehicles, OJ 1970, L 76/1.

[19] See, e.g., Directive 92/43 of 21 May 1992 on the conservation of natural habitats of wild fauna and flora, OJ 1993, L 206/7.

[20] See, e.g., Directive 79/409 of 2 April 1979 on the conservation of wild birds, OJ 1979, L 103/1.

integration, were taken on the basis of both Articles 100 and 235 of the Treaty.[21]

In Case C-300/89, *Commission* v. *Council* (the 'Titanium Dioxide' case), the Court of Justice was confronted with one of these borderline cases.[22] The Commission asked the court to annul Council Directive 89/249 on pollution caused by waste from the titanium dioxide industry because it was based on Article 130S whereas it should have been based on Article 100A. With respect to the legal basis of Directive 89/249, the Council and the Commission were offering conflicting theories. The Council argued that in order to define the correct legal basis of a Community act pursuing at the same time different goals sought by different Treaty provisions, it was necessary to determine the 'centre of gravity', understood in the sense of the 'general objective' of the act. For the Council, the 'general objective' of the Directive was to suppress the pollution produced by waste coming from the fabrication of titanium dioxide.[23] The Commission also made reference to the concept of 'centre of gravity' but it understood it in the sense of 'content' or 'object' of the act. For the Commission, this 'object' was the improvement in the conditions of competition in the titanium dioxide industry.[24]

The court went beyond these approaches, saying that with regard to both its objective and content, Directive 89/249 was concerned inextricably with both environmental protection and the disparities in the conditions of competition.[25] However, being unable to reconcile the different voting rules and procedures of Articles 100A and 130S, the Court of Justice had to opt for one of these provisions at the expense of the other.[26] The court based its choice on Articles 130R(2) and 100A(3) of the

---

[21] See, e.g., Directive 84/360 of 28 June 1984 on the combating of air pollution from industrial plants, OJ 1984, L 188/20; Directive 84/361 of 6 December 1984 on the supervision and control within the Community of the transfrontier shipments of hazardous waste, OJ 1984, L 326/1; Directive 75/442 of 15 July 1975 on waste, OJ 1975, L 194/39.

[22] [1991] ECR I-2,867 noted by Kramer L. in *European Environmental Law Casebook* (London: Sweet & Maxwell, 1994) at 21; C. Barnard, *European Law Review* 17 (1993), 127; H. Somsen, *Common Market Law Review* 29 (1992), 149; J. Robinson, *Journal of Environmental Law* 4 (1993), 112. See also S. Crosby, 'The Single Market and the Rule of Law', *European Law Review* 16 (1991), 451.

[23] [1991] ECR I-2,867 at 2,875–7.

[24] *Ibid.* at 2,871–3. It should be noted that the Commission has always fought for a instrumentalist/objectivist approach against the theological/subjectivist approach of the Council. On this aspect, see K. Bradley, 'L'Arrêt Dioxide de Titane – Un Jugement de Salomon?' *Revue Trimestrielle de Droit Européen* (1992), 609, 616.

[25] Judgment of the court at para. 14.

[26] In Case 165/87, *Commission* v. *Council* [1988] ECR 5,545, 5,561, the Court of Justice ruled

Treaty. Article 130R(2) provides that 'environmental-protection requirements shall be a component of the Community's other policies'. According to the court, that principle implies that a Community measure
should not be based on Article 130S for the sole reason that it also
pursues environmental-protection objectives. The court then recalled that
environmental provisions can be a burden upon the firms to which they
apply and, in the absence of harmonization of national provisions, can
result in distortions of competition. It follows that action which aims at
the approximation of national measures concerning methods of production in a given sector of industry contributes to the establishment of the
internal market and, hence, falls within the scope of Article 100A.[27]
Finally, the court drew attention to Article 100A(3) which requires the
Commission to take as a base 'a high level of protection' in matters
relating to environmental protection. This provision indicates that the
environmental objectives mentioned at Article 130R can be pursued
effectively by way of harmonization measures based on Article 100A. For
the foregoing reasons, which are not entirely convincing,[28] the court
decided that Directive 89/249 should have been based on Article 100A and
therefore annulled it.[29]

The principal consequence of the *Titanium Dioxide* decision appeared to
be that every time Article 100A is applicable in a given situation, it must
be applied. Article 100A would thus become the legal basis for all borderline cases and Article 130S would only be used for all the measures which
do not imply the harmonization of national regulations related to

---

that to the extent the competence of an institution resides in two provisions of the
Treaty, the institution must base the corresponding act on both provisions. In the
Titanium Dioxide case, this jurisprudence could not apply as the voting rules and
procedures contained in Article 100A and 130S cannot be reconciled. As we have seen,
Article 130S requires a unanimous decision of the Council after consultation of the
European Parliament, whereas Article 100A requires a decision of a qualified majority
and the use of the co-operation procedure. A combined application of Articles 100A
and 130S would therefore empty the procedure of co-operation of its substance which,
for the court, 'reflects at a Community level, a fundamental democratic principle,
according to which the people participate in the exercise of power by means of a
representative assembly': judgment of the court at para. 20. This language was first
used in Case 139/79, *Maizena* v. *Council* [1980] ECR 3,393, 3,424; and Case 138/79, *Roquette
Frères* v. *Council* [1980] ECR 3,333, 3,360.

[27] Judgment of the court at para. 27.
[28] The various arguments developed by the Court of Justice seem at best to defeat the
argument that all environmental measures must be adopted under Article 130S.
However, they clearly fail to indicate why Article 100A should be preferred over Article
130S when both provisions are applicable.
[29] Judgment of the court at para. 25.

product or process standards and which do not govern the free movement of goods or the conditions of competition in the internal market. However, far from being settled by the *Titanium Dioxide* decision, the question of the articulation of Articles 100A and 130S of the Treaty re-emerged in two further cases. First, in Case C-155/91, *Commission v. Council* (The '*Waste Directive*' case), the court was asked by the Commission to annul Council Directive 91/156 on waste on the ground that it had been wrongly based on Article 130S of the Treaty.[30] According to the Commission, the Directive would have the dual object of protecting the environment and promoting the functioning of the internal market. It would therefore fall, *ratione materiae*, within the scope of both Articles 130S and 100A and, following the *Titanium Dioxide* decision, it should be based on Article 100A only. The court rejected this argument: following its objective and content, Directive 91/156 sought to ensure the management of waste in conformity with the requirements of environmental protection.[31]

The court also rejected two specific arguments made by the Commission in order to justify the application of Article 100A. First, the Commission had argued that Directive 91/156 promoted the free movement of waste to be recycled and imposed conditions consistent with the internal market on the movement of waste to be disposed. The court disagreed, referring to the *Belgian Waste* case where it had earlier recognized that the principle of correction of environmental damage at source implies that it is up to each region, commune or local entity to take appropriate measures in order to ensure the collection, treatment and disposal of its waste, and that waste should therefore be eliminated as near as possible to its place of production. For the court, the implementation of this restrictive orientation constituted the object of Directive 91/156, which could not therefore be considered as seeking to ensure the free movement of waste within the Community.[32]

Second, the Commission argued that Directive 91/156 harmonizes the conditions of competition both at the level of industrial production and elimination of waste. Although the court admitted that certain dispositions of the directive have an impact on the functioning of the internal market, it found that this was not sufficient to render Article 100A applicable.[33] Indeed, the use of Article 100A is not justified when the

---

[30] Case C-155/91, *Commission v. Council* [1993] ECR I-939; noted by D. Geradin, *European Law Review* 18 (1993), 418–26; A. Wachsmann, *Common Market Law Review* 30 (1993), 1,051; N. de Sadeleer, *Journal of Environmental Law* 5 (1993), 293.

[31] Judgment of the court at para. 9.

[32] *Ibid.* at para. 15.   [33] *Ibid.* at para. 19.

measure to be adopted has only incidentally the effect of harmonizing market conditions inside the Community.[34] For the court, Directive 91/156 is precisely one of these measures. In this regard, Directive 91/156 must be distinguished from Directive 89/429 on the pollution caused by waste from the titanium dioxide industry. The latter is clearly aimed at equalizing the conditions of competition in that sector. In these conditions, the court judged that Directive 91/156 was validly adopted on the basis of Article 130S of the Treaty.[35]

The approach adopted by the Court of Justice in the *Waste Directive* case was subsequently confirmed in Case C-187/93, *Parliament* v. *Council* (the '*Transfer of Waste Regulation*' case).[36] In that case, the court was asked by the Parliament to annul Regulation 259/93 on the supervision and control of shipments of waste into and out of the Community[37] because it was based on Article 130S whereas it should have been based on Articles 100A and 113 of the Treaty.[38] The court rejected the Parliament's petition and confirmed that Article 130S was the proper legal basis for Regulation 259/93. In order to reach that conclusion, the court once again made reference to the objective and content of the challenged act. With regard to the objective of Regulation 259/93, the court found that it results from its preamble that the system it establishes for the surveillance and control of the transfer of waste between member states is designed to improve the

---

[34] See also Case C-70/88, *Parliament* v. *Council* [1991] ECR I-4,529 (holding that a directive fixing the maximum admissible levels of contamination for specific foodstuffs has only a marginal effect on the harmonization of the conditions for the free movement of goods and is therefore validly based on Article 31, Euratom).

[35] It should be noted that the Commission had also asked the Court of Justice to declare void Directive 91/689 of 12 December 1991 on hazardous waste (OJ 1991, L 377/20) as it should have been based on Article 100A rather than Article 130S (Action brought on 16 March 1992 by the Commission of the European Communities against the Council of the European Communities, Case C-86/92, OJ 1992, C 97/7). The Commission, however, withdrew its application to the Court of Justice when the judgment on Directive 91/156 of 19 March 1991 was issued.

[36] [1994] ECR I-2,857.

[37] OJ 1993, L 30/1.

[38] The court declared the Parliament's action inadmissible as far as it was based on the exclusion of Article 113 from the legal basis of the challenge Regulation. Following the Court of Justice's case law, the Parliament is entitled to challenge an act adopted by the Council or the Commission only to the extent that such a challenge aims at preserving its prerogatives (see, e.g., Case C-316/91, *Parliament* v. *Council* [1994] ECR I-625 at para. 12). However, at the time Regulation 259/93 was adopted, Article 113 made no provision for the participation of the Parliament in the elaboration of the acts provided for in this article. The exclusion of Article 113 from the legal basis of the challenged Regulation could not therefore have undermined the prerogatives of the Parliament: judgment of the court at paras. 14–16.

quality of the environment.[39] This system must also be seen in the broader context of the waste-management measures adopted by the Council pursuant to Directive 91/156. In this regard, the court recalled that pursuant to its objective and content Directive 91/156 ensures the management of waste in conformity with the requirements of environmental protection and cannot be seen as implementing a system designed to ensure the free movement of waste within the Community.[40]

With regard to the content of Regulation 259/93, the court noted that it prescribes the conditions to which transfers of waste between member states are submitted and the procedures that must be followed in order to authorize such transfers. The court underlined that these conditions and procedures had been adopted in conformity with the principles of proximity, priority for recovery and self-sufficiency at Community and national level. In order to implement these principles, they allowed member states to take measures to prohibit generally or partially or to object systematically to shipments of waste.[41] In these conditions, the court concluded that, contrary to the Parliament's position, Regulation 259/93 had as its object the furthering of environmental protection and could not be seen as designed to facilitate the transfer of waste in the Community.[42] Regulation 259/93 had therefore been validly adopted under Article 130S. Finally, the court indicated that its conclusion could not be contradicted by the fact that, in approximating the conditions pursuant to which transfers of waste take place, Regulation 259/93 may have an effect on the functioning of the internal market.[43] Indeed, as already decided in the *Waste Directive* case, the recourse to Article 100A is not justified when the Community act in question has only incidentally the effect of harmonizing market conditions. This was the case here. The objective of Regulation 259/93 was not to define the characteristics that waste must possess to circulate freely, but to provide for a harmonized system of procedures pursuant to which the circulation of waste can be reduced to protect the environment.[44]

---

[39] *Ibid.* at para. 18.   [40] *Ibid.* at para. 20.

[41] See Article 4.3.a.1. This provision confirms the restrictive orientation adopted by the court in the *Belgian Waste* case. On the relationship between Regulation 259/93 and the *Belgian Waste* case, see my comments in *European Law Review* 18 (1993), 418, 426.

[42] Judgment of the court at para. 23.   [43] *Ibid.* at para. 24.

[44] Clearly, the court provides here an answer to those who might say that its view of Article 100A is too narrow: 'internal market' is not necessarily synonymous with 'completely free trade' and in the case of 'dangerous' goods such as waste, the establishment of the internal market may well imply the adoption of strict or even, in some cases, restrictive trade rules. See, e.g., A. Schmidt, 'Transboundary Movement of

Following the *Waste Directive* and the *Transfer of Waste Regulation* decisions, the Court of Justice's approach to the legal basis of environmental regulation can be summarized as follows. Community environmental measures having a direct impact on the establishment or functioning of the internal market must be based on Article 100A of the Treaty. Among such measures are those which harmonize regulations related to specific products and specific industries. Community measures having an indirect or incidental impact on the internal market process must be based on Article 130S.[45] Among such measures are anti-pollution regulations of a general character such as environmental quality standards or general waste-management regimes. Community environmental measures having no impact on the internal market must also be based on Article 130S of the Treaty.

A more difficult question, of course, is how to reconcile the *Waste Directive* and the *Transfer of Waste Regulation* decisions with the *Titanium Dioxide* decision, which promoted a broad application of Article 100A. One way of reconciling these cases is to say that in favouring Article 130S over Article 100A in the two later cases, the court did not in fact overrule *Titanium Dioxide* but rather refined it.[46] The *Titanium Dioxide* decision established the rule that for measures concerned with both environmental protection and the internal-market process, Article 100A should be applied. The court did not, however, specify the degree of connection with the internal market that was necessary to render Article 100A applicable. The *Waste Directive* and the *Transfer of Waste Regulation* decisions

Waste under EC Law: The Emerging Regulatory Framework', *Journal of Environmental Law* 4 (1992), 57, 68. Although the court did not contradict this view, it said that recourse to Article 100A was only justified when the ultimate objective of the act is to promote the free movement of the good(s) in question, which is not the case with regard to Regulation 259/93. On this aspect, see also Advocate-General Jacobs' opinion at paras. 44–7.

[45] From a practical standpoint, a different solution would have created a lot of confusion. Indeed, since the entry into force of the SEA, the Council has adopted a large body of environmental measures under Article 130S. See, e.g., Directive 90/219 of 23 April 1990 on the contained use of genetically modified micro-organisms, OJ 1990, L 117/1; Directive 88/610 of 24 November 1988 amending Directive 82/501 of 24 June 1982 on major-accident hazards of certain industrial activities, OJ 1988, L 336/14; Directive 88/609 of 24 November 1988 on the limitation of emissions of certain pollutants into the air from large combustion plants, OJ 1988, L 336/1. As these measures undoubtedly affect the functioning of the internal market, a wide interpretation of the scope of Article 100A would have made them susceptible to challenge.

[46] For a similar view, see M. Schemmel and B. de Regt, 'The European Court of Justice and the Environmental Protection Policy of the European Community', *Boston College International and Comparative Law Review* 17 (1994), 53, 67.

simply filled this lacuna by indicating that an incidental connection with the internal market was not sufficient for the application of Article 100A. Reconcilable with *Titanium Dioxide* or not, the test introduced in the *Waste Directive* and the *Transfer of Waste Regulation* cases may not always be easy to apply in practice.[47] In this context, it is interesting to see whether the amendments brought about by the TEU offer any solution to the debate over the proper legal basis for Community environmental action.

Unfortunately, the TEU complicates rather than simplifies the legislative process for Community environmental action. While the SEA provided for two distinct procedures for environmental action, the TEU has increased the number of legislative procedures to no less than four:

1. Article 100A: qualified-majority voting in the Council and co-decision with the Parliament for those matters related to the establishment of the internal market;
2. Article 130S(1): qualified majority in the Council and co-operation procedure with the Parliament; this represents the standard legislative procedure for the adoption of Community environmental legislation;
3. Article 130S(2): unanimous voting in the Council and consultation with the Parliament for a limited number of exceptions; and
4. Article 130S(3): qualified-majority voting in the Council and co-decision with the Parliament for the adoption of general action programmes.

The existence of these various procedures is likely to lead to two kinds of legal-basis litigation.[48] First, the tension between Article 100A and 130S as the proper legal basis for borderline cases is still present. Conflicts are particularly likely to occur between Article 100A and Article 130S(1) which contains the general regime for the adoption of environmental-

---

[47] See Emiliou, 'Opening the Pandora's Box' at 499. It should be noted that this test was also used by the court to distinguish between the application of Article 130S and other Treaty provisions, such as Articles 43 and 113, which may, in a number of circumstances, constitute a basis for measures that affect the environment. See Case C-405/92, *Mondiet* v. *Islais* [1993] ECR I-6,133 (holding that, although it also aimed at the protection of the environment, Regulation 345/92 banning the use of driftnets of more than 2.5 km in length was rightly based on Article 43 since its principal objective was to ensure the conservation and rational exploitation of fish stocks, which is part of the Community fishery policy); Case C-62/88, *Greece* v. *Council* [1990] ECR I-1,527 (holding that, although it also aimed at the protection of the environment, Regulation 3955/87 on trade in radioactively contaminated products had been rightly based on Article 113 since according to its aim and content the regulation intended to regulate trade between the Community and the non-member states and therefore came within the common commercial policy of the Community).

[48] See K. Lenaerts, 'The Principle of Subsidiarity and the Environment in the European Union: Keeping the Balance of Federalism', *Fordham International Law Journal* 17 (1994), 846, 874.

protection legislation. Although both provisions now imply the use of qualified-majority voting, two differences subsist. First, Article 130S(1) involves the use of the co-operation procedure whereas Article 100A implies the use of the co-decision mechanism. Second, Article 130T permits member states to maintain or introduce measures stricter than those adopted under Article 130S(1), whereas it is subject to discussion whether Article 100A(4) permits member states to *maintain* and *introduce* stricter national measures or only allows them to *maintain* previously existing measures stricter than those adopted under Article 100A.[49] As Article 100A gives the Parliament a more central role in the legislative process than Article 130S(1), one can expect it to favour the use of the former over the latter. The presence of this 'democratic' element should also induce the court to favour Article 100A over Article 130S(1) when the object of Community action relates even-handedly to the functioning of the internal market and environmental protection. By contrast, the Council should prefer Article 130S(1) since it guarantees member states the power to adopt stricter standards than Community ones, provided they are compatible with the Treaty. It is more difficult to speculate on the position of the Commission. On the one hand, as Article 100A seems to ensure more uniformity than Article 130S(1), the Commission will probably favour the use of the former. On the other hand, if the co-decision procedure implied by Article 100A proves to be excessively burdensome, the Commission may decide to opt for the faster co-operation procedure contained in Article 130S(1).

Legal-basis litigation may also occur over the scope of the different legislative procedures contained in the first, second and third paragraphs of Article 130S. First, the scope of Article 130S(3) appears to be quite limited and this provision should not create too much difficulty of interpretation.[50] By contrast, drawing a line between Article 130S(1) and 130S(2) may not always be easy. In particular, the imprecise language used to define the exceptions contained in Article 130S(2) may generate a great deal of confusion.[51] Once again, because of the differences in the

---

[49] See discussion at pp. 134–9 below.

[50] It should be noted, however, that the choice of the Commission to base its 'Proposal for an Action Programme for Integrated Groundwater Protection and Management' on Article 130S(3) has been criticized by several member states on the ground it should have been based on Article 130S(2). See 'EU Groundwater Proposal Heads for Legal Wrangle', *Environment Watch*, 19 July 1996, 15.

[51] For example, Article 130S(2) provides for unanimity voting with regard to measures concerning the 'management of water resources'. It is not clear, however, whether this ambiguous formula covers only the quantitative aspects of water policy or also its

legislative procedures they provide for, disagreement is likely to appear between Community institutions over the scope of these provisions. As it provides for qualified-majority voting and the use of the co-operation procedure, Article 130S(1) should be generally favoured by the Commission and the Parliament. On the other hand, the Council could be tempted to give a broader interpretation to Article 130S(2) which remains the only provision to guarantee a veto right to the member states. Sooner or later, the Court of Justice may therefore be asked to draw a line between the respective scope of these provisions.

The principles of subsidiarity and proportionality

Once the Community has found a sufficient legal basis for its environmental regulation, further questions arise as to whether it should act (necessity of Community action) and, if so, to what extent (intensity of Community action).[52] These questions must be addressed with reference to the second and third paragraphs of Article 3B of the TEU which read:

In the areas which do not fall within its exclusive jurisdiction, the Community shall take action, in accordance with the principle of subsidiarity, only if and in so far as the objectives of the proposed action cannot be sufficiently achieved by the member states and can therefore, by reason of the scale and effects of the proposed action, be better achieved by the Community.

Any action by the Community shall not go beyond what is necessary to achieve the objectives of the Treaty.[53]

The second paragraph of Article 3B contains the principle of subsidiarity *sensu stricto*. Pursuant to this principle, it also contains a test designed to assess the need for Community action. The third paragraph contains the principle of proportionality which can be seen as part of the principle of subsidiarity *sensu lato* and which is designed to shape the nature and intensity of Community action when, pursuant to the principle of subsidiarity, such an action is deemed to be necessary. The

qualitative aspects. This issue may quickly become of central importance since Community directives on water quality usually have very important financial consequences for the member states. Such directives are also often criticized on the ground of subsidiarity. See p. 97 below. It is therefore likely that a certain number of member states will invoke Article 130S(2) to oppose the amendment of existing water quality directives or the adoption of any new directives through the qualified majority procedure contained in Article 130S(1).

[52] This paragraph draws heavily on Lenaerts, 'The Principle of Subsidiarity' at 875.
[53] References to the idea of subsidiarity can also be found in the preamble, as well as in Articles A, B and F of the TEU.

principles of subsidiarity and proportionality, as well as the potential limits they impose on Community environmental action, will be discussed successively below.[54]

Since its insertion in the TEU, the principle of subsidiarity has received considerable attention.[55] It has indeed been seen by many as a general safeguard against excessive Community intervention in the increasing number of fields where the Community has the power to take action.[56] Such an interpretation of the principle of subsidiarity has in turn generated fears that the principle may severely impede Community action. In this regard, it should be noted that the principle of subsidiarity does not reorganize the division of powers between the Community and the member states which, as already observed, flows solely from the Treaty provisions conferring powers on the Community institutions. It is, however, clearly designed to have some influence on the *exercise* of the powers received from the Treaty by these institutions.

Article 3B(2) indicates that the principle of subsidiarity does not apply when the competence of the Community is exclusive.[57] It would only

[54] Since these principles involve different enquiries, I will treat subsidiarity and proportionality as two separate though related concepts. For a similar approach, see the conclusions adopted by the European Council in its Edinburgh Meeting of 11–12 December 1992 (reprinted in *Europe*, 13–14 December 1994). It should be noted, however, that in its Communication to the Council and the European Parliament on the Principle of Subsidiarity of 27 October 1992 (reprinted in *Europe*, 30 October 1992), the Commission suggested that subsidiarity is the broader concept, consisting of two branches, one being the 'need-for-action' test and the other being the requirement of proportionality proper. Under such an approach, proportionality is merely a 'species of subsidiarity'. See, e.g., G. Bermann, 'Taking Subsidiarity Seriously: Federalism in the European Community and the United States', *Columbia Law Review* 94 (1994), 331.

[55] See generally K. Lenaerts and P. van Ypersele, 'Le Principe de Subsidiarité et son Contexte: Etude de l'Article 3B du Traité CE', *Cahiers de Droit Européen* (1994), 3. See also G. Strozzi, 'Le Principe de Subsidiarité dans la Perspective de l'Union Européenne: Une Enigme et Beaucoup d'Attentes', *Revue Trimestrielle de Droit Européen* (1994), 374; M. A. Gaudissart, 'La Subsidiarité: Facteur de (Dés)intégration Européenne?' *Journal des Tribunaux* (1993), 173; N. Emiliou, 'Subsidiarity: An Effective Barrier against "the Entreprises of Ambition"?' *European Law Review* 17 (1992), 383; D. Cass, 'The Word that Saves Maastricht? The Principle of Subsidiarity and the Division of Powers within the Community', *Common Market Law Review* 29 (1992), 1,107; A. Toth, 'The Principle of Subsidiarity in the Maastricht Treaty', *Common Market Law Review* 29 (1992), 1,079; V. Constantinesco, 'La Subsidiarité Comme Principe Constitutionel de l'Union Européenne', *Aussenwirtschaft* (1991), 439; M. Wilke and H. Wallace, 'Subsidiarity: Approaches to Power-Sharing in the European Community', Royal Institute for International Affairs Discussion Papers No. 27 (1990).

[56] See Lenaerts and van Ypersele, 'Le Principe de Subsidiarité' at 7*ff.*

[57] The exclusive competence of the Community in a field means that member states are not entitled to act, even in the absence of Community action. It is generally admitted that the fields over which the Community has an exclusive competence are limited in

apply to matters over which the Community and the member states have a concurrent jurisdiction, including environmental protection.[58] Article 3B(2) also indicates that the exercise of shared competences is conditioned by the insufficiency of member states' action and by the greater efficiency of Community action 'by reason of the scale and effects of the proposed action'. Taken literally, Article 3B(2) provides, however, that it is only when member states are incapable of acting effectively that Community action will be more efficient and should therefore take place.[59] Under such an interpretation, the test of subsidiarity contained in Article 3B(2) seems to be more restrictive than the test that was contained in Article 130R(4) of the SEA, which represented the first reference to the idea of subsidiarity in the Treaty.[60] Article 130R(4) established a form of competition between the Community and the member states whereby the Community was entitled to act provided its action was more efficient than the action of the member states taken separately (test of comparative efficiency). Article 3B(2) would therefore considerably weaken the position of the Community as, contrary to Article 130R(4), action would have to be taken at the lowest efficient level and not at the most efficient level.[61] As pointed out by Lenaerts, such a literal interpretation of Article 3B(2) is, however, unsatisfactory since, in a number of circumstances, it would

---

number. According to the Court of Justice case law, such an exclusive competence would only exist in the context of the common commercial policy (Opinion 1/75 [1975] ECR 1,355, 1,364) and the policy conservation of the biological resources of the sea (Case 804/79, *Commission* v. *United Kingdom* [1981] ECR 1,045, paras. 17–18; Joined Cases 3, 4 and 6/76, *Kramer et al.* [1976] ECR 1,279, paras. 39–41).

[58] See, e.g., Kramer, *EC Treaty and Environmental Law* (London: Sweet & Maxwell, 1995) at 100–1 ('Both the Community and the member states are "competent" or empowered to take action on environmental issues . . . The Treaty assigns no particular area of environmental legislation exclusively to the Community or exclusively to the member states . . . Consequently, the interrelationship between the Community's and the member states' competencies is flexible, dynamic and complementary.').

[59] See Article 3B(2): 'the Community shall take action only *if* . . . the objectives of the proposed action cannot be sufficiently achieved by the member states and can *therefore* . . . be better achieved by the Community' (emphasis added). A literal interpretation of this provision seems to indicate that it is only when the means at the disposal of the member states are ineffective, that the Community should be entitled to take action. See Lenaerts and van Ypersele, 'Le Principe de Subsidiarité' at 47*ff.*

[60] Although Article 130R(4) generated some controversy, its practical importance proved to be limited and it imposed little restraint on Community environmental action. For a good discussion on Article 130R(4), see L. Kramer, *EEC Treaty and Environmental Protection* (London: Sweet & Maxwell, 1990) at 71.

[61] See H. Bribosia, 'Subsidiarité et Répartition des Compétences entre la Communauté et les Etats Membres', *Revue du Marché Unique Européen* (1992), 165.

prevent 'economies of scale' from being realized by taking action at Community rather than member state level.[62]

In its Communication to the Council and the European Parliament of 27 October 1992, the Commission clearly rejected a literal interpretation of Article 3B(2) and described the principle of subsidiarity as involving 'a test of *comparative efficiency* between Community action and that of the member states'.[63] The Commission also enunciated the factors that have to be taken into account in the context of this test, including 'the effect of the scale of the operation (transfrontier problems, critical mass, etc.), the cost of inaction, the necessity of maintaining a reasonable coherence, the possible limits on action at national level (including cases of potential distortion where some member states were able to act and others were not able to do so) and the necessity of ensuring that competition is not distorted within the common market'.[64]

This 'common sense' approach was endorsed by the European Council in its conclusions adopted at the Edinburgh meeting of 11 December 1992 where it defined the principle of subsidiarity as 'the principle that the Community should only take action where an objective can be *better* attained at the level of the Community than at the level of the individual Member States'.[65] The Council also enunciated three guidelines which should be used in examining whether a Community action fulfils the requirements of subsidiarity:

- the issue under consideration has transnational aspects which cannot be satisfactorily regulated by action by the Member States; and/or

---

[62] See Lenaerts, 'The Principle of Subsidiarity' at 876.

[63] See Communication of the Commission to the Council and the European Parliament on the Principle of Subsidiarity of 27 October 1992 (reprinted in *Europe*, 30 October 1992).

[64] In its Fifth Environmental Action Programme, the Commission combined the principle of subsidiarity with the wider concept of 'shared responsibility' which is said to involve 'not so much a choice of action at one level to the exclusion of others but, rather, a mixing of actors and instruments at the appropriate levels without calling into question the division of competences between the Community, the Member States, local and regional authorities'. See *Towards Sustainability*, OJ 1993, C 138/5, 17. Pursuant to this interpretation, there would be no area where the Community would be totally excluded. The Commission seems, however, to indicate that, within the general context of Community action, regulatory powers and responsabilities between the Community and the member states should be divided depending on an evaluation of their respective comparative advantages in exercising these powers and fulfilling these obligations. As will be seen below, this seems to involve a question of proportionality rather than subsidiarity *sensu stricto*.

[65] See conclusions adopted by the European Council in its Edinburgh Meeting of 11–12 December 1992 (reprinted in *Europe*, 13–14 December 1994).

- actions by Member States alone or lack of Community action would conflict with the requirements of the Treaty (such as the need to correct distortion of competition or avoid disguised restrictions on trade or strengthen economic and social cohesion) or would otherwise significantly damage Member States' interests; and/or
- the Council must be satisfied that action at Community level would produce clear benefits by reason of its scale or effects compared with action at the level of the Member States.[66]

Placed in an environmental context, these guidelines seem to allow the Community to take a wide range of environmental actions.[67] The first guideline can safely be used to justify the need for Community action when such an action aims at regulating *pollution spillovers* such as pollution of international rivers, transboundary air pollution, and the pollution caused by cross-border transfers of waste.[68] Pollution spillovers involve transnational aspects which, according to the first guideline, 'cannot be satisfactorily regulated by action by member states'.[69] Moreover, in the (unlikely) event that both Community and member states appear to be equally able to deal with such spillovers, the third guideline still gives preference to Community action when such an action is more efficient than action undertaken at the level of the member states. The second guideline also justifies the need for Community action when inconsistent national environmental regulations are likely to create barriers to intra-Community trade or distortions of competition between member states (*economic spillovers*). The need for Community action in the form of harmonization of environmental product and process standards cannot be doubted – although the nature and extent of such actions may be debated.

---

[66] *Ibid.*

[67] See Lenaerts, 'The Principle of Subsidiarity' at 879ff.

[68] On the concept of spillovers and the various kinds of spillovers that may arise in the environmental context, see R. Stewart, 'Environmental Law in the United States and the European Community: Spillovers, Cooperation, Rivalry, Institutions', *University of Chicago Legal Forum* (1992), 39, 45.

[69] It is indeed unlikely that pollution spillovers can be solved through decentralized actions. Since interstate externalities are not usually imposed symmetrically, polluter states have little incentive to take into account the environmental costs that accrue to out-of-state residents. On the contrary, the fact that the environmental costs of certain practices only accrue to out-of-state residents may be a factor encouraging states not to regulate these practices. In this context, economic efficiency requires centralized legislation to correct the interstate externalities. See R. van den Bergh, 'The Subsidiarity Principle in European Community Law: Some Insights from Law and Economics', *Maastricht Journal of European and Comparative Law* 1 (1994), 337.

The above discussion reveals that, in the specific area of environmental protection, the European Council guidelines on the application of the subsidiarity principle contain 'an extremely low threshold with regard to the assessment of the need for Community action'.[70] It should be noted that this corresponds with the traditional economic theory of federalism pursuant to which the 'appropriate locus of regulation is the jurisdiction whose geographical coverage internalizes the major impacts of the public policy in question'.[71] Applying this approach to environmental protection, Community action would therefore be justified every time it aims at preventing or remedying the spillovers that may be created by inadequate and/or inconsistent member state environmental policies.[72]

When the need for Community action has been recognized, questions still arise as to the nature and intensity of such an action. Article 3B(3) of the Treaty states that Community action 'shall not go beyond what is necessary to achieve the objectives of the Treaty'. This provision echoes the principle of proportionality which is the subject of a well-established case law of the Court of Justice. As we have seen in Part 1, this principle has been essentially developed by the Court of Justice in order to assess the validity of member states' actions restricting the free movement of goods (or any other freedom protected by the Treaty) in order to further a legitimate national objective. In a variety of circumstances, the court has also referred to the principle of proportionality in order to evaluate the validity of Community measures, which, although they had been adopted to further objectives included in the Treaty, entered into conflicts with

---

[70] Lenaerts, 'The Principle of Subsidiarity' at 880.

[71] See W. Wils, 'Subsidiarity and EC Environmental Policy: Taking People's Concerns Seriously', *Journal of Environmental Law* 6 (1994), 85, 88. citing Emerson in 'The Appropriate Level of Regulation in Europe: Local, National or Community Wide?' *Economic Policy* (1989), 467–72. See also R. van den Bergh, M. Faure and J. Lefevere, 'The Subsidiarity Principle in European Environmental Law: An Economic Analysis', paper prepared for the Conference on the Law and Economics of the Environment, Oslo, 8–9 June 1995; J. Pelkmans, 'Regulation and the Single Market: An Economic Perspective' in Siebert (ed.), *The Completion of the Internal Market* (Tübingen: Mohr, 1989) at 388.

[72] On the other hand, it seems that, in the absence of spillovers, the Community should generally refrain from taking action. Decentralized decision-making is indeed expected to foster more efficient policy choices. For example, the Commission has indicated that it did not see, under the subsidiarity principle, the need to take action at Community level in order to: take care of erosion problems in the Greek municipality of Kiato (answer to written question No. 583/93 of Mr S. Kostopoulos, OJ 1993, C 264/40); protect environmental crisis areas (answer to written question E-2393/94 of Mr A. Alavanos, OJ 1995, C 75/40).

other Treaty objectives[73] or general principles of law, such as fundamental rights.[74]

In the conclusions to its Edinburgh meeting, the European Council expressly referred to this case law.[75] The European Council, however, appeared to add a new dimension to the principle of proportionality which it interpreted as requiring that Community action should not affect member states' residual powers more than is necessary in order for the Community to be able to act effectively towards the achievement of its objective.[76] The competing value to be protected by this expression of the principle of proportionality is clearly perceived, namely the sovereignty of the member states and of their subnational authorities.[77] In this regard, the Council declared that 'Community measures should leave as much scope for national action as possible, consistent with securing the aim of the measure and observing the requirements of the Treaty' and that 'where appropriate and subject to the need for proper enforcement, Community measures should provide Member States with alternative ways to achieve the objectives of the measures'.[78] The European Council also indicated that the Community 'should legislate only to the extent

---

[73] See, e.g., Case 37/83, Rewe-Zentral [1984] ECR 1,229 (court examining the compatibility with Articles 30 to 36, 43, 100 and 190 of Directive 77/93 on protective measures against the introduction into the member states of harmful organisms or plants or plant products).

[74] See, e.g., Case 44/79, Hauer [1979] ECR 3,727 (court questioned on the validity of a Community measure which had been adopted in order to promote a common organization of the wine market which was deemed to be incompatible with the right to ownership contained in Article 1 of the first Protocol to the European Convention on Human Rights).

[75] See conclusions adopted by the European Council in its Edinburgh Meeting of 11–12 December 1992 (reprinted in Europe, 13–14 December 1994).

[76] According to Lenaerts and van Ypersele, this new dimension of the principle of proportionality (designed to protect member states' sovereignty) would find its origin in the second rather than the third paragraph of Article 3B. On the other hand, Article 3B(3) would only contain the general principle of proportionality developed by the Court of Justice in its case law. See Lenaerts and van Ypersele, 'Le Principe de Subsidiarité' at 31. Although theoretically attractive, this view is not confirmed by the Communication to the Council and the European Parliament on the Principle of Subsidiarity of 27 October 1992 (reprinted in Europe, 30 October 1992) and by the conclusions adopted by the European Council in its Edinburgh Meeting of 11–12 December 1992 (reprinted in Europe, 13–14 December 1994), which amalgamated the two expressions of the principle of proportionality in Article 3B para. 3.

[77] See Lenaerts, 'The Principle of Subsidiarity' at 883. This shows the close connection between the subsidiarity and proportionality principles, the ultimate aim of both of which being to offer a general safeguard against excessive Community intervention.

[78] See conclusions adopted by the European Council in its Edinburgh Meeting of 11–12 December 1992 (reprinted in Europe, 13–14 December 1994).

necessary' and when a legislative intervention is necessary 'directives should be preferred to regulation and framework directives rather than detailed directives'.[79] Finally, the Council marked its preference for the setting of minimum standards, leaving member states free to adopt stricter national measures.

As understood by the European Council, the requirement of proportionality contained in Article 3B(3) has always been present in some form in Community environmental action. The development of Community action in the environmental field has indeed only been allowed by the member states provided it would not go beyond certain limits. This can be observed by the adoption of numerous safeguard clauses allowing member states to adopt stricter standards than Community standards, a practice institutionalized by the SEA in Article 130T. Community environmental law has also been developed through the adoption of directives, an instrument which relies on the member states for its implementation and thus offers them considerable flexibility of interpretation.[80] For the same reason, the enforcement of Community environmental law has generally been left to the member states under the general supervision of the Commission.[81]

Article 3B(3) and the European Council guidelines will nevertheless have a strong influence on the development of Community environmental law, working in favour of less regulatory density in Community environmental legislation[82] and, as far as possible, the adoption of non-uniform rather than uniform solutions.[83] In this regard, it is suggested that, in practice, the principle of proportionality will have a more lasting influence on the development of Community environmental law than the principle of subsidiarity *sensu stricto* which, for reasons expressed above,

---

[79] *Ibid.*
[80] See Article 189(3) of the Treaty.
[81] See generally R. Macrory, 'The Enforcement of Community Environmental Laws: Some Critical Issues', *Common Market Law Review* 29 (1992), 347.
[82] The Commission has already taken initiatives in that direction. For example, in its Report to the European Council on the adaptation of Community legislation on the subsidiarity principle of 24 November 1993 (COM (93) 545 final), the Commission announced that it will make the necessary legislative proposals to replace six directives on water quality by framework directives, reoriented 'towards compliance with essential quality and health parameters, leaving member states free to add secondary parameters as they fit': *ibid.* at 16.
[83] For example, Council Directive 96/61 of 24 September 1996 concerning integrated pollution prevention and control, OJ 1996, L 257/26, allows for national differences in the regulation of industrial processes since it provides that emissions limits for air, water and soil pollutants will have to be adopted by national rather than Community authorities.

does not appear to impose serious limitations on Community intervention in that field. But what will be the practical implications of the application of the principle of proportionality to Community environmental action? First, a clear advantage of the principle of proportionality is that it will strengthen the role of the member states in the general context of Community environmental action. It will also give the member states increased flexibility in the attainment of Community environmental goals. Such flexibility is an important factor in the context of the current process of Community enlargement as a result of which states with domestic environmental policies at very different stages of development will have to agree on a set of environmental rules.[84] On the other hand, the danger of such an approach is that, by offering increased space for national divergences in environmental regulation, it may have the effect of reducing the effectiveness of Community environmental action[85] and of encouraging regulatory competition.[86] In this context, a central task for the Community will be to find an adequate balance between the Community interest in uniform regulations and the member states' interest in local autonomy and environmental diversity.

Finally, I should briefly deal with the question of whether and to what extent the principles of subsidiarity and proportionality are justiciable.[87] In its conclusions to the Edinburgh meeting, the European Council declared that 'the interpretation [of the principle of subsidiarity] as well as the review of compliance with it by the Community institutions are subject to the control of the Court of Justice'.[88] This leaves little doubt that the principle of subsidiarity is justiciable. On the other hand, serious

---

[84] See T. Schultz and C. Crockett, 'Developing a Unified European Environmental Law and Policy', *Boston College International and Comparative Law Review* 14 (1991), 301.

[85] See, e.g., R. Stewart, 'Antidotes for the "American Disease"', *Ecology Law Quarterly* 20 (1993), 85, 91 ('The more specific the directives, the more definite the obligations of the member states to adopt and implement national measures carrying out these directives. Such precision prevents member states from exercising discretion to protect local industry, which would undermine effective environmental protection.').

[86] See, e.g., N. Reich, 'Competition between Legal Orders: A New Paradigm for EC Law', *Common Market Law Review* 29 (1992), 861, 889 ('Community law based on the principle of subsidiarity encourages decentralized measures which, of necessity, will be divergent and then favour competing choices . . . [S]ubsidiarity may lead to "distortions of competition", and therefore needs careful monitoring by the European court as "umpire".').

[87] See generally A. Toth, 'Is Subsidiarity Justiciable?' *European Law Review* 19 (1994), 268.

[88] By way of contrast, the European Council declared that subsidiarity 'cannot be regarded as having direct effect'. This indicates that individual litigants in national courts cannot invoke subsidiarity to avoid the application of otherwise valid Community measures. See conclusions adopted by the European Council in its

doubts have been expressed as to whether the Court of Justice is fitted for the delicate task of deciding whether a particular Community measure is compatible with the principle of subsidiarity. Most authors see this task as involving policy choices which exceed the proper judicial function.[89] The prevalent view is therefore that the court should confine itself to procedural grounds and to verify whether the Community legislative authorities have sufficiently explained why there is a need for Community action.[90] The same cautious note applies to the principle of proportionality which in the new dimension given to it by Article 3B(3) as interpreted by the Edinburgh European Council also involves delicate political judgments.

Harmonization of environmental standards

Having discussed the power of the Community to legislate in the environmental field as well as the potential limits that may be placed on this power by the principles of subsidiarity and proportionality, it is now important to examine how, in the areas of product standards, process standards and waste, the Community has concretely attempted to reconcile the competing interests of trade and environmental protection through or in the context of its legislative action.

In this regard, it should be noted from the outset that the objective of this section is not to provide an exhaustive description of the numerous legislative instruments adopted by the Community in the areas mentioned. Instead, my objective is to illustrate through a number of examples (i) how the harmonization of environmental standards can provide a solution, or at least a useful complement to judicial intervention, with regard to most kinds of tension occurring between trade and environmental protection; but also (ii) the various difficulties that the Community legislature may encounter when it attempts to harmonize such standards at a high level of environmental protection.[91]

Edinburgh Meeting of 11–12 December 1992 (reprinted in *Europe*, 13–14 December 1994).

[89] See, e.g., Toth, 'The Principle of Subsidiarity' at 283; Bermann, 'Taking Subsidiarity Seriously' at 390; Emiliou, 'Subsidiarity' at 402.

[90] See, e.g., Bermann, 'Taking Subsidiarity Seriously' at 390.

[91] Note that the various areas of environmental regulation discussed in this section (product standards, process standards and waste) are not examined in the same order as in Part 1. In Part 1, the order of examination of these areas of regulation was essentially based on the degree of restriction imposed by member state environmental measures on intra-Community trade. In this context, I started by examining member

Product standards

As has been seen, inconsistent member state product standards may impede intra-Community trade and create market fragmentation. The Community, however, possesses two institutional means of dealing with this problem.[92] As has been seen in the first Part of this study, the first means of dealing with the impediments to the free movement of goods created by inconsistent member state product standards is through selective judicial invalidation of such standards (negative harmonization). Using the free-trade provisions of the Treaty, the Court of Justice can invalidate member state standards that unduly burden intra-Community trade. The second means of dealing with divergent product standards is through the adoption of Community legislation setting uniform standards for all member states. This technique of positive harmonization has been generally perceived as an instrument of prime importance for ensuring the free movement of products between member states and has been used to regulate the environmental characteristics of a large number of products, such as cars,[93] fuels,[94] chemicals,[95]

state measures regulating waste since such measures often impose import or export bans between member states. Member state product and process standards were then examined since their effect is not to ban intra-Community trade in certain categories of goods but merely to make such a trade more difficult or to distort it. By contrast, in this second Part, product and process standards will be first examined. Because they concern wide categories of goods or industrial activities, Community harmonization of such standards is of central importance to the establishment of the internal market and the legislative intervention of the Community has been extremely extensive. On the other hand, until recently, the Community legislative intervention in the area of waste has been more marginal. In this context, it appears more logical to start by examining Community intervention in the areas of product and process standards and then in the area of waste.

[92] For a good discussion on these two means, see J. M. Sun and J. Pelkmans, 'Regulatory Competition in the Single Market', *Journal of Common Market Studies* 33 (1995), 67.

[93] See, e.g., Directive 70/220 of 20 March 1970 on the measures to be taken against air pollution by gases from positive-ignition engines of motor vehicles, OJ 1970, L 76/1 and its amendment directives.

[94] See, e.g., Directive 85/210 of 20 March 1985 on the approximation of the laws of the member states relating to the lead content of petrol, OJ 1985, L 96/25 and its amendment directives; Directive 75/716 of 24 November 1975 on the approximation of the laws of the member states relating to the sulphur content of certain liquid fuels, OJ 1975, L 307/22 and its amendment directives.

[95] See, e.g., Directive 90/220 of 23 April 1990 on the deliberate release into the environment of genetically modified organisms, OJ 1990, L 117/15; Directive 76/769 of 27 July 1976 on the restrictions on the marketing and use of certain dangerous substances and preparations, OJ 1976, L 262/201 and its amendment directives; Directive 67/548 of 27 June 1967 on the classification, packaging and labelling of dangerous substances, OJ 1967, L 196/1 and its amendment directives.

pesticides,[96] noise-generating equipment,[97] batteries and accumulators[98] and packaging.[99]

In addition to the fact that it facilitates intra-Community trade, one advantage of the harmonization of product standards is that it can be used to upgrade the level of environmental soundness of the products that are traded within the Community and ensure that a minimum level of protection is applied in all member states. Although nothing prevents the Community from adopting harmonization directives that further both free trade and environmental protection, some tension may nevertheless exist between economic and environmental objectives.[100] While environmental protection requires the adoption of strict standards, all that is needed to satisfy the requirements of economic integration is that standards be uniform (or at least subject to a maximum requirement). In some circumstances, member states may therefore agree on harmonization directives that further economic integration but, because they contain standards that are too lax, represent a set-back for environmental protection.

Against this background, the objective of this section is to examine whether environmental requirements have been at the core of Community regulation of products or whether such requirements have been merely ancillary to the economic objectives sought by such regulation. A related issue is to what extent the institutional changes brought about by the SEA and the TEU have influenced the taking into account of environmental requirements in product-standards harmonization. Although these issues are relevant to all areas of product regulation, their importance can perhaps be best illustrated by a brief survey of Community legislation in the area of motor-vehicle-exhaust emissions. The regulation of motor-vehicle-exhaust emissions is an area where the economic and environmental interests at stake are enormous and where Community

---

[96] See, e.g., Directive 91/414 of 15 July 1991 concerning the placing of plant-protection products on the market, OJ 1991, L 230/1; Directive 78/631 of 26 June 1978 on the classification, packaging and labelling of dangerous preparations (pesticides), OJ 1978, L 206/13.

[97] See, e.g., Directive 84/534 of 17 September 1984 on the permissible sound power level of tower cranes, OJ 1984, L 300/130; Directive 84/533 of 17 September 1984 on the permissible sound power levels of compressors, OJ 1984, L 300/123.

[98] See Directive 91/157 of 18 March 1991 on batteries and accumulators containing certain dangerous substances, OJ 1991, L 78/38.

[99] See Directive 94/62 of 20 December 1994 on packaging and packaging waste, OJ 1994, L 365/14.

[100] See O. Lomas, 'Environmental Protection, Economic Conflict and the European Community', *McGill Law Journal* 33 (1988), 506.

intervention has generated bitter conflicts between member states. More-over, as will be seen below, important lessons can be learned from the evolution of this area of regulation.

The Community's involvement in the regulation of motor-vehicle-exhaust emissions started at the end of the 1960s when it realized that the adoption of inconsistent exhaust emission limits by the member states were likely to fragment the Community market in cars.[101] In order to avoid such a fragmentation, the Community adopted in 1970 a Directive setting limits for emissions of carbon monoxide and unburnt hydrocarbons.[102] A subsequent directive of 1977 imposed limit values on emissions of nitrogen oxides (NO_x).[103] The focus of these measures, which were adopted under Article 100 of the Treaty, was clearly economic.[104] Rather than imposing compulsory minimum emission limits, the Com-munity opted for a strategy of optional harmonization pursuant to which member states must ensure market access to vehicles which comply with Community standards but are free to allow on their territory the operation of vehicles that do not meet such standards.[105] Community

[101] France and Germany had indeed adopted legislation regulating motor-vehicle-exhaust emissions. See French Ordinance of 31 March 1969, *Journal Officiel*, 17 May 1969 and German Ordinance of 14 October 1968, *Bundesgesetzblatt*, 18 October 1968.

[102] Council Directive 70/220 of 20 March 1970 on the approximation of the laws of the member states relating to measures to be taken against air pollution by gases from positive-ignition engines of motor vehicles, OJ 1970, L 76/1.

[103] Directive 77/102, OJ 1977, L 32/32.

[104] As a matter of fact, these measures were adopted in the context of the General Programme for Elimination of Technical Obstacles to Trade of 28 May 1969, OJ 1969, C 76/1, as updated on 17 December 1973, OJ 1973, C 117/1. See P. J. Slot, *Technical and Administrative Obstacles to Trade* (Leiden, Sijthoff, 1975) at 101*ff*.

[105] Optional harmonization is the strategy generally used by the Community when it regulates the environmental characteristics of products. See, e.g., the directives harmonizing noise-emission limits for products, such as Directive 78/1015 of 23 November 1978 on the approximation of the laws of the member states on the permissible sound level and exhaust systems of motorcycles, OJ 1978, L 349/21 and Directive 77/311 of 25 March 1977 on the approximation of the laws of the member states relating to the driver-perceived noise level of wheeled agricultural or forestry tractors, OJ 1977, L 105/1. Optional harmonization has often been criticized as giving preference to economic interests at the expense of environmental ones. Indeed, it allows member states to maintain lower national standards and leaves businesses free to comply either with the more stringent Community or the more liberal national standards. As pointed out by Rehbinder and Stewart, the negative impact of the optional harmonization strategy is, however, tempered by considerations of economies of scale. Because of the export-oriented nature of industry, producers will often have an incentive to comply with stricter Community standards. As a result, optional harmonization may have the same result as total harmonization. See E. Rehbinder and R. Stewart, 'Environmental Protection Policy' in Cappelletti *et al.* (eds.), *Integration through Law* (Walter de Gruyter, 1985), vol. I, at 209.

standards thus functioned as a ceiling rather than a floor: the only obligation that was required from the member states was not to adopt stricter standards than Community ones.[106]

In the middle of the 1980s, the increasing awareness of the problems created by acid rain motivated the Commission to put forward proposals involving stricter emission limits similar to those already existing in the United States. A number of member states, including Germany, Denmark and the Netherlands, supported the Commission proposals for more stringent limits. These proposals were, however, strongly opposed by other member states, such as France, Italy and the United Kingdom which felt that these new limits would operate to the detriment of their car-manufacturing industries. In particular, they feared that small and inexpensive cars, which represented the major part of their production, would be rendered commercially unattractive if they had to be fitted with catalytic converters in order to comply with stricter emission requirements.[107] In March 1985, the Council found a compromise solution, subject to the reservation of Denmark (the so-called 'Luxembourg compromise').[108] The original feature of that compromise was the decision to split the European car fleet into three categories (small, medium and large), according to their cubic capacity, making it possible to impose different limit values for each category of vehicles. According to the compromise, only the limits for large cars would be stringent enough to require the use of catalytic converters. On the other hand, compliance with the limits imposed for small and medium cars could be ensured through the use of less expensive technologies, such as 'lean-burn' engines.[109] The conflict between member states over the scope and the level of stringency of the new emission limits appeared to be solved and a Directive reflecting the compromise should have been adopted in November 1985. Denmark, however, decided to maintain its objections because it considered that the new emission limits proposed in the compromise were too lax. As a consequence, the unanimity required by Article 100, the legal basis then proposed for the directive, could not be

---

[106] See D. Vogel, 'Environmental Protection and the Creation of the Single Market', paper prepared for delivery at the 1992 Annual Meeting of the American Political Science Association, 3–6 September 1992, at 64.

[107] Lomas, 'Environmental Protection' at 526.

[108] See S. Johnson and G. Corcelle, *The Environmental Policy of the European Communities* (London: Graham & Trotman, 1989) at 128.

[109] Lomas, 'Environmental Protection' at 526. On this occasion, Denmark threatened to use the safeguard clause contained in Article 100A(4) but did not do it because the Community eventually adopted stronger legislation.

achieved.[110] The impasse reached as a result of the Danish objections was finally broken at a meeting of the Council on 21 July 1987, where the Council was for the first time able to use Article 100A, which only required voting at a qualified majority.[111] A directive based on the Luxembourg compromise was then formally adopted by the Council on 3 December 1987.[112]

The Luxembourg compromise provided that new stricter emission limits for vehicles below 1.4 litres would have to be fixed by the Council in 1987 on a proposal from the Commission.[113] A Commission proposal providing for such stricter limits was sent to the Council on 10 February 1988.[114] The Council reached a common position on this proposal at its meeting of 24 November 1988. The position incorporated the limit values which the Commission proposed for reducing emissions. Under the procedure of co-operation, the text of the directive still had to be communicated to the Parliament so that it could give its opinion. By an overwhelming majority, the Parliament rejected the common position in favour of stricter US standards.[115] The Commission followed the opinion of the Parliament and strengthened its proposal accordingly.[116] At its meeting of 8 June 1989, the Council finally adopted emission limits equivalent to those existing in the United States.[117]

If, as indicated by its legal basis (Article 100A), the trade objective is still clearly present, Directive 89/458 was probably the first directive on car emissions to contain a strong environmental component. First, the preamble of this directive clearly recognized 'the major role played by pollutant emissions from motor vehicles and their contribution to the

---

[110] See Johnson and Corcelle, *The Environmental Policy of the European Communities* at 129.
[111] See Lomas, 'Environmental Protection' at 531.
[112] Directive 88/76 of 3 December 1988 amending Directive 70/220 of 20 March 1970, OJ 1988, L 36/1. It should be noted that the emission limits contained in this directive fell short of the standards imposed in the United States at that time. Although the initial objective of the Commission was to impose standards similar to US standards, the Council finally adopted standards 'whose ultimate effect on the environment is equivalent to that of standards for vehicle emissions in force in the United States': see preamble of Directive 88/76 of 3 December 1988.
[113] See Article 4 of Directive 88/76 of 3 December 1988.
[114] OJ 1988, C 56/9.
[115] OJ 1989, C/120. For a comparison of US and EC standards, see Comment, 'Small Automobiles Causing Large Air Pollution Problems on a Global Basis: The European Economic Community Can Learn and Live from United States Legislation', *Dickinson Journal of International Law* 8 (1990), 313.
[116] OJ 1989, C 134/8.
[117] Directive 89/458 of 18 July 1989 amending, with regard to European emission standards for cars below 1.4 litres, Directive 70/220 of 20 March 1970, OJ 1989, L 226/1.

gases responsible for the greenhouse effect' and declared that the emissions of carbon dioxide of such vehicles should therefore 'be stabilized and subsequently reduced'.[118] Second, Directive 89/458 abandoned the strategy of optional harmonization for a strategy of total harmonization of exhaust-emission limits.[119] Contrary to earlier directives, Community standards therefore represent not only a ceiling but also a floor below which no member state can go. Third, Directive 89/458 authorized member states to adopt tax incentives in order to encourage the sale of cars complying with the new stricter limits before the implementation dates set for such limits.[120] Finally, Directive 89/458 declared that, before the end of 1990, the Council should align the limit values for the emission of cars with an engine equal or superior to 1.4 litres to the standards adopted for small cars.[121] The Council adopted such limit values in Directive 91/441[122] and, together with the Parliament, lowered them in Directive 94/12.[123]

The evolution of Community legislation in the area of motor-vehicle-exhaust emissions presents a number of important lessons which are generally applicable to other areas of product regulation. First, although economic objectives may induce member states to adopt measures that have a positive impact on the environment, the interests of economic integration and environmental protection are not always coterminous.[124] As already noted, while economic integration only requires that standards be uniform or at least contain a maximum requirement, environmental protection requires the adoption of compulsory minimum standards, set up at a high level of protection. Economic objectives may thus very well be pursued at the expense of environmental ones. For example, although the Luxembourg compromise avoided the fragmentation of the European car market, it offered little progress for environmental protection. In some respect, it even presented a set-back for the environment since it pre-empted some member states, such as Denmark, from adopting more protective standards. Second, although Article 100A was first used to

---

[118] See the twelfth recital of Directive 89/458 of 18 July 1989.

[119] See Article 2 of Directive 89/458 of 18 July 1989. The strategy of optional harmonization had been already partly abandoned in Directive 88/76 of 3 December 1988. See Articles 3 and 4 of that directive.

[120] Article 3 of Directive 89/458.   [121] *Ibid.* at Article 5.

[122] Directive 91/441 of 26 June 1991 amending Directive 70/220 of 20 March 1970, OJ 1991, L 242/1.

[123] Directive 94/12 of 23 March 1994 amending Directive 70/220 of 20 March 1970, OJ 1994, L 100/42.

[124] See Lomas, 'Environmental Protection' at 532.

break the Danish resistance to the adoption of lax emission limits, this provision has since permitted the adoption of much stricter emission limits. Because it permits isolating those member states opposed to environmental progress, the qualified-majority-voting system contained in this provision strongly favours the adoption of stricter environmental legislation. In this context, one should welcome the generalization of this system of voting to all environmental law-making procedures by the TEU.[125] Third, the evolution of motor-vehicle-exhaust emissions legislation in the Community also illustrates the important role played by the Parliament in the area of environmental protection through the procedure of co-operation.[126] In this regard, the new procedure of co-decision introduced in Article 100A by the TEU should generally favour the adoption of more stringent environmental product regulation.[127] The search for progressive solutions rather than the lowest common denominator is therefore likely to guide harmonization in this area.

A question so far little explored in the legal literature is to what extent the 'New Approach' to harmonization of technical standards will have a substantial impact on the harmonization of the environmental product standards.[128] The central characteristic of this New Approach is that harmonization should be limited to the adoption of 'essential requirements' necessary for ensuring the free movement throughout the Community of a particular product.[129] The task of drawing up on the basis of

[125] See Article 130S(1) of the Treaty. See, however, the exceptions contained in Article 130S(2).

[126] The Parliament has traditionally been in favour of strong environmental measures. See, e.g., P. Sands, 'EC Environmental Legislation Law: The ECJ and Common-Interest Groups', *Modern Law Review* 53 (1990), 685, 691.

[127] On this aspect, see K. Collins, 'Plans and Prospects for the European Parliament in Shaping Future Environmental Policy', *European Environmental Law Review* (1995), 74.

[128] The text of reference with regard to the New Approach is Council resolution of 7 May 1985 on a new approach to technical harmonization of standards, OJ 1985, C 136 at 1. Generally on the New Approach, see D. Waelbroeck, 'L'Harmonisation des Règles et des Normes Techniques dans la CEE', *Cahiers de Droit Européen* (1988), 243; and J. Pelkmans, 'The New Approach to Technical Harmonization and Standardization', *Journal of Common Market Studies* 25 (1986), 249.

[129] The New Approach relies on the concept of 'mutual recognition' according to which a product which is lawfully produced and marketed in one member state must be admitted in another member state except when the latter can refer to essential or mandatory requirements. See Case 120/78, *Rewe Zentral AG* v. *Bundesmonopolverwaltung für Branntwei* [1979] ECR 649. The harmonization of those essential requirements would therefore be necessary and sufficient to ensure the free movement of goods throughout the Community. See generally A. Mattera, 'L'Article du Traité CEE, la Jurisprudence "Cassis de Dijon" et le Principe de Reconnaissance Mutuelle', *Revue du Marché Unique Européen* (1992), 13.

those essential requirements the detailed specifications for the particular product is left to European standards organizations, such as the Comité Européen de Normalisation (CEN).[130] If a product meets those specifications, it benefits from a presumption that it satisfies the Community's essential requirements and it can therefore move freely throughout the Community.[131] The principal advantage of the New Approach is that it thus avoids the need for the Community to have recourse to extremely detailed directives that may require lengthy negotiations and result in the adoption of costly and inefficient regulation.[132] The New Approach seems also to be in conformity with the guidelines of the Edinburgh European Council according to which the Community 'should only legislate to the extent necessary' and 'Community measures should leave as much scope for national decision as possible'.[133] In this context, the New Approach appears to be a more 'proportionate' method of intervention.

Prima facie, it seems that the New Approach could be usefully applied to regulate the environmental characteristics of products capable of generating pollution.[134] For example, harmonization of noise emission limits for products is essentially a technical matter which could be regulated by standardization bodies. In this area, the Community has always based the

---

[130] Generally on CEN, see S. Farr, *Harmonization of Technical Standards in the European Community* (London: Chancery, 1992) at 33.

[131] For some examples of New Approach directives, see Directive 90/396 of 29 June 1990 on the approximation of the laws of the member states relating to appliances burning gaseous fuels, OJ 1990, L 196/15; Directive 89/392 of 14 June 1989 on the approximation of the laws of the member states relating to machinery, OJ 1989, L 183/9; Council Directive 89/106 of 21 December 1989 on the approximation of the laws, regulations and administrative provisions of the member states relating to construction products, OJ 1989, L 40/12. As pointed out by Kramer, although these directives do not directly concern environmental protection, the technical standards they set up may nevertheless have important effects on the environment since they deal with matter such as, air emissions from water-heating installations, asbestos pipes or copper pipes for drinking water use, or construction material containing PVC. See Kramer, *EC Treaty and Environmental Law* at 38.

[132] See, e.g., R. Dehousse, 'Integration v. Regulation? On the Dynamics of Regulation in the European Community', *Journal of Common Market Studies* 30 (1992), 383, 392. On the difficulties which surround the 'traditional' harmonization process, see also A. Dashwood, 'Hastening Slowly: The Community's Path Towards Harmonization' in Wallace, Wallace and Webb (eds.), *Policy-Making in the European Community* (London: Wiley, 1983), 177, 201.

[133] See pp. 96–7 above.

[134] For a good discussion of the role of standardization of bodies in the environmental field, see R. Hunter, 'Standardization and the Environment', *International Environmental Reporter*, 10 March 1993 at 185. See also J. Salter, 'Environmental Standards and Testing', *European Environmental Law Review* (1993), 276.

standards it adopted on the standards established by the ISO (International Standards Organization) and the ICAO (International Civil Aviation Organization).[135] The New Approach seems also appropriate for the elaboration of common criteria for the life-cycle analysis and the recycling methods of products or parts of products, such as packaging.[136] On the other hand, it is not certain that member states will be ready to rely on the New Approach where the nature and the level of stringency of the standards adopted may have great economic implications, such as in the context of vehicle exhaust emissions or the composition of certain chemical substances.[137] When great economic interests are at stake, they may prefer to negotiate every single aspect of the matters at hand.[138]

More generally, it seems that one must be very careful about excessive delegation of regulatory powers to standardization bodies.[139] Contrary to legislatures or traditional regulatory agencies, these bodies are not politically accountable and, due to the relative secrecy in which they operate, are not generally well suited for ensuring that the views of all affected parties are heard and taken into account in the standardization process.[140] A further inconvenience of relying on standardization bodies is that the technical experts doing most of the substantive work are typically representatives of companies interested in the field and that supervision by the Commission is inadequate or non-existent. In the absence of proper democratic control, there is therefore a serious danger of industry dominating the standardization process within these bodies.[141]

---

[135] See Johnson and Corcelle, *The Environmental Policy of the European Communities* at 221.

[136] See, e.g., Article 10 of Directive 94/62 of 20 December 1994 on packaging and packaging waste which expressly encourages the development of European standards with regard to these matters, OJ 1994, L 365/14.

[137] See, e.g., Stewart, 'Environmental Law in the United States and the European Community' at 35.

[138] See, *mutatis mutandis*, the Commission Report on the adaptation of Community legislation on the subsidiarity principle of 24 November 1993 (COM 93 (545) final) at 7, where the Commission notes that attempts at simplification of Community legislation that do not satisfy the criteria of proportionality 'risk encountering resistance from national administrations which, because of the lack of mutual confidence, are anxious to obtain the most detailed regulations possible'.

[139] See Hunter, 'Standardization and the Environment' at 189.

[140] See Kramer, *EC Treaty and Environmental Law* at 38. See also 'Environmentalists Criticize EU Standardization Move', *Environment Watch*, 21 June 1996 at 19.

[141] See A. McGee and S. Weatherill, 'The Evolution of the Single Market – Harmonization or Liberalization', *Modern Law Review* 53 (1990), 578, 585 (arguing that as a result of the New Approach the regulated has become the regulator).

Process standards

Community legislation harmonizing environmental process standards can be justified under two separate rationales. Firstly, process-standards harmonization may be used to remove the distortions of competition that may occur when member states adopt different requirements regulating industrial processes. It may therefore contribute to the establishment and subsequent functioning of the internal market. Secondly, harmonization of process standards may also be used to control the pollution that is generated by the industrial processes that are used in the manufacture of products and to ensure that a minimum level of environmental protection is applied in all member states. Though conceptually distinct, these rationales are usually both present in directives harmonizing processes and, as has been seen in the Court of Justice's legal-basis case law, it is generally difficult to determine in specific cases which of the economic or environmental rationales is dominant.[142]

Although Community legislation harmonizing industrial processes can be justified on solid economic and environmental grounds, there are, however, obstacles to the adoption of such legislation. Contrary to the case of products where member states share a common interest in harmonization in order to avoid market fragmentation,[143] member states do not always share a common interest in harmonizing environmental processes.[144] On the one hand, harmonization will be clearly favoured by the member states which have already adopted strict process standards on a domestic basis. If these member states want to avoid their producers suffering a competitive disadvantage in relation to the producers located in member states applying less stringent standards, it is important for them to ensure that standards equivalent to their standards are applied throughout the Community. On the other hand, member states applying less stringent process standards will usually oppose harmonization.[145] In

---

[142] See Case C-300/89, *Commission* v. *Council* [1991] ECR 2,867 (holding that with regard to its objectives and content Directive 89/428 on pollution caused by waste from the titanium dioxide industry was concerned inextricably with both environmental protection and the conditions of competition).

[143] Member states may, however, disagree over the level of stringency of the standards resulting from such a harmonization.

[144] See Rehbinder and Stewart, 'Environmental Protection Policy' at 11.

[145] As will be seen below, the opposition of these member states will be particularly strong when they are able to absorb or externalize the environmental costs generated by such processes on other member states. One should also note that, in theory, member states that import goods but do not produce them should also oppose harmonization. In the absence of pollution spillovers, harmonization would be detrimental to their interests since their citizens would bear the costs of control (in

the absence of harmonization, they can continue to market their (usually cheaper) products in other member states even though the industrial processes used to manufacture them have been less controlled.[146] Divergences in the level of pollution control between member states can be based on differences in the relative availability of jobs and economic opportunities, differences in the capacity of the environment to absorb pollution, differences in the subjective values of the citizens of these member states, or any combination of these three factors.

The difficulty of reaching agreement over harmonization of environmental process standards can be illustrated by the negotiations that led to the adoption of Directive 88/609 on the limitation of certain pollutants into the air from large combustion plants.[147] These negotiations started when, in December 1983, the Commission sent to the Council a proposal for substantial reductions in the emissions of SO_2 and NO_x from large combustion plants in order to curb the environmental damage caused by acid rain.[148] This proposal was strongly supported by Germany which, following domestic pressures, had unilaterally adopted measures to reduce the emissions from its combustion plants. As these measures were placing a heavy burden on its domestic industry, it was imperative for Germany to convince its European partners to agree on the adoption of comparable measures at Community level.[149] The Commission proposal, which was based on Articles 100 and 235 of the Treaty, required that the total emissions from existing plants with over 50 megawatts thermal output should be reduced by 60 per cent in the case of SO_2 and 40 per cent in the case of NO_x by 1995, compared with the reference period of 1980. The proposal also laid down mandatory uniform emission limits for new plants.

If the Commission proposal created few difficulties from a technological standpoint,[150] it was nevertheless opposed by a number of member states. For example, the United Kingdom was opposed to the Commission

terms of higher prices for products) but enjoy none of the benefits (in terms of fairer conditions of competition and better environmental protection). See Rehbinder and Stewart, 'Environmental Protection Policy' at 11.

[146] This is the case because member states may not exclude products from other member states on the ground they have been produced in factories applying process standards that are laxer than their standards.

[147] OJ 1988, L 336/1, amended by Directive 94/66, OJ 1994, L 337/83.

[148] OJ 1983, C 49/1.

[149] See Lomas, 'Environmental Protection' at 521.

[150] The know-how necessary to achieve the emission reductions required existed at the time of the proposal.

proposal because it would have meant surrendering the competitive advantage arising from its geographical location. Being an island exposed to Atlantic weather systems and westerly winds, the United Kingdom was able to disperse air pollution more easily than other member states and, hence, could preserve the integrity of its environment at a lesser cost for industry.[151] The United Kingdom was therefore firmly against any type of uniform reductions. Other member states, such as Greece, Ireland, Portugal and Spain,[152] were concerned that the reductions in emissions it required would have a negative impact on their domestic industry and would generally impede their economic development.[153] The struggle between contending interests paralysed the decision-making process and it was only in June 1988, more than four and a half years after the initial Commission proposal, that the member states managed to agree on a common position. Directive 88/609 on the emissions from large combustion plants was eventually adopted on 24 November 1988 on the basis of Article 130S of the Treaty.

The various compromises that were made to overcome the objections from individual member states complicated the structure of the Directive and essentially provided for non-uniform emission reductions among member states. With regard to existing plants, Directive 88/609 requires overall reductions for SO_2 and NO_x and fixes implementation dates for such reductions.[154] However, different reduction targets are set for each member state[155] and a number of member states, including Greece, Ireland and Portugal, are even authorized to increase their emissions.[156] In order to increase flexibility, the sharing of emissions among the different installations within a member state is left to the discretion of the member states.[157] With regard to new plants, Directive 88/609 also fixes emission limit values differentiated according to the size of the

---

[151] Lomas, 'Environmental Protection' at 535.

[152] Portugal and Spain had joined the Community on 1 January 1986.

[153] See Lomas, 'Environmental Protection' at 522.

[154] Directive 88/609 of 24 November 1988 provides that the member states are to reduce emissions of SO_2 in three phases (1993, 1998 and 2003) and emissions of NO_x in two phases (1993 and 1998). See Article 3 and Annexes I and II of the Directive.

[155] For example, while Belgium, France, Germany and the Netherlands are to reduce their emissions of SO_2 by 40 per cent by 1993, 60 per cent by 1998 and 70 per cent by 2003 and their emissions of NO_x by 20 per cent by 1993 and 40 per cent by 1998, the United Kingdom will only reduce its emissions of SO_2 by 20, 40 and 60 per cent and its emissions of NO_x by 15 and 30 per cent: *ibid.*

[156] *Ibid.*

[157] See Article 3.2.

installations.[158] It also gives Spain a special authorisation until 1999 to authorize the entry into service of more combustion plants.[159]

It is subject to question whether the differentiated approach taken by Directive 88/609 with regard to the emission reductions to be applied by the member states is compatible with the requirements of a common market.[160] Contrary to the initial Commission proposal,[161] the directive clearly fails to create equal conditions of competition with regard to the operation of large combustion plants. On the other hand, a clear advantage of Directive 88/609 is that it takes into consideration the economic, energy and environmental situation of the individual member states. Because of several enlargements, the Community is no longer composed of a small group of states at relatively similar stages of economic and social development. There may therefore be circumstances where the level of environmental protection sought by the most economically advanced member states may impose excessive sacrifices, in terms of implementation costs and loss of economic opportunities, to the least economically developed member states. This problem is now expressly acknowledged in Article 130S(5) of the Treaty. This provision, which represents a counterpart to the extension of the qualified-majority-voting procedure to Article 130S(1) of the Treaty by the TEU, provides that when a Community environmental measure adopted under Article 130S(1) involves costs that are deemed disproportionate to the public authorities of a member state, the Council may provide for temporary derogations in favour of that member state.[162] In addition, or as an alternative to such derogations, the Council may grant to the affected member state financial assistance from the Cohesion Fund to be established under Article 130D of the Treaty.[163]

---

[158] See Article 4.   [159] See Article 5.3.

[160] Examples of a differentiated approach can also be found in other areas of Community law. For discussions on the legal issues generated by such an approach, see C. D. Ehlermann, 'How Flexible is Community Law? An Unusual Approach to the Concept of "Two Speeds"', *Michigan Law Review* 82 (1984), 1,274; E. Grabitz and B. Langenheine, 'Legal Problems Related to a Proposed "Two-Tier" System of Integration within the Community', *Common Market Law Review* 18 (1981), 33.

[161] The preamble to the Commission draft directive stated that disparities between member states in 'the obligations imposed in respect of large combustion plants . . . [were] liable to create unequal conditions of competition and this would have direct effect on the Common Market': see OJ 1983, C 49/1.

[162] Prior to the entry into force of the TEU, Article 130S relied on a unanimity voting system which guaranteed a veto right to the member states economically affected by a Community provision.

[163] This fund was established by the Council in Regulation 1164/94, OJ 1994, L 130/1. In conformity with the Protocol on economic and social cohesion annexed to the TEU,

In addition to the problem of burden-sharing, a controversial issue with regard to the harmonization of environmental process standards relates to which regulatory technique is used for such a harmonization.[164] The two main regulatory techniques at the disposal of the Community for regulation of industrial processes are environmental quality standards and effluent standards.[165] Environmental quality standards prescribe the level of pollution which must not be exceeded, without specifying any maximum level of discharge into the atmosphere by industry. Such standards present the advantage of creating a 'partnership' between the Community and the member states. The Community sets quality standards with reference to relatively objective criteria, such as what is needed to protect human health or public welfare. Then, the member states have the freedom and the responsibility to make determinations about how to limit pollution of individual sources to what is allowed under Community standards. On the other hand, environmental quality standards may be perceived as inequitable, in that they give a competitive advantage to industries located in regions that are less polluted or that are better able to absorb pollution.[166] Effluent standards specify, usually

the granting of financial assistance to member states from the Cohesion Fund is subject to two conditions: firstly, that they have a per capita gross national product of less than 90 per cent of the Community average (currently only Greece, Ireland, Portugal and Spain fulfil that condition); and, secondly, that they have a programme leading to the fulfilment of the conditions of economic convergence as set out in Article 104(C) of the Treaty. Contrary to what was proposed by some environmentalists, financial assistance from the Cohesion Fund is not subject to 'green conditionality', i.e., member states are not obliged to show a good environmental record in order to benefit from such assistance. Generally on the environmental 'impact' of the Cohesion Fund, see D. Wilkinson, 'Using the European Union's Structural and Cohesion Funds for the Protection of the Environment', *Review of European Community and International Environmental Law* 3 (1994), 119.

[164] See Rehbinder and Stewart, 'Environmental Protection Policy' at 216.

[165] A third strategy is for the Community to impose a limitation on total loadings of emissions. This strategy, which is not common in Community environmental law, has nevertheless been used in Directive 88/609 of 24 November 1988 on the limitation of certain pollutants into the air from large combustion plants to regulate emissions from existing installations. See pp. 100–12 above. Such a strategy offers more flexibility than the adoption of effluent standards since member states are free to allocate pollution among their installations. On the other hand, it offers less flexibility than environment quality standards since it does not take into account the absorptive capacity of local environments.

[166] Since environmental quality standards only prescribe the level of pollution which must not be exceeded in a given atmosphere, the member states whose atmosphere is relatively unpolluted or better able to absorb pollution will be able to attain such standards by allowing more emissions than the member states that do not benefit from such natural locational advantages. Because their compliance costs will be

with reference to the 'Best Available Techniques' (BAT), the maximum allowable emissions of a substance into the atmosphere by industry. They may therefore be perceived as more equitable since they deny industries located in less polluted areas the competitive advantage they would enjoy under a system of quality standards.[167] On the other hand, equality in treatment of pollution sources regardless of their location tends to have an 'overkill' effect and thus may be inefficient from an economic standpoint.

The most extensive discussion about environmental quality and effluent standards arose in the context of Directive 76/464 on pollution caused by certain dangerous substances discharged into the aquatic environment.[168] Directive 76/464 divides the dangerous substances into two categories: a 'black list' including the substances considered to be the most dangerous for the aquatic environment and a 'grey list' covering other substances which are considered to have a less harmful effect.[169] The point of contention in the proposal originally made by the Commission concerned the regime of control to be adopted with regard to black-list substances. The Commission proposed that effluent standards should be fixed in implementing directives, for each substance on the list. All member states agreed on the proposed method, except the United Kingdom which proposed instead that water quality standards be applied for the discharge of individual substances.[170] The United Kingdom wanted to exploit a natural locational advantage. Since it enjoys a system of short, free-running rivers, in many locations, water quality standards could be met by very generous emission limits involving little or no abatement costs for the industries concerned.[171] Environmental production costs

maintained comparatively low, this in turn will generally strengthen the competitiveness of the producers located in these member states.

[167] Under a system of effluent standards, all pollution sources must respect the same emission limits regardless of the nature of the atmosphere into which the discharges are made. The same emission limits therefore apply to all producers wherever located in the Community.

[168] OJ 1976, L 129/23. For discussions on this directive, see D. Taylor, G. Diprose and M. Duffy, 'EC Environmental Policy and the Control of Water Pollution: The Implementation of Directive 76/464 in Perspective', *Journal of Common Market Studies* 24 (1986), 225; Guruswamy et al., 'The Development and Impact of an EEC Directive: The Control of Discharge of Mercury to the Aquatic Environment', *Journal of Common Market Studies* 22 (1983), 71; J. T. Farquhar, 'The Policies of the European Community Towards the Environment – The "Dangerous Substance" Directive', *Journal of Planning and Environmental Law* (1983), 145.

[169] See lists I and II in the Annex of the Directive.

[170] Lomas, 'Environmental Protection' at 516.

[171] *Ibid.* at 518.

could thus be minimized, thereby making local economy more competitive.[172]

After lengthy negotiations, a compromise was eventually found whereby effluent standards would be the rule but a member state could, under strict conditions, opt for an alternative system of water quality standards.[173] The attitude taken by the United Kingdom during the negotiations was nevertheless severely criticized.[174] According to these criticisms, the British position was motivated purely by economic self-interest and, because it prevented thorough equalization of the conditions of competition in the industries concerned, it was contrary to the requirements of the common market. On the other hand, the adoption of a pure system of effluent standards would have imposed costly burdens on the regions of the Community with waters with a high absorptive capacity and prevented them from exploiting their natural locational advantages. From an economic standpoint, there were therefore some merits in the British position.[175]

The controversy over which regulatory technique should be used for the Community harmonization of industrial processes has never been totally resolved[176] and has recently reappeared with force in the context of the

[172] David Vogel quotes a British official arguing against the adoption of effluent standards: 'Italy economically benefits from the amount of sunshine that it receives every year. Why should not our industry be able to take similar advantage of our long coastline . . . and rapidly flowing rivers?': D. Vogel, *National Styles of Regulation: Environmental Policy in Great Britain and the United States* (Ithaca: Cornell University Press, 1986) at 103.

[173] See Article 6 of the Directive. For a similar kind of compromise, see Directive 89/428 of 21 June 1989 on the pollution caused by waste from the titanium dioxide industry, OJ 1989, L 201/59 (providing for emissions standards, but authorizing member states to make use of quality objectives 'in such a way that the effects in terms of protecting and avoiding distortions of competition are equivalent to that of the directive').

[174] See, in particular, Lomas, 'Environmental Protection' at 534.

[175] Interestingly enough, the Commission has recognized in its recent Communication on 'European Community Water Policy' (COM (96) 59) that effluent standards may entail excessive costs compared with the environmental benefits they may achieve ('a strict emission limit values approach can in some circumstances lead to unnecessary investments without significant benefits to the environment').

[176] The Community has indeed subsequently made use of both environmental quality and effluent standards. For some examples of directives applying environmental quality standards, see Directive 85/203 of 7 March 1985 on air quality standards for nitrogen dioxide, OJ 1985, L 87/1; Directive 80/779 of 15 July 1980 on air quality limit values and guide values for sulphur dioxide and suspended particulates, OJ 1980, L 229/30; Council Directive 78/659 of 18 July 1978 concerning the quality of water for freshwater fish, OJ 1978, L 281/47. For some examples of directives fixing effluent standards, see Directive 94/67 of 16 December 1994 on the incineration of hazardous waste, OJ 1994, L 365/34; Directive 89/369 of 8 June 1989 on the prevention of air

negotiations on the draft directive on integrated pollution prevention and control.[177] The objective of this draft directive, which contains the new Community strategy for the regulation of industrial processes, is the prevention of industrial pollution at source. In order to attain this objective, the system established by the draft directive would operate a prior-authorization procedure, whereby industrial installations would apply to the competent authority in the appropriate member state for a permit to operate.[178] The conditions of the permit would include emission limit values for the pollutant substances to be emitted from the installations authorized to operate.[179]

As in the case of Directive 76/464, there is a strong disagreement between member states on how these limit values should be set.[180] For certain northern member states, these limit values should be fixed at Community level on the basis of the 'Best Available Techniques' (i.e., technology-based effluent standards). In particular, German industry and the German government insist on the creation of a level playing field within the Community.[181] Industries in other member states should bear the costs of installing state-of-the-art pollution-abatement technologies which the German industries have already borne pursuant to strict domestic standards. On the other hand, southern member states and the United Kingdom argue that these limit values should be adopted at member state level pursuant to more flexible Community environmental quality standards. The advantage that these member states see in this approach is that, contrary to technology-based effluent standards, environmental quality standards permit them to take into account their environmental circumstances and, hence, their natural locational advan-

---

pollution from new municipal waste-incineration plants, OJ 1989, L 163/32; Directive 88/609 of 24 November 1988 on the limitation of emissions of certain pollutants into the air from large combustion plants (with regard to new plants), OJ 1988, L 336/1.

[177] Commission proposal for a Council Directive on integrated pollution prevention and control, OJ 1993, C 311/6.

[178] See Articles 3 to 7 of the draft directive.

[179] See Articles 8 and 9 of the draft directive.

[180] See 'Industrial Pollution: "Philosophical" Problems Subsist on IPPC Directive', *Europe Environment*, 7 March 1995 at 2.

[181] In order to put forward its views, the German government produced in September 1994 a revised draft of the draft directive earlier proposed by the Commission. See European Council Document 9049/1/94 Env 201 Rev 1(d). For a discussion of this revised draft, see J. Schnutenhaus, 'Integrated Pollution Prevention and Control: New German Initiatives in the European Environment Council', *European Environmental Law Review* (1994), 323.

tages when they set the emission limits applicable to their installations.[182]

The common position reached by the Council in November 1995 attempts to reconcile these competing positions. Pursuant to this common position, which has now been formally adopted by the Council and has become binding law,[183] the emission limit values included in the permits granted by the member states to the controlled installations would be:

based on the best available techniques, without prescribing the use of any technique or specific technology, but taking into account the technical characteristics of the installation concerned, its geographical location and the local environmental conditions.[184]

This provision has been strongly criticized by the European Parliament on the ground that it would lead to different levels of environmental protection in the Community.[185] In response to these criticisms, the Environment Commissioner has, however, made clear that the Commission could not allow permitting authorities to abuse the flexibility built into this provision by giving local producers an unfair competitive advantage.[186] In this regard, the Commissioner has indicated that the Commission will not hesitate to propose to the Council uniform emission limit values if such authorities were tempted to deregulate the environment. In the present political context, which is dominated by the principles of subsidiarity and proportionality, one can wonder, however, whether sufficient consensus could be found in the Council to adopt such uniform limits.

---

[182] Because their environment is generally less polluted than the environment of the more industrialized northern member states, southern member states should indeed be able to attain Community environmental quality standards by imposing more generous emission limits than the northern member states. This should in turn give to producers located in southern member states a competitive advantage over those located in northern member states. See pp. 113–14 above.

[183] Directive 96/61 of 24 September 1996 concerning integrated pollution prevention and control, OJ 1996, L 257/26.

[184] See Article 9.4 of the Common Position.

[185] See 'Parliament Approves IPPC Proposal, Sends Measure to Council for Final Action', *International Environmental Reporter*, 29 May 1996, at 431.

[186] See 'Bjerregaard Defends Flexibility in IPPC Directive', *Environment Watch*, 7 June 1996, at 13.

Waste

As we have seen in the *Belgian Waste* case, the disposal of waste is an environmental issue involving important trade aspects.[187] Every year, millions of tons of waste cross Community internal borders.[188] One central reason for such shipments is economic: waste produced in one member state tends to be transferred to another member state if the cost of disposal in that member state plus the transport cost is less than the cost of disposal in the member state of origin.[189] Cost disparities in waste disposal primarily result from variations in the legal requirements for disposal applied by member states. Harmonization of waste-disposal standards on a Community basis should tend to reduce these cost disparities and, hence, the incentives for producers to transfer their waste to other member states.[190] Harmonization will not, however, lead to uniform prices. The cost of disposal also depends on non-regulatory factors, such as the cost of land and labour, and on the type of installations that are compatible with the geographical constraints of the member states.[191] Although the harmonization of waste-disposal standards may reduce transfrontier shipments of waste, it will not prevent them.[192] It follows that, in addition to harmonized waste-disposal standards, there is also a need for some form of control on the transfrontier shipments of waste.

Harmonization of waste-disposal standards

The first Community instruments designed to bring about some harmonization of waste-disposal practices were Directives 75/442 on

---

[187] I will deal exclusively here with waste transfers occurring between member states. It is, however, common practice for the member states to send their waste to third countries and, in particular, less developed countries. See generally B. Huntoon, 'Emerging Controls on Transfers of Waste to Developing Countries', *Law and Policy of International Business* 21 (1989), 247.

[188] For some figures, see 'A Community Strategy for Waste Management', Communication from the Commission to the Council and the Parliament, 18 September 1989, SEC (89) 934 final, at 3. See also J. Vallette and H. Spalding, *The International Trade in Waste – A Greenpeace Inventory* (Washington, DC: Greenpeace USA, 5th edn, 1990).

[189] See p. 70 above. See also N. de Sadeleer, *Le Droit Communautaire et les Déchets* (Paris; Brussels: LGDJ/Bruylant, 1995) at 447.

[190] 'A Community Strategy for Waste Management' at 20.

[191] Moreover, as will be seen below, the Community has used minimum-harmonization schemes in the area of waste management. As a result, even after Community harmonization, disparities in waste-disposal standards may remain between member states since the latter retain the power to adopt stricter standards than Community standards. See p. 121 below.

[192] 'A Community Strategy for Waste Management' at 21.

waste[193] and 78/319 on toxic and dangerous waste.[194] Taken together, these two directives, which were adopted on the basis of Articles 100 and 235 of the Treaty, created the basic framework for the Community's regulation of the disposal of waste.[195] They required member states to take the necessary measures to ensure that waste is disposed without endangering human life or the environment. To this end, they envisaged a broad range of disposal and recovery activities involving waste and toxic and dangerous waste. However, the vague terms contained in these directives led to inconsistent implementation in the member states.[196] In particular, the vagueness of the definition of the concepts of 'waste' and 'toxic and dangerous waste' represented an important weakness.[197] The definition of 'waste' contained in Directive 75/442 was circular[198] and the definition in Directive 78/319 of 'toxic and dangerous waste' effectively delegated the determination of whether a waste was covered to national authorities.[199] As a result, national divergences remained.

In 1991, the Community overhauled its waste-management legislation

---

[193] OJ 1975, L 194/39.

[194] OJ 1978, L 84/43.

[195] The Community has also adopted a number of directives regulating specific categories of waste. See, e.g., Directive 86/278 of 12 June 1986 on the protection of the environment, and in particular of the soil, when sewage sludge is used in agriculture, OJ 1986, L 181/6; Directive 76/403 of 6 April 1976 on the disposal of polychlorinated biphenyls and polychlorinated terphenyls, OJ 1976, L 108/41; Directive 75/439 of 16 June 1975 on the disposal of waste oils, OJ 1975, L 194/23. For an overview of Community action in the area of waste, see J. P Hannequart, *Le Droit Européen des Déchets* (Brussels: IBGE, 1993); E. Morgan de Rivery and F. Note-Pinte, 'La Gestion des Déchets Industriels – Action Passée, Présente et Future de la Communauté', *Revue du Marché Commun* (1992), 414.

[196] This induced the Commission to start a large number of proceedings against non-complying member states. See Case C-45/91, *Commission v. Greece* [1992] ECR I-2,508; Case C-33/90, *Commission v. Italy* [1991] ECR I-5,987; Case C-48/89, *Commission v. Italy* [1990] ECR I-2,425; Case 239/85, *Commission v. Belgium* [1986] ECR 3,645; Case 69/81, *Commission v. Belgium* [1982] ECR 163.

[197] Generally on this issue, see J. Fluck, 'The Term "Waste" in EU Law', *European Environmental Law Review* (1994), 79; P. de Bruycker and P. Morrens, 'Qu'est ce qu'un Déchet dans l'Union Européenne?' *Aménagement – Environnement* (1993/3), 154; J. T. Smith, 'The Challenge of Environmentally Sound and Efficient Regulation of Waste – The Need for Enhanced International Understanding', *Journal of Environmental Law* (1993), 91, 93.

[198] Article 1(a) of Directive 75/442 of 15 July 1975 defined 'waste' as any substance which the holder 'disposes of or is required to dispose of pursuant to the provisions of national law in force'. In turn, Article 1(b) defined 'disposal' as 'the collecting, sorting, transport and treatment of *waste* as well as its storage or tipping above or under ground' (emphasis added). The circularity of these definitions is readily apparent.

[199] See Article 1(b) of Directive 78/319 of 20 March 1978.

with the adoption of Directives 91/156 on waste[200] and 91/689 on hazardous waste.[201] These directives, which are based on Article 130S of the Treaty, are designed to amend Directives 75/442 and 78/319 respectively. They first attempt to clarify the definition of the concept of 'waste'[202] and 'hazardous waste'.[203] They also strengthen the licensing requirements for those who handle, transport, dispose or recycle waste. In keeping with the Council Resolution on waste policy of 7 May 1990,[204] which emphasized the importance of the principle of self-sufficiency, Directive 91/156 requires member states to establish an integrated network of disposal installations, enabling 'the Community as a whole to become self-sufficient in waste disposal and the member states to move towards that aim individually'.[205] Given their character of 'framework' directives, Directives 91/156 and 91/689 provide, however, little detail on the technical standards that are applicable to the installations involved in waste-disposal activities. These standards are to be elaborated in subsequent directives.

To date, the Community has only adopted one such directive, Directive 94/67 on the incineration of hazardous waste.[206] The purpose of this directive is to establish strict uniform site design and operational criteria for all hazardous-waste-incineration facilities as well as for industrial plants which incinerate a proportion of hazardous waste as a fuel supplement. It should be noted that, in its original proposal, the Commission had chosen Article 100A as the legal basis for this directive.[207] The Commission insisted in the preamble of the proposed directive that

---

[200] OJ 1991, L 78/32.

[201] OJ 1991, L 377/20.

[202] Article 1.4 of Directive 91/689 of 12 December 1991 defines 'hazardous waste' as waste featuring on a list to be drawn up following a technical committee procedure. This list can now be found in Council Decision 94/404 establishing a list of hazardous waste pursuant to Article 1(4) of Council Directive 91/689 of 12 December 1991 on hazardous waste, OJ 1994, L 356/14.

[203] Article 1 of Directive 91/156 of 18 March 1991 defines 'waste' as any 'substance or object' falling within certain broad categories outlined in Annex I, 'which the holder discards, or intends or is required to discard'. Uncertainties, however, remain since the directive does not define 'discard'.

[204] OJ 1990, C 122/2.

[205] Article 5.1 of Directive 91/156 of 18 March 1991. Article 7 of the Directive also requires member states to draw up waste-management plans and to take measures which are necessary to prevent movements of waste which are not in accordance with those plans.

[206] OJ 1994, L 365/34.

[207] Proposal for a Council Directive on the incineration of hazardous waste (92/C 130/01), COM (92) 9 final, SYN 406, OJ 1992, C 130/1.

'differences in national provisions applicable to the incineration of hazardous waste . . . may distort competition, affect the free movement of goods, and give rise to differences in the protection of human health and the environment'.[208] However, following its victory in the *Waste Directive* case, the Council removed from the preamble all mention of the internal market, and decided to base this Directive on the new Article 130S(1) procedure. It should be noted that this change of legal basis could have an impact on the movement of waste between member states. As will be seen below, Article 130T authorizes member states to adopt stricter standards than Community standards adopted under Article 130S.[209] A member state could therefore use this provision in order to adopt stricter incineration standards than those contained in Directive 94/67. This could in turn give an incentive to producers located in that member state to incinerate their hazardous waste in other member states applying laxer Community standards.

On 23 April 1991, the Commission also sent to the Council a proposal for a Directive on the landfill of waste.[210] In its original version, which was based on Article 100A, this proposal was designed to harmonize the technical standards for the landfill of waste on a high level of environmental protection. The proposal set detailed standards regarding all aspects of landfilling activities: licensing requirements, waste-acceptance procedure, etc. After four years of negotiations, the common position reached by the member states' environment ministers is, however, rather unsatisfactory.[211] Based on Article 130S rather than Article 100A as originally proposed by the Commission, the draft directive only represents a loose regulatory framework. Pursuant to the requirement of proportionality, it only contains minimum standards and leaves considerable discretion to national authorities. It also contains myriad exemptions to its rules. If this common position were to be formally adopted,[212] one can expect to see important disparities in the technical standards applied to landfills in

---

[208] See the eleventh recital of the proposed directive.
[209] See pp. 134–5 below.
[210] OJ 1991, C 190 at 1; amended COM (93) 275, 10 June 1993.
[211] See Common Position No. 4/96 adopted by the Council on 6 October 1995 with a view to adopting Council Directive 96/_ on the landfill of waste, OJ 1996, C 59/1.
[212] In this regard, it should be noted that the European Parliament has formally rejected this common position because it felt that it was not stringent enough to ensure adequate environmental protection. This means that in practice the Council needs to agree unanimously if they wish to 'confirm' this common position. This is, however, an unlikely scenario since a number of member states initially voted against this common position. See 'Parliament Rejection Dooms EU Landfill Directive', *Environment Watch*, 7 June 1996, at 3.

the member states, thereby maintaining incentives for transfrontier shipments of waste towards the least strictly regulated landfills.[213]

The foregoing analysis reveals that, so far, Community harmonization of waste-disposal standards has been relatively broad in scope but relatively low in intensity. Directives 91/156 and 91/689 only provide a broad framework for the regulation of waste-disposal activities. They must be completed by further directives containing detailed technical standards applicable to waste-disposal activities. As illustrated by the negotiations on the draft Directive on the landfill of waste, there seems to be a movement away from a strict Community harmonization of waste-disposal standards. This movement seems to be partly motivated by the idea of proportionality contained in Article 3B(3) of the Treaty. As will be seen below, there is also an increasing consensus between member states that waste disposal is essentially a problem to be regulated by national authorities according to national interests.

Regulation of transfrontier movements of waste

In addition to adopting rules governing the management of waste activities, the Community has adopted legislation specifically regulating transfrontier shipments of waste. The first Community measure to tackle the issue of waste transfers was Directive 84/361 on the supervision and control of the transfrontier shipment of hazardous waste.[214] This Directive, which was based on Articles 100 and 235 of the Treaty, was adopted essentially as a result of the continuing increase in the volume of transfrontier shipments of hazardous waste and the numerous accidents which have occurred.[215] Based on the principle of prior informed consent, it aimed at establishing a complete and uninterrupted chain of supervision and control when hazardous waste was shipped across national

---

[213] It should also be noted that, after more than five years of discussion, the member states have not yet managed to agree on the Commission proposal for a directive on civil liability for damage caused by waste. OJ 1989, C 251 at 3, amended OJ 1991, C 192/6. See also the Commission Green Paper on remedying environmental damage, COM (93) 47 final, 14 March 1993.

[214] OJ 1984, L 326/31. For an analysis of this directive, see C. de Villeneuve, 'Les Mouvements Transfrontières de Déchets Dangereux (Convention de Bâle et Droit Communautaire)', *Revue du Marché Commun* 340 (1990), 568; M. Kelly, 'International Regulation of Transfrontier Hazardous Waste Shipments: A New EEC Environmental Directive', *Texas International Law Journal* 21 (1985), 85.

[215] Of particular significance was the Seveso incident in which forty-one barrels of highly toxic, dioxin-contaminated waste were transported illegally from Italy to France undetected and dumped in a barn in the Northern part of France. For details, see U. Wasserman, 'The Seveso Affair', *Journal of World Trade Law* 17 (1983), 371.

borders between member states.[216] Because of its limited scope and a poor implementation record by the member states, this Directive had, however, limited success in controlling transfrontier shipments of waste.[217]

Since May 1994, Directive 84/361 has been replaced by Regulation 259/93 on the transfrontier shipments of waste.[218] This regulation, which is intended to implement the Basle[219] and Lomé IV[220] Conventions, regulates comprehensively the transnational movements of waste, whether hazardous or not, within, into and out of the Community.[221] As far as intra-Community shipments of waste are concerned, the central objective of Regulation 259/93 is to ensure prior notification and consent for waste shipments to member state 'Competent Authorities', enabling them to be informed of the particular type of movement, and disposal or recovery of waste, so that they can take all necessary measures for the protection of health and the environment, including the possibility of raising objections to shipments. The bases on which member state authorities may object to a waste shipment vary depending on the shipment's purposes (i.e., disposal or recovery). While in the case of waste destined for recovery, objection may be made to a planned shipment only on reasoned grounds which relate to the particular shipment concerned,[222] member states may

---

[216] See Articles 3 and 4 of the directive.

[217] See A. Schmidt, 'Transboundary Movements of Waste Under EC Law: The Emerging Regulatory Framework', *Journal of Environmental Law* 4 (1992), 57, 61.

[218] OJ 1993, L 30 at 1. Individual firms have attacked Regulation 259/93 on the ground that the different restrictions it imposes on the movements of waste would be contrary to Articles 30ff of the Treaty. The Court of First Instance rejected their application. See Case T-475/93, *Buralux and Others* v. *Council*, judgment of 17 May 1994, unreported. This judgment was subsequently confirmed by the Court of Justice. See Case C-209/94, *Buralux and Others*, judgment of 15 February 1996, unreported.

[219] Reprinted in ILM 28 (1989), 567. The Basle Convention was approved on behalf of the Community by Council Decision 93/98, OJ 1993, L 38 at 1. Generally on this Convention, see K. Kummer, *International Management of Hazardous Wastes: The Basel Convention and Related Legal Rules* (Oxford: Oxford University Press, 1995).

[220] Reprinted in ILM 29 (1990), 788. For a discussion on the Lomé IV Convention and its implications, see C. Hilz, *The International Toxic Waste Trade* (New York: van Nostrand Reinhold, 1992) at 153ff.

[221] For good discussions on Regulation 259/93, see J. Sommer, 'Les Déchets, de l'Autosuffisance et de la Libre Circulation des Marchandises', *Revue du Marché Commun* (1994), 246; N. de Sadeleer, 'La Libre Circulation des Déchets et le Marché Unique Européen', *Revue du Marché Unique Européen* (1994), 71; A. Skroback, 'Even a Sacred Cow Must Live in a Green Pasture: The Proximity Principle, Free Movement of Goods, and Regulation 259/93 on the Transfrontier Waste Shipments within the EC', *Boston College International and Comparative Law Review* 17 (1994), 85; J. P. Hannequart, 'Le Règlement Européen sur les Mouvements de Déchets', *Aménagement – Environnement* (1993/2), 67.

[222] See Article 7.4 of Regulation 259/93.

introduce general or partial prohibitions, or make systematic objections to shipments of waste for disposal.[223] In this regard, Article 4.3.a.1 of the regulation indicates that:

In order to implement the principles of proximity, of priority for recovery and of self-sufficiency at Community and national levels . . . Member States may take measures in accordance with the Treaty to prohibit generally or partially or to object systematically to shipments of waste [for disposal]. Such measures shall immediately be notified to the Commission who will inform the other Member States.[224]

This provision, which was seen as a victory by environmentalists as well as a number of member states,[225] has two main effects. First, Article 4.3.a.1 protects member states from being pre-empted from adopting restrictions on the transfrontier shipments of waste. The absence of such a provision in a regulation organizing a comprehensive system for waste control would have excluded the possibility of member states adopting alternative systems of control such as general or partial prohibitions on imports or exports of waste.[226] Regulation 259/93 should not therefore be seen as a complete harmonization of the rules governing the transfer of waste, but as a sort of organized 'renationalization' of that matter. Second, Article 4.3.a.1 extends to all categories of waste (with the exception of those for recycling) the restrictive approach taken by the *Belgian Waste* case as regards restrictions on the shipments of non-hazardous waste.[227] In this regard, there is little doubt that the *Belgian Waste* case has been a decisive factor in the insertion of Article 4.3.a.1 in Regulation 259/93. This case was decided at a time when the member states were actively negotiating the regulation and, obviously, gave a strong argument to those who favoured

---

[223] The absence of general prohibitions on shipments of waste for disposal does not prevent member states from making objections to specific shipments of such waste. See Article 4.3.

[224] Article 4.3.a.2 provides, however, that such objections shall not apply to hazardous waste produced in a member state in such a small quantity per year that the provision of new specialized disposal installations in that member state would be uneconomic.

[225] See, in particular, the enthusiastic declarations made by the Belgian and French environment ministers, reported in *Europe*, 16 October 1992, at 12–13.

[226] This aspect was made clear in the *Belgian Waste* case where the Court of Justice ruled that, as far as they concerned the transfer of hazardous waste, the Walloon restrictions were pre-empted by Directive 84/361 of 6 December 1984 which organized a comprehensive system of control for such waste.

[227] This provision also confirms the approach earlier adopted by the Community in Articles 4 and 7 of Directive 91/156 of 18 March 1991 (strongly emphasizing the need for self-sufficiency at national level).

allowing member states to object systematically to certain categories of shipments of waste.[228]

Contrary to the original objective of the Commission,[229] Regulation 259/93 does not therefore provide for the establishment of a 'common market' for waste where shipments of waste would move, under the supervision of uniform rules, to the most adequate disposal installations wherever such installations are located in the Community. Instead, Regulation 259/93 adopts a restrictive approach to the movements of waste enabling each member state to close off its borders to such movements in order to implement the principles of proximity and self-sufficiency. As we have seen, it is because of this restrictive approach that, in the *Transfer of Waste Regulation* case,[230] the Court of Justice ruled that Regulation 259/93 had been rightly based on Article 130S of the Treaty rather than on Article 100A as originally proposed by the Commission.

A central question at this stage is whether, in allowing member states to act unilaterally to restrict transfrontier movements of waste, Regulation 259/93 will have a positive impact on the fight led by the Community against what is often referred to as 'waste tourism'.[231] This question is extremely controversial.[232] On the one hand, fear has been expressed that restrictions on the movements of waste on the grounds of proximity and self-sufficiency could in fact hide protectionist measures.[233] For example, member states wishing to ban the importation of waste might pretend

---

[228] See my comments in *European Law Review* 18 (1993), 418, 426.

[229] The fifth recital of the Commission proposal stated that '[w]hereas the completion of the internal market by 1 January 1993 will remove internal frontiers, in particular as regards the movement of waste, and implies that there must be new procedures for the supervision and control of waste shipments as this will no longer be possible at frontiers . . .'. See Amended Proposal for a Council Regulation on the supervision and control of shipments of waste within, into and out of the European Community, OJ 1992, C 115 at 4. The Commission proposal referred to the principle of proximity as a potential limitation on waste transfers. However, this principle was understood in a pure 'geographical' sense and it applied to movements of waste between member states but also within one member state. See Article 4.3. The principle of self-sufficiency was mentioned as a long-term objective in the preamble, but was not mentioned in the substantive part of the proposed regulation.

[230] Case C-187/93, *Parliament v. Council* [1994] ECR 2,857.

[231] See A. Schmidt, 'Trade in Waste Under Community Law' in Cameron, Demaret and Geradin (eds.), *Trade and the Environment – The Search for Balance* (Cameron & May, 1994) at 184.

[232] D. Chalmers, 'Community Policy on Waste Management – Managing Environmental Decline Gently', *Yearbook of European Law* 14 (1994), 257.

[233] See J. T. Smith and J. Sarnoff, 'Free Commerce and Sound Waste Management: Some International Comparative Perspectives', *International Environmental Reporter*, 8 April 1992, 207, 212.

that adequate facilities exist nearer in the member states of origin. Conversely, member states that have invested public funds in the development of waste-management facilities might be tempted to deny export approvals in order to capture a market for such facilities.[234] Fear has also been expressed by industry commentators that a strict application of the principles of proximity and self-sufficiency could considerably impede the integrated waste-management schemes developed by certain companies.[235] Industrial companies operating in several member states often use one or a limited number of waste-disposal sites to ensure the proper disposal of their company's waste throughout the Community. Sending their waste to be disposed at these sites may, however, involve movements over considerable distances and, in a number of cases, across national borders. A strict application of the principles of proximity and self-sufficiency could clearly upset these schemes.

On the other hand, it has been argued that, to the extent exports of waste are rendered more difficult, member states will have to adopt appropriate measures to prevent or limit the production of waste on their territory.[236] It has been argued that limited bans on the transfrontier movement of waste on the ground of self-sufficiency could help alleviate the problems created by the shortage of adequate waste-disposal facilities in a number of member states.[237] As is well known, this shortage usually

[234] In this regard, it is important to note that Article 4.3.a.1 makes it clear that if in order to implement the principles of proximity and self-sufficiency member states adopt partial or total prohibitions on the movements of waste, they can only do so 'in accordance with the Treaty'. National restrictions adopted under Article 4.3.a.1 must therefore be compatible with Articles 30 to 36 of the Treaty. In light of the Court of Justice judgments in Case 172/82, *Interhuiles* [1983] ECR 555 and Case 118/86, *Nertsvoederfabriek* [1987] ECR 3,883, it seems unlikely that export bans motivated by protectionist purposes may be justified on the ground that they comply with Article 4.3.a.1 of Regulation 259/93.

[235] See G. Williamson, 'The EU's New Regulation on Waste Shipments: Content and Concerns Arising from Practical Implementation', *Environment Watch*, 6 May 1994, at 6.

[236] See de Sadeleer, *Le Droit Communautaire* at 490.

[237] This point is remarkably summarized by P. von Wilmowsky in 'Waste Disposal in the Internal Market: The State of Play after the ECJ's Ruling on the Walloon Import Ban', *Common Market Law Review* 30 (1993), 541, 552: 'The siting of waste disposal has become a considerable political problem in all EC countries, because the local population regularly resists the setting up of such plants. While all the social costs for waste disposal are concentrated on the municipality where the site is located, the advantages are spread over the whole geographical collection area. This conflict is not only evident at local level; it can also be found on the level of regions and countries. The political leaders will try to escape the political costs caused by debates with local protest movements. Any access to disposal facilities opened on the basis of the free movement of goods constitutes an inducement to avoid the political problems

stems from the fact that, in a market where waste circulates freely, it is tempting for member state, regional and local authorities to avoid the political cost of setting up 'loathsome' waste-disposal facilities by sending their waste to other jurisdictions which have set up these facilities (the 'not-in-my-backyard' or 'NIMBY' syndrome).[238] In this context, by preventing member states from free-riding on the efforts of other member states, limited bans on the movements of waste could give a strong incentive to all member states to provide for an adequate supply of waste-disposal services within their borders.

As these conflicting assessments make clear, it is too early to evaluate the impact of Regulation 259/93 on the problems created by the transfrontier shipments of waste. Given the controversial nature of some of its provisions, and in particular Article 4.3.a.1, it is likely that the application of this regulation will generate litigation over the validity of restrictions on the movement of waste. In this context, the burden will fall on the Court of Justice to define clearly the boundaries within which member states may restrict the movement of waste in order to implement the principles of proximity and self-sufficiency.

The question of pre-emption

A question of central importance with regard to the relationship between trade and environmental policies is whether, once the Community has legislated, member states remain free to adopt stricter environmental standards than Community standards. From a policy standpoint, this question, which generally relates to the doctrine of pre-emption, is not easy to answer.[239] On the one hand, allowing member states to adopt

    involved in the authorization of waste-disposal sites and instead seek refuge with those EC partners who demand such sacrifices. As the temptation to take a free ride on the siting efforts of others exists to the same degree for every region of every country, there arises a negative conflict with regard to siting, with a resulting undersupply of disposal services right across the Community.'

[238] Generally on the NIMBY syndrome, see D. Mazmanian and D. Morell, 'The "NIMBY" Syndrome: Facility-Siting and the Failure of Democratic Discourse' in Vig and Kraft (eds.), *Environmental Policy in the 1990s* (Washington, DC: CQ Press, 1990).

[239] On the question of pre-emption generally, see E. Cross, 'Pre-emption of Member State Law in the European Community: A Framework for Analysis', *Common Market Law Review* 28 (1992), 447. See also S. Weatherill, *Law and Integration in the European Union* (Oxford: Clarendon Press, 1995), Chapter 5; S. Weatherill, 'Beyond Pre-emption? Shared Competence and Constitutional Change in the European Community' in O'Keeffe and Twomey (eds.), *Legal Issues of the Maastricht Treaty* (London: Wiley, 1993); M. Cappelletti and D. Golay, 'The Judicial Branch in the Federal and Transnational Union: Its Impact on Integration' in Cappelletti *et al.* (eds.), *Integration through Law*

more protective standards than Community standards seems desirable since it permits them to provide for particular local needs and to ensure a higher level of environmental protection on their territory. On the other hand, there may be circumstances where stricter member state standards disrupt the harmony of the Community regulatory scheme. Stricter standards may also have the effect of reintroducing the kind of trade distortions that the Community attempted to remove by adopting uniform legislation.[240] In this context, it is of central importance to examine how the tension between the Community interest in preserving the uniformity of its legislation and the member states' interest in better providing for local needs has been resolved in Community law.

Once again, it is useful to distinguish between the Community legislation adopted in the period prior to the SEA and Community legislation adopted in the period following the SEA; since the SEA introduced provisions allowing, under certain conditions, member states to apply environmental measures that are more stringent than Community measures (Articles 130T and 100A(4)). Separate attention will not be devoted to the period following the TEU since Articles 130T and 100A(4) have not been modified by this new instrument.

Pre-emption prior to the Single European Act

Prior to the entry into force of the SEA, pre-emption questions were sometimes solved in advance by the Community legislature when it expressly indicated whether the effect of Community legislation was to deprive member states of the power to adopt stricter standards or whether it only imposed minimum standards. In this regard, the degree of uniformity required by Community legislation has usually varied depending on the areas that were regulated.

Where the area to be regulated is that of product standards, the Community has generally expressly pre-empted member states from adopting stricter national standards. Since varying product standards impede intra-Community trade and create market fragmentation, the adoption of maximum standards pursuant to total[241] or

(Walter de Gruyter, 1985), vol I, at 318–21; M. Waelbroeck, 'The Emergent Doctrine of Community Pre-emption – Consent and Redelegation' in Sandalow and Stein (eds.), *Courts and Free Markets* (Oxford University Press, 1982) at 548.

[240] T. Joseph, 'Preaching Heresy: Permitting Member States to Enforce Stricter Environmental Laws than the European Community', *Yale Journal of International Law* 20 (1995) at 277.

[241] Total harmonization means that all member states will apply the same (Community) standards for the product in question. For examples of total-harmonization directives,

optional[242] harmonization regimes has been perceived as necessary to ensure the unrestricted movement of products between member states. It should be noted, however, that in a limited number of circumstances the Community has allowed member states to adopt stricter product standards than Community standards.

First, some directives contain 'safeguard clauses' following which, if a member state establishes that a product presents a danger to humans or the environment even though it complies with Community rules, it may provisionally prohibit or make subject to special conditions the marketing of that product on its territory.[243] The member state in question must immediately inform the Commission of the measures taken. The Commission then consults the other member states concerned to try to obtain their agreement. If the Community believes it necessary, the protective measures of the individual member state will be replaced by a Community provision in order to re-establish a uniform rule. If, on the other hand, it regards such measures as unjustified, the Commission will initiate proceedings against the member state in question in respect of breach of the Treaty. Until the Community decides on a common set of rules on the matter, or the court declares the member state's provisions

---

see Directive 78/631 of 26 June 1978 on the approximation of the laws of the member states relating to the classification, packaging and labelling of dangerous preparations (pesticides), OJ 1978, L 206/13; Directive 77/728 of 7 November 1977 on the approximation of the laws, regulations and administrative provisions of the member states relating to the classification, packaging and labelling of paints, varnishes, printing inks, adhesives and similar products, OJ 1977, L 303/3; Directive 73/173 of 4 June 1973 on the approximation of the laws of the member states relating to solvents, OJ 1973, L 189/7.

[242] As already noted, optional harmonization means that member states must ensure market access to products which comply with Community standards but are free to allow on their territory the sale and operation of products that do not meet such standards. Optional harmonization therefore provides for a regulatory ceiling above which no member state can go. For some examples of optional harmonization directives, see Directive 70/220 of 20 March 1970 on the measures to be taken against air pollution by gases from positive-ignition engines of motor vehicles, OJ 1970, L 76/1 and its amendment directives; Directive 78/1015 of 23 November 1978 on the approximation of the laws of the member states on the permissible sound level and exhaust systems of motorcycles, OJ 1978, L 249/21.

[243] See, e.g., Article 15 of Directive 90/220 of 23 April 1990 on the deliberate release into the environment of genetically modified organisms, OJ 1990, L 117/15; Article 5(2) of Directive 87/18 of 18 December 1987 on the harmonization of laws, regulations and administrative provisions relating to the application of the principles of good laboratory practice and the verifications of their application for tests of chemical substances, OJ 1987, L 15/29; Article 23 of Directive 67/548 of 27 June 1967 on the approximation of laws, regulations and administrative provisions relating to the classification, packaging and labelling of dangerous substances, OJ 1967, L 196/1.

invalid, the member state which adopted the safeguard measures may maintain them.[244]

Another technique used in product regulations to enable more extensive measures to be taken by individual member states is the granting of an 'express authorization' allowing member states to adopt, within a certain margin, stricter standards than the minimum Community harmonized standards.[245] For example, Directive 78/611 on lead content of gasoline set up a harmonized minimum level of 0.40 g/l for lead in gasoline, but permitted member states to establish a stricter lead level as low as 0.15 g/l.[246] This system was confirmed in Directive 85/210.[247] Directive 85/210 also stated the objective that 'Member States shall, as soon as they consider appropriate, reduce to 0.15 g/l the permitted lead-compound content, calculated in terms of lead, of leaded petrol put on their markets'.[248] As pointed out by Kramer, Directive 85/210 leads therefore to a 'Community with different speeds for the introduction of a certain policy'.[249]

With regard to environmental process standards, Community legislation has generally provided for minimum harmonization, i.e., the Community sets minimum standards and the member states are free to maintain or adopt more stringent requirements.[250] The rationale for such an approach is that, on the one hand, the adoption of minimum process standards may be necessary to address important environmental problems and/or to remove the distortions of competition that may arise

---

[244] This safeguard procedure has now been institutionalized in Article 100A(5) of the Treaty which states that, in appropriate cases, measures of harmonization based on Article 100A 'include a safeguard clause authorizing the member states to take, for one or more of the non-economic reasons referred in Article 36, provisional measures subject to a Community control procedure'. See also Article 130R(2)(2) discussed at note 271 below.

[245] L. Kramer, *Focus on European Environmental Law* (London: Sweet & Maxwell, 1992) at 191.

[246] Article 2 of Directive 78/611 on the approximation of the laws of the member states concerning the lead content of petrol, OJ 1987, L 197/19.

[247] Article 2.3 of Directive 85/210 on the approximation of the laws of the member states concerning the lead content of petrol, OJ 1985, L 96/25.

[248] *Ibid.*

[249] Kramer, *Focus on European Environmental Law*, 191.

[250] See, e.g., Directive 87/217 of 15 March 1987 on the prevention and reduction of environmental pollution by asbestos, OJ 1987, L 85/40; Directive 80/778 of 15 July 1980 relating to the quality of water intended for human consumption, OJ 1980, L 229/11; Directive 78/176 of 20 February 1978 on waste from the titanium-dioxide industry, OJ 1978, L 54/19; Directive 76/464 of 4 May 1976 on pollution caused by certain dangerous substances discharged into the aquatic environment of the Community, OJ 1976, L 129/23.

when member states adopt inconsistent process standards. On the other hand, there is no strong Community interest in preventing member states going beyond these minimum standards.[251] If the principal objective of Community legislation is to address a particular environmental problem, there seems to be no reason why member states should be prevented from adopting more protective provisions than those provided for at Community level. Similarly, if the principal objective of Community legislation is to ensure that fair conditions of competition are applied in certain industries, allowing stricter national standards will not affect this objective since only domestic producers will be affected by such stricter standards.

In the area of waste, Directive 78/319 on toxic and dangerous waste, now amended by Directive 91/689,[252] contained a provision clearly indicating that member states were entitled to take more stringent measures than those provided for in the directive.[253] Such an approach is not surprising since Directive 78/319 did not directly deal with the movement or, more generally, the trade aspects of toxic and dangerous waste, but rather aimed at providing some harmonization of the industrial processes involved in the disposal of such waste. Perhaps more surprising was the absence of a similar provision in Directive 75/442 on waste.[254] Directives 75/442 and 78/319 were indeed clearly linked and generally pursued the same objectives and structure. Directive 84/361 on the transfrontier shipments of hazardous waste also failed to indicate whether it was exhaustive or only provided for minimum standards.[255] Some elements of an answer to this question can, however, be found in the *Belgian Waste* case, where, although it did not entirely exclude the possibility for member states to impose stricter requirements on the transfers of hazardous waste, the Court of Justice ruled out the possibility for member states to impose a global ban on imports of such waste.[256]

---

[251] Rehbinder and Stewart, 'Environmental Protection Policy' at 211.

[252] It should be noted that this paragraph is of pure historical interest since all the Directives mentioned have now been amended.

[253] See Article 8 of the Directive, OJ 1978, L 84/43. See also Article 12 of Directive 86/278 of 12 June 1986 on the protection of the environment, and in particular of the soil, when sewage sludge is used in agriculture, OJ 1986, L 181/6.

[254] OJ 1975, L 194/1. Directive 76/403 of 6 April 1976 on the disposal of PCBs and PCTs, OJ 1976, L 108/41 and Directive 75/439 of 16 June 1975 on the disposal of waste oils, OJ 1975, L 194/23, also fail to indicate whether they pre-empt member states to adopt stricter measures or not.

[255] OJ 1984, L 326/31.

[256] See Case C-2/90, *Commission* v. *Belgium*, [1992] ECR I-4,431. The court considered that the fact Directive 84/361 of 6 December 1984 had opted for a system of prior

In the absence of legislative guidance on the issue of pre-emption, the Court of Justice may be asked to infer the pre-emptive effect of Community legislation over more exacting member state legislation. It is indeed a basic rule of Community law that, even in the absence of an express pre-emption provision, the adoption of a Community measure of harmonization may have the effect of prohibiting member states from adopting more stringent measures on the basis of the 'police powers' recognized in Article 36, or the rule of reason.[257] In this context, the Court of Justice's task is to analyse the Community legislation in question in order to determine whether it 'occupies the field' or if it leaves space for further member state action.[258] For example, in *Ratti*, the court was questioned by an Italian court on the compatibility with Directive 79/173 on solvents of an Italian law imposing more stringent requirements than those contained in that directive.[259] Emphasizing the exhaustive nature of Directive 79/173, the court declared that it was a consequence of the system introduced by this directive 'that a Member State may not introduce into its national legislation conditions which were more restrictive than those laid down in the directive in question, or which are even more detailed or in any event different'.[260] Similarly, in Case 278/85, *Commission* v. *Denmark*, the Court of Justice ruled that it was clear from the scheme of Directive 67/548 on dangerous substances and preparations 'that the Community legislature has laid down an exhaustive set of rules governing the notification, classification, packaging and labelling of substances, both new and old, and that it has not left Member States any scope to introduce other measures in their national legislation'.[261] By contrast, in *Nijman*, the court found that Directive 79/117 prohibiting the placing on the market and the use of plant-protection products con-

---

notification of itself excluded the possibility of member states adopting an alternative system of control such as a general prohibition on imports.

[257] This rule has been applied in a large number of cases. See, e.g., Case C-241/89, *SARPP* [1990] ECR I-4,695; Case 190/87, *Moormann BV* [1988] ECR 4,689; Case 29/87, *Dansk Denkavit Aps* [1988] ECR 2,965; Case 72/83, *Campus Oil* [1984] ECR 2,727; Case 227/82, *van Bennekom* [1983] ECR 3,883; Case 251/78, *Denkavit* [1979] ECR 3,369; Case 5/77, *Tedeschi* [1977] ECR 5; Case 46/75, *Bauhuis* [1977] ECR 5. Generally see J. Currall, 'Some Aspects of the Relation Between Articles 30–6 and Article 100 of the EEC Treaty, with a Closer Look to Optional Harmonization', *Yearbook of European Law* 3 (1984), 187–91.

[258] It goes without saying that, pursuant to the principle of supremacy of Community law, even when the Community has chosen not to 'occupy the field', stricter member state measures may nevertheless be invalidated when they conflict with the objectives of Community legislation. See Case 106/77, *Simmenthal* [1978] ECR 629, 643.

[259] Case 148/78 [1979] ECR 1,629.

[260] *Ibid.* at 1,643.

[261] Case 278/85 [1987] ECR 4,069, at 4,087.

taining certain active substances did not fully harmonize national rules covering the marketing and use of plant-protection products.[262] As a consequence, the Netherlands was entitled to rely on Article 36 of the Treaty to justify legislation prohibiting Improsol, a plant-protection product which was not listed in Directive 79/117. Similarly, in *Enichem*,[263] the court ruled that the scope of Directive 75/442 on waste was not as broad as to prevent member states from imposing prohibitions on the right to sell or use plastic bags and other non-biodegradable containers. Nothing in Directive 75/442 prevented member states from regulating that matter.

In the absence of well-defined criteria indicating in which circumstances pre-SEA Community environmental legislation is to be considered exclusive, it is difficult to assess how much latitude is left to the member states in the areas where the Community has legislated. As will be seen below, the entry into force of new or amendment directives based on Articles 100A or 130S will bring about some clarification on the scope of Community intervention.[264] In the absence of adoption of new directives, the doctrine of pre-emption will remain of central importance to determine the scope of pre-SEA Community environmental legislation. In this regard, there seem to be good reasons for the Court of Justice to impose limits on its use of the doctrine of pre-emption. First, there may be circumstances where adoption of stricter national standards is necessary to protect particular local needs.[265] For obvious reasons, the Community cannot take into account all local human or geographical circumstances when it legislates. In invalidating all member state interventions in areas where the Community has legislated, an extensive application of the pre-emption doctrine could leave a series of local needs unfulfilled. Second, far-reaching implied pre-emption could also prevent member states from acting as 'laboratories' for new regulatory solutions.[266] This would be unfortunate as, due to its relatively limited technical and administrative

---

[262] Case 125/88 [1989] ECR 3,533, at 3,546.

[263] Case 380/87, *Enichem Base* [1989] ECR 2,491.

[264] See, however, pp. 135–9 above (pointing out the uncertainties surrounding the application of Article 100A(4)).

[265] This idea can be found, for example, in Lord Templeman's speech in *Regina v. London Boroughs Transport Committee ex parte Freight Transport Association Limited, et al.* [1992] 1 CMLR; [1991] 3 All ER 915 ('London's environmental traffic problems cannot be solved, although they can be ameliorated by Council Directives to control every vehicle at all times throughout the Community').

[266] See, *mutatis mutandis*, Justice Brandeis' famous opinion in *New State Ice Co. v. Liebmann*, 285 US 262, 311 (1932), quoted at note 206, p. 182 above.

resources,[267] the Commission often relies on solutions developed at member state level as a basis for Community regulation.[268] Adoption of a strict pre-emption doctrine would therefore deprive the Community of a useful source of innovation for better environmental protection. Finally, and perhaps more fundamentally, support for a limitation of the doctrine of pre-emption can also be found in the principles of subsidiarity and proportionality, which, applied in the pre-emption context, could form the basis of a presumption in favour of national measures.[269]

Pre-emption following the Single European Act

The SEA considerably modified the principles at play. In addition to clearly recognizing the competence of the Community to act in the environmental field, the SEA established new provisions allowing member states to take more stringent measures than Community measures.

The new provisions in the Treaty: Articles 130T and 100A(4)

Article 130T states:

The protective measures adopted in common pursuant to Article 130S shall not prevent any member state from maintaining or introducing more stringent measures compatible with the Treaty.

Article 130T has a limited field of application. It only applies to measures adopted on the basis of Article 130S, i.e., Community environmental measures having no or only an incidental connection with the internal market process. The use of Article 130T is also subject to some limitations. First, only 'more stringent' protective measures are permitted under that provision.[270] As a result, the member states may not adopt measures of a 'different' nature than the Community measure in ques-

---

[267] This is particularly true with regard to environmental protection. DG-XI, the Directorate-General in charge of environmental protection, has a staff of about 150 officials (as of 1990), who have a budget of about 55 million ECU at their disposal (i.e., approximately 0.1 per cent of the total Commission budget of about 55 billion ECU). By way of comparison, the US Environmental Protection Agency has about 15,000 officials. For additional figures, see Kramer, *Focus on European Environmental Law* at 58.

[268] See Rehbinder and Stewart, 'Environmental Protection Policy' at 213.

[269] For a similar opinion, see Cross, 'Pre-Emption of Member State Law' at 470. See also S. Weatherill in *European Law Review* 19 (1994), 55, 65.

[270] It should be noted that Article 130R(2)(2) of the Treaty states that, where appropriate, harmonization measures may include 'a safeguard clause allowing Member States to take provisional measures, for non-economic environmental reasons, subject to a Community inspection procedure'. Like Article 100A(5), this provision essentially confirms the long-standing Community practice of including safeguard clauses in certain categories of environmental measures.

tion.[271] As pointed out by Kramer, it is important that the rules adopted by the individual member state are of the same type as the Community rules in order to maintain the possibility for the Community and the other member states to align on the standards of the more stringent member state and to re-establish uniform legislation throughout the Community.[272] Second, the more stringent measures adopted under Article 130T must also be compatible with the Treaty. This indicates the continuing importance of Court of Justice scrutiny under Articles 30 to 36 of the Treaty. Community environmental rules provide the floor, whereas Articles 30 to 36 provide the ceiling.[273]

A differently worded safeguard clause applies to environmental measures taken in the framework of achieving the internal market. Article 100A(4) provides:

If, after the adoption of a harmonisation measure by the Council acting by a qualified majority, a Member State deems it necessary to apply national provisions on grounds of major needs referred to in Article 36, or relating to protection of the environment or the working environment, it shall notify the Commission of these provisions.

The Commission shall confirm the provisions involved after having verified that they are not means of arbitrary discrimination or a disguised restriction on trade between Member States.

By way of derogation from the procedure laid down in Articles 169 and 170, the Commission or any Member State may bring the matter directly before the Court of Justice if it considers that another Member State is making improper use of the powers provided in this Article.

This clause, which specifically mentions environmental protection as one of the admissible grounds for derogation with respect to harmonization measures taken on the basis of Article 100A, has given rise to considerable controversy, in particular concerning its potentially adverse effects on the establishment of the internal market.[274] One of the major

---

[271] See Opinion of Advocate-General Jacobs in Case C-187/93, *Parliament v. Council* [1994] ECR I-2,857, 2,867 ('it may be unclear when measures adopted by a Member State are to be regarded as more stringent versions of the Community measures and when they are on the contrary to be regarded as measures of an entirely different kind, and hence not permitted by Article 130T').

[272] See Kramer, *Focus on European Environmental Law* at 102.

[273] Weatherill, *Law and Integration* at 25.

[274] For discussions on Article 100A(4), see generally B. Langeheine, 'Le Rapprochement des Législations Nationales selon l'Article 100A du Traité: L'Harmonisation Communautaire face aux Exigences de Protection Nationale', *Revue du Marché Commun* (1989), 347; P. Pescatore, 'Some Critical Remarks on the Single European Act', *Common*

criticisms against Article 100A(4) is that it appears to act against the pre-emption theory discussed above. In spite of the existence of a harmonization measure based on Article 100A, this provision expressly authorizes member states to rely on Article 36 of the Treaty to safeguard what they consider to be their 'major needs'. Article 100A(4) therefore creates the possibility that obstacles to trade are maintained even after the adoption of a Community measure of harmonization.

Problems also arise from the poor drafting of the provision. For example, it is not apparent from Article 100A(4) whether a member state may introduce new national provisions, or whether it can only maintain provisions which were already in force before the Community measure of harmonization was adopted. Kramer argues that 'the maintenance of existing stricter national measures is permitted in the case of majority decisions, but not the introduction of new measures of this nature'.[275] On the other hand, according to Flynn: 'Article 100A(4) by no means rules out the possibility of a member state wishing to raise its standard after the adoption of a measure.'[276] Since the text is inconclusive, this issue will require clarification by the Court of Justice.

The use of Article 100A(4) is subject to some limitations. First, it only applies to the harmonization measures covered by Article 100A, and only those which are adopted by a qualified majority.[277] Secondly, only national provisions which are 'justified' on the grounds referred to in paragraph 4 (i.e., those indicated in Article 36, the working environment and the environment in general) may be applied. Thirdly, the national provisions in question must be notified to the Commission which must then verify that they comply with the criteria deriving from the Court of Justice's case law on Article 36 and the rule of reason, i.e., the provisions must be necessary, proportionate and not constitute a means of arbitrary discrimination or a disguised restriction on trade between member states.

Market Law Review 24 (1987), 9, 12; C. D. Ehlermann, 'The Internal Market Following the Single European Act', Common Market Law Review 24 (1987), 361, 381; L. Kramer, 'The Single European Act and Environmental Protection: Reflections on Several New Provisions in Community Law', Common Market Law Review 24 (1987), 659, 678; J. Flynn, 'How Will Article 100A(4) Work? A Comparison With Article 93', Common Market Law Review 24 (1987), 689.

[275] Kramer, 'The Single European Act' at 681.

[276] Flynn, 'How Will Article 100A(4) Work?' at 696. See also C. Gulman, 'The Single European Act – Some Remarks from a Danish Perspective', Common Market Law Review 24 (1987), 31, 38.

[277] This does not mean, however, that Article 100A(4) can only be invoked by the member states which were outvoted. See D. Wyatt and A. Dashwood, European Community Law (London: Sweet & Maxwell, 3rd edn, 1993) at 365.

In the event of a persistent disagreement between the Commission (or another member state) and a dissenting member state, the court will decide under an accelerated procedure whether the dissenting member state is justified in relying on Article 100A(4).

To date, the only example of formal use of Article 100A(4) by a member state arose in the context of Council Directive 91/173,[278] which amended Directive 76/769.[279] The object of Directive 91/173, adopted in March 1991, was to harmonize the laws of the member states with regard to the restrictions on the use of pentachlorophenol (PCP), a substance used mainly for the preservation of wood, presenting adverse effects to man and the environment. As a rule, Directive 91/173 prohibited the placing on the market of substances and preparations containing more than 0.1 per cent of PCP, subject to some exceptions. On 2 August 1991, Germany sought to apply Article 100A(4) in order to preserve its more stringent national provisions.[280] On 2 December 1992, the Commission decided to confirm the German provisions concerning PCP pursuant to Article 100A(4),[281] but on 9 February 1993, France asked the Court of Justice to declare void this Commission decision.[282] First, the French government alleged an infringement of Article 100A(4) as the Commission had confirmed the German provisions even though the information forwarded was not sufficient to establish that the conditions indicated in that provision were fulfilled. Secondly, the French government argued that by failing to state clearly the reasons for its decision, the Commission had violated Article 190 of the Treaty. In its judgment, the Court of Justice concentrated on this second argument.[283] The Court recalled that Article 190 required that the measures concerned should contain a statement of the reasons which had led the Community institution in question to adopt them, so that the Court can exercise its power of review and so that the member states and the individuals concerned may learn the conditions under which the Community institutions have applied the rules of

---

[278] OJ 1991, L 85/34. See generally S. Dwyer, 'EC Directive 91/173 Pertaining to Dangerous Substances: When May a Member State Impose Environmental Restrictions which are Stricter than those Mandated by the European Community?' *Boston College International and Comparative Law Review* 17 (1994), 127.

[279] OJ 1976, L 262/201. During the negotiations of Directive 88/76 of 3 December 1988 on motor-vehicle-emission standards, Denmark threatened to use Article 100A(4), but the procedure was not carried through the state of confirmation by the Commission.

[280] *Agence Europe*, 6 June 1992, at 13.

[281] Communication of the Commission (92/C 334/04), OJ 1992, C 334/8.

[282] OJ 1993, C 70/11.

[283] Case C-41/93, *France v. Commission* [1994] ECR I-1,829.

the Treaty.[284] The Court held that, in this case, that requirement was not satisfied. An analysis of the Commission decision revealed that the Commission had confined itself to describing in general terms the content and the aim of the German provisions and to stating that those rules were compatible with the Treaty, without explaining the reasons of fact and law on account of which it considered that all the conditions contained in Article 100A(4) were fulfilled.[285] On these grounds, the court annulled the Commission's decision on the German provisions concerning PCP.[286]

The Court judgment does little to clarify the uncertainties surrounding the application of Article 100A(4). From a substantive point of view, it would have been more interesting if the Court had examined whether the actual conditions governing the application of Article 100A(4) were fulfilled in the case in point. If one lesson can be learned from the case, it is perhaps that the Court of Justice is not ready to allow a broad interpretation of Article 100A(4) which, despite the current claims for national (environmental) diversity in the light of the principle of

---

[284] Judgment of the Court at para. 34.

[285] *Ibid.* at para. 36.

[286] Since the adoption by the Court of Justice of its judgment, three important events have occurred. First, on 14 September 1994, the Commission adopted a decision re-authorizing Germany to maintain its more restrictive rules on the use and sale of PCP on the basis of Article 100A(4). See Commission Decision 94/783 concerning the prohibition of PCP notified by the Federal Republic of Germany, OJ 1994, L 316/43. In order to comply with the judgment of the court, this decision states in greater detail the reasons why the stricter German rules can be justified under Article 100A(4). For an argument that this new decision nevertheless violates Article 100A(4), see R. Sloan and P. Carbonnel, 'Exemptions from Harmonization Measures under Article 100A(4): The Second Authorization of the German Ban on PCP', *European Environmental Law Review* (1995), 45. Second, on 12 November 1994, the Commission published a notice indicating that it had requested that a report be prepared to enable it to assess whether a total ban on the use and sale of PCP could be imposed. See consultation notice on the forthcoming review of Community policy on pentachlorophenol (PCP), OJ 1994, C 315/4. This report, which was released by the Commission on 27 February 1996, highlights the risks posed by PCP but also underlines that data are lacking to evaluate the environmental dangers of chemical substitutes. Moreover, it makes it clear that member states are split over whether to tighten restrictions on PCP further: eight countries favour a total ban, while the initial reaction of six others was that the *status quo* should prevail. See 'European Commission Report on PCP', *Europe Environment*, 19 March 1996 at 3. Finally, on 31 January 1995, Denmark formally requested a derogation on the basis of Article 100A(4) to be authorized to apply its stricter regulations on the use of PCP. The Commission is still considering whether to grant such an authorization. The Commission decision allowing this derogation was published on 19 March 1996, OJ 1996, L 68/32.

subsidiarity,[287] it clearly considers as a derogation from the objective of the creation of the internal market, one which must therefore be interpreted restrictively.[288]

Articles 130T and 100A(4) and the Court of Justice legal-basis case law

As we have seen, prior to the adoption of the SEA, total or optional schemes of harmonization were generally used with regard to the regulation of product standards, whereas minimum harmonization schemes were generally applied to the regulation of processes and the management of waste.[289] Taking into account the Court of Justice's legal-basis case law, it is now interesting to see whether the introduction of Articles 130T and 100A(4) in the Treaty by the SEA has had an impact on these traditional regulatory schemes.

It has already been noted that Article 130T may be only applied to measures adopted under Article 130S, whereas Article 100A(4) may be applied to measures adopted under Article 100A. Further, taken together, the *Titanium Dioxide*, the *Waste Directive* and the *Transfer of Waste Regulation* cases suggest that Article 130S should be essentially used for Community environmental measures having no or only an incidental connection with the internal-market process, whereas Community environmental measures having a direct impact on this process should be based on Article 100A exclusively.[290] According to this distribution, Community measures regulating product standards should be based on Article 100A since the harmonization of such standards is a necessary step to the completion of the internal market. The escape clause contained in Article 100A(4) is applicable to such measures but, as the *PCP* case seems to indicate, it should be narrowly interpreted.[291]

With regard to process standards, the Court of Justice's legal-basis case law suggests that a distinction be made between Community measures primarily designed to protect the environment and Community measures primarily designed to equalize the conditions of competition with regard to specific industries. The former type of measure, which represents the

---

[287] See, e.g., Somsen's comments in *European Environmental Law Review* (1994), 238. ('in the age of subsidiarity, it was not all that extravagant to predict that the court would be sympathetically inclined towards diversification of environmental standards, even if this would be at the expense of the internal market').

[288] See, in particular, paras. 19–24 of the court's judgment. See also paras. 4–6 of Advocate-General Tesauro's opinion.

[289] See pp. 128–31 above.   [290] See pp. 80–8 above.   [291] See pp. 137–9 above.

vast majority of directives regulating process standards, should be based on Article 130S and Article 130T and should permit member states to adopt more protective national measures. In this regard, Article 130T essentially consolidates traditional Community practice. By contrast, Community measures primarily designed to regulate the conditions of competition in certain industries should be adopted under Article 100A since they share a close connection with the establishment of the internal market. In theory, Article 100A(4) is therefore applicable. It is submitted, however, that, as far as it places restrictions on the capacity of member states to adopt stricter national standards, this provision has no role to play in the area of process standards. As we have seen, what matters in this area is the establishment of minimum requirements in order to prevent member states from adopting unduly lax standards in order to give a competitive advantage to their producers.[292] By contrast, the adoption of maximum requirements is not necessary to attain that objective. This is exactly why pre-SEA process-standards directives were only providing for minimum harmonization even when regulating the conditions of competition was their main objective.[293] In this context, there should be no restrictions on the member states' capacity to maintain or even adopt stricter standards than Community standards.[294]

In the area of waste management, the *Waste Directive* and the *Transfer of Waste Regulation* cases suggest a similar distinction between Community waste-management measures primarily designed to harmonize the conditions of competition and measures primarily designed to protect the environment. The same cases, however, indicate that, because their impact on the internal market process is generally incidental, Community waste-management measures should be primarily considered as environmental-protection measures.[295] Consequently, such measures should be

---

[292] See pp. 130–1 above.

[293] *Ibid.*

[294] One way of avoiding confusion would be for the Community legislature to indicate expressly in legislation harmonizing process standards on the basis of Article 100A that Community standards only represent minimum standards. For an example of an environmental directive based on Article 100A which expressly authorizes member states to adopt stricter standards, see Article 6.6 of Directive 94/62 of 20 December 1994 on packaging and packaging waste, OJ 1994, L 36/14 (allowing member states to maintain or adopt stricter standards than Community standards 'on condition that these [standards] avoid distortions of the internal market and do not hinder compliance by other Member States with the Directive').

[295] As has been seen, following its victory in the *Waste Directive* and the *Transfer of Waste Regulation* cases, the Council decided to modify the legal basis of the proposed

based on Article 130S and Article 130T should permit member states to adopt more stringent measures.

In conclusion, the introduction of Articles 130T and 100A(4) into the Treaty by the SEA has in practice brought about little change to the regulatory patterns traditionally used by the Community in the pre-SEA period. As we have seen, pre-SEA product-standards legislation usually imposed maximum requirements on the member states. Since the adoption of the SEA, such legislation is based on Article 100A and, contrary to the situation prior to the SEA, Article 100A(4) authorizes, under certain conditions, member states to apply stricter standards than Community standards. However, the escape clause contained in Article 100A(4) has been used very little by the member states. The dire predictions of a number of commentators, such as Pescatore,[296] about the threat this provision created on the establishment of the internal market have proved to be unfounded.[297] On the other hand, Article 100A(4) played an extremely useful psychological role in that its presence in the SEA helped to overcome the reluctance of some member states, such as Denmark, to give up their veto in the legislative process.[298]

Since the adoption of the SEA, Community legislation regulating industrial processes and the management of waste is generally based on Article 130S and Article 130T and permits member states to adopt stricter national measures. Although Article 130T was seen as a great victory by some environmentalists, this provision merely confirms pre-SEA Community practice where such matters were generally regulated pursuant to minimum harmonization schemes. It is only when Community legislation governing such matters has a direct impact on the internal-market process that it should be based on Article 100A and that stricter national measures should be limited to the restrictive conditions contained in Article 100A(4). It should be noted, however, that in practice no waste management[299] directive has been based on Article 100A and there has been only one process-standards directive, the now famous titanium

---

Directives on the landfill of waste and the incineration of hazardous waste and to apply Article 130S rather than Article 100A.

[296] See pp. 135–6 above.

[297] For an attempt at explanation of why these commentators have been wrong, see Wyatt and Dashwood, *European Community Law* at 367.

[298] *Ibid.* at 364.

[299] Directive 94/62 of 20 December 1994 on packaging and packaging waste OJ 1994, L 365/14 is based on Article 100A. This directive should, however, be seen as regulating product standards rather than the management of waste.

dioxide directive,[300] based on that provision. As in the pre-SEA period, minimum harmonization therefore remains the rule in the areas of industrial processes and waste management.

[300] See Directive 89/428 on procedures for harmonizing the programmes for the reduction and eventual elimination of pollution caused by the titanium-dioxide industry, annulled by Case C-300/89, *Commission* v. *Council* [1991] ECR I-2,867 and replaced by Directive 92/212, OJ 1992, L 409/11.

6   Harmonization in United States law

This chapter, which is devoted to United States law, follows the same subdivisions as those adopted in the context of European Community law. The first two sections deal with important institutional questions. The first section addresses the question of the existence of a constitutional basis for federal environmental action. The second section then discusses, in parallel to the Community principles of subsidiarity and proportionality, whether the federal government's exercise of regulatory authority over environmental matters is limited in any significant way out of respect for the states' residual sphere of competence over these matters. Having discussed the power of the federal government to act in the environmental field, as well as the potential limits imposed on the exercise of such power, the third section examines how in the areas of product standards, process standards and waste the federal government has attempted to balance trade and environmental objectives through or in the context of its legislative action. Finally, the fourth section deals with the question of pre-emption, i.e., whether, once the federal government has legislated, states may adopt stricter standards than federal standards or if federal standards are exhaustive.

The principle of attributed powers

Like the EC Treaty, the US Constitution is founded on a system of limited, attributed powers pursuant to which the states remain the ordinary bearer of sovereignty, while the federal government has only the powers entrusted to it by the Constitution.[1] Given the absence of a reference to environmental protection in the US Constitution, the power to regulate

---

[1] US Constitution, Tenth Amendment.

the environment should belong to the states, which benefit from residual powers. However, as will be seen below, the US Constitution provides Congress with several law-making powers that have been so broadly extended by a series of Supreme Court decisions 'that virtually any conceivable measure intended to protect the environment can readily be sustained under one or more of the grants of authority to Congress'.[2]

In practice, the most significant source of Congressional authority for environmental action is to be found in the federal power to regulate interstate commerce (the 'Commerce Clause').[3] First, it is generally admitted that physical transport of pollutants across states amounts to interstate commerce, thereby justifying federal legislation attempting to control transboundary pollution.[4] However, even when pollution takes place at a purely intrastate level, the power to regulate commerce can still provide a basis for federal intervention.[5] Congress might indeed rationally conclude that the adverse effects of intrastate pollution on human health, farm animals and fish, crops and natural resources have a depressive effect on production and consumption related to interstate markets.[6]

[2] See A. Rosenthal, 'The Federal Power to Protect the Environment: Available Devices to Compel or Induce Desired Conduct', *Southern California Law Review* 45 (1982), 397, 398. See also R. Findley and D. Farber, *Environmental Law in a Nutshell* (St Paul, Minn.: West Publishing Co., 1992) at 60; R. Stewart, 'Pyramids of Sacrifice? Problems of Federalism in Mandating State Implementation of National Environmental Policy', *Yale Law Journal* 86 (1977), 1,196, 1,222; S. Edelman, 'Federal Air and Water Control: The Application of the Commerce Power to Abate Interstate and Intrastate Pollution', *George Washington Law Review* 23 (1965), 1,067. Generally on the extension of federal legislative powers in the area of social regulation, see W. Eskeridge and J. Ferejohn, 'The Elastic Commerce Clause: A Political Theory of American Federalism', *Vanderbilt Law Review* 47 (1995), 1,355; T. Sandalow, 'The Expansion of Federal Legislative Authority' in Sandalow and Stein (eds.), *Courts and Free Markets* (Oxford University Press, 1982) at 49.

[3] US Constitution, Article 1, para. 8, clause 3. The breadth of the power to regulate interstate commerce as a source of regulatory authority for Congress is illustrated in *Hodel* v. *Virginia Surface Mining and Reclamation Association Inc.*, 452 US 264 (1981) ('The court must defer to a Congressional finding that a regulated activity affects interstate commerce, if there is any rational basis for such a finding.'). See also *Hodel* v. *Indiana*, 452 US 314 (1981) (rejecting the use of a quantitative test to determine whether the effect of the regulated activity on the interstate commerce is important).

[4] See *United States* v. *Bishop Processing Co.*, 287 F. Supp. 624 (Md 1968), affirmed, 423 F. 2d 469 (4th Cir.), cert. denied, 398 US 904 (1970). See also *Bethlehem Steel Corp.* v. *Train*, 544 F. 2d 657, 663 (3rd Cir. 1976); *Sierra Club* v. *EPA*, 544 F. 2d 1,114, 1,139 (1976), cert. denied, 430 US 959 (1977); *United States* v. *Ashland Oil & Transportation Co.*, 504 F. 2d 1,317, 1,325 (6th Cir. 1974); *South Terminal Corp.* v. *EPA*, 504 F. 2d 646, 677 (1st Circ. 1974).

[5] See Stewart, 'Pyramids of Sacrifice?' at 1,222.

[6] It should be noted that when the pollution damage is attributable to emissions from a large number of small sources, Congress can regulate these sources on a 'class basis'. See *Wickard* v. *Filburn*, 317 US 111, 127–9 (1942). See also *Perez* v. *United States*, 402 US 146 (1971).

Congress can also invoke the power to regulate interstate commerce to harmonize environmental product standards in order to facilitate interstate trade and to avoid market fragmentation. Facilitating interstate trade in cars and avoiding market fragmentation of the car market by inconsistent state regulations was, for example, the dominant rationale for the adoption of federal motor-vehicle-exhaust-emission limits.[7] The Commerce Clause can also be used by Congress to harmonize environmental process standards in order to eliminate the potential competitive advantage enjoyed by producers situated in states with lax standards over firms located in states enforcing stringent standards and thus ensure that interstate commerce takes place in fair conditions of competition.[8] As will be seen below, the equalization of the conditions of competition was the main rationale for the adoption of uniform air- and water-pollution standards by the federal government.[9]

In some cases, courts have even recognized that a tenuous link with interstate commerce was sufficient to validate Congressional action. For example, in *Palila* v. *Hawaii Department of Land and Natural Resources*, a district court reasoned that the existence of a 'national program to protect and improve the natural habitats of endangered species preserves the possibility of interstate commerce in these species and the interstate movements of persons, such as amateur students of nature or professional scientists who come to a state to observe and study these species'.[10] It then concluded that the power of Congress to regulate interstate commerce offered an appropriate basis for the adoption of the federal Endangered Species Act.[11]

---

[7] See discussion at pp. 156–62 below.

[8] A similar rationale was used in *United States* v. *Darby*, 312 US 100, 115 (1941) to justify imposition of federal minimum wage and maximum hours requirements. See also *NRLB* v. *Jones & Laughlin Steel Corp.*, 301 US 1 (1937).

[9] See pp. 162–7 below.

[10] 471 F. Supp. 985, 995 (D. Hawaii 1979), affirmed, 639 F. 2d 495 (9th Cir. 1981) (rejecting a claim from the State of Hawaii that the federal government had no authority to regulate purely indigenous species). See also *United States* v. *Byrd*, 609 F. 2d 1,204, 1,210 (7th Cir. 1979) (holding that Congress may extend its regulatory control of navigable waters under the Commerce Clause to wetlands which adjoin or are contiguous to intrastate lakes that are used by interstate travellers for water-related recreational purposes). Since the federal government has the authority to protect indigenous species, it is *a fortiori* competent to protect migratory species. See, e.g., *Leslie Salt Co.* v. *United States*, 896 F. 2d 354, 360 (9th Cir. 1990), cert. denied, 111 S. Ct 1,089 (1991) (holding that the Commerce Clause is broad enough to extend the Army Corps of Engineers' jurisdiction to local waters which may provide habitat to migratory birds and endangered species).

[11] Codified in 16 USC 1,531–44 (1985 and Supp. 1995). For another illustration of the

It is open to question whether the district court's reasoning in *Palila* would be compatible with the recent Supreme Court judgment in *United States* v. *Lopez*[12] where for the first time in sixty years the Supreme Court struck down a federal statute on the ground that it violated the Commerce Clause.[13] In *Lopez*, the Supreme Court found that the federal Gun-Free School Zone Act of 1990, a statute which made it a federal offence 'for any individual knowingly to possess a firearm at the place that the individual knows, or has reasonable cause to believe, is a school zone',[14] was unconstitutional because it intruded into a area of traditional state concern and did not regulate a commercial activity.[15] This case indicates that the Commerce Clause is not a plenary delegation of powers to Congress and that only federal legislation that has a clearly identifiable impact on interstate commerce will be validly justified under the Commerce Clause.[16] It seems therefore that, in the future, wide interpretations of the Commerce Clause such as the one of the district court in *Palila* are less likely to be accepted by the Supreme Court.

Three additional sources of authority for Congress to legislate in the environmental field should also be mentioned. One is to be found in Article IV(3), clause 2 of the Constitution which grants Congress the power to 'dispose of and make all needful Rules and Regulations respecting the Territory and other Property belonging to the United States' (the 'Property Clause'). Congress can find authority in this clause to enact laws necessary for the protection of the environmental resources located in the land

Commerce Clause as a source of federal power to protect wildlife, see the Marine Mammal Protection Act, 16 USC paras. 1,361–407, at 1,361(5)(B) (1985 and Supp. 1995) (Congress reasoning that disruption of populations of marine mammals that are not themselves the subject of commerce may disturb ecosystems, thereby affecting populations of animals that are the subject of commerce).

[12] 115 S. Ct 1,624 (1995). Generally on *Lopez*, see D. Regan, 'How to Think About the Federal Commerce Power and Incidentally Rewrite *United States* v. *Lopez*', *Michigan Law Review* 94 (1995), 554.

[13] The last Supreme Court decisions finding federal statutes incompatible with the Commerce Clause dated back from the early New Deal Era. See, e.g., *Carter* v. *Carter Coal Co.*, 298 US 238 (1936); *Railroad Retirement Board* v. *Alton RR Co.*, 295 US 330 (1935), *A. L. A. Schechter Poultry Corp.* v. *United States*, 295 US 496 (1935); *Hammer* v. *Dangenhart*, 247 US 251 (1918).

[14] 18 USC para. 922(q)(1)(A) (1988 and Supp. V 1993).

[15] For attempt to evaluate this impact, see J. Dwyer, 'The Commerce Clause and the Limits of Congressional Authority to Regulate the Environment', *Environmental Law Reporter* 25 (1995), 10,421.

[16] Specifically, the *Lopez* court identified 'three broad categories of activity that Congress may regulate under its commerce power': (i) 'the channels of interstate commerce'; (ii) 'the instrumentalities of interstate commerce, or persons or things in interstate commerce', and (iii) 'activities having a substantial relation to interstate commerce'.

owned by the federal government.[17] Another source of authority for federal environmental action is to be found in Article I(8), clause 1 of the Constitution which provides that Congress can 'lay and collect Taxes, Duties, Imports and Excises, to pay the Debts and provide for the Common Defence and general Welfare of the United States'.[18] These taxing and spending powers authorize Congress to adopt pollution taxes and provide for environmental subsidies. They also allow it to condition the receipt of federal grants by state or local authorities to the implementation of environmental-protection programmes.[19] A final source of Congressional authority to legislate in the environmental field can be found in the Treaty power.[20] In *Missouri v. Holland*, the Supreme Court held that, even if the absence of appropriate enumerated power otherwise prevented Congress from adopting legislation to protect the migration of wild birds, the Migratory Bird Treaty of 1876 between the United States and Canada provided a valid basis for Congressional action in the field in question.[21] By negotiating a Treaty and obtaining the requisite consent of the Senate, the President may therefore endow Congress with a source of legislative authority independent of the powers enumerated in the Constitution.[22]

---

[17] See *Kleppe v. New Mexico*, 426 US 529 (1976) (holding that the Wild Free-Roaming Horses and Burros Act was a constitutional exercise of Congress' power under the Property Clause as applied to wild horses and burros residing on federally owned lands within a state); *Alaska v. Andrus*, 429 F. Supp. 958 (D. Alaska 1977) (holding that under the Property Clause the federal government retains the right to control wildlife management on federal lands).

[18] For an early illustration of the use of the federal taxing powers to regulate the environment, see the Esch-Hughes Act of 1912, Pub. L. No. 62-112, 37 Stat. 81 (levying a prohibitive tax on matches containing white phosphorous and prohibiting the importation and exportation of the same).

[19] See E. Rehbinder and R. Stewart, 'Environmental Protection Policy' in Cappelletti, Seccombe and Weiler (eds.), *Integration through Law* (Walter de Gruyter, 1985), vol. I, at 43.

[20] US Constitution, Article 2, para. 2.

[21] 252 US 426 (1920). In that case, a prior attempt by Congress in 1913 to adopt legislation designed to protect migratory birds had been held unconstitutional by two lower courts which did not deem the commerce power to be applicable. See *United States v. Shauver*, 214 F. 154 (D. Arkansas 1914) and *United States v. McCullogh*, 221 F. 288 (D. Kansas 1915). For a more recent reference to the Treaty power as a source of authority for environmental legislation, see *Palila v. Hawaii Department of Land and Natural Resources*, 471 F. Supp. 985, 995 (D. Hawaii 1979).

[22] See L. Tribe, *American Constitutional Law* (Minolea, NY: Foundation Press, 2nd edn, 1988) at 227. See also D. Wirth, 'A Matchmaker's Challenge: Marrying International Law and American Environmental Law', *Virginia Journal of International* Law 32 (1992), 379, 387.

Need for and intensity of federal environmental action

As we have seen in the preceding section, the federal government enjoys very broad powers to take action in the environmental field. The objective of this section is to discuss, with reference to the Community principles of subsidiarity and proportionality, whether the federal government's exercise of legislative or regulatory authority over environmental matters is limited in any significant way out of respect for the states' residual sphere of autonomy over these matters.

First, it should be observed that US constitutional law does not contain any judicially enforceable mechanism designed to protect the residual powers of the states against excessive federal intervention in areas of shared competence, among which figures environmental protection.[23] The working assumption in the United States seems to be that influence through the political process, rather than judicially imposed limits, is to be the primary means by which the states should protect themselves against excessive Congressional exercise of delegated powers.[24] According to Herbert Weschler, who was perhaps the strongest supporter of this view, 'the national political process in the United States – and especially the role of states in the composition and selection of the central government – is intrinsically well adapted to retarding or restraining new intrusion by the center on the domain of the states'.[25] The corollary of

[23] See G. Bermann, 'Taking Subsidiarity Seriously: Federalism in the European Community and the United States', *Columbia Law Review* 94 (1994), 331, 403.

[24] See H. Weschler, 'The Political Safeguards of Federalism: The Role of States in the Composition and Selection of the National Government', *Columbia Law Review* 54 (1954), 543. See also B. La Pierre, 'Political Accountability in the National Political Process – The Alternative to Judicial Review of Federalism Issues', *Northwestern University Law Review* 80 (1985), 577; J. Choper, 'The Scope of National Power vis-à-vis the States: The Dispensability of Judicial Review', *Yale Law Journal* 86 (1977), 1,552. Recent years have, however, witnessed growing concern over the impact of broad federal intervention on the balance of federalism and some authors have strongly complained of the 'uncritical acceptance in many quarters of the notion that the federal government is the best level of government at which to establish regulatory programs'. See B. Gray, 'Regulation and Federalism', *Yale Journal on Regulation* 1 (1984), 93. As a result, numerous studies have attempted to develop principles designed to determine the circumstances in which federal action is to be preferred over state action. See, e.g., R. Pierce, 'Regulation, Deregulation, Federalism, and Administrative Law: Agency Power to Pre-empt State Regulation', *University of Pittsburgh Law Review* 46 (1985), 607; S. Foote, 'Beyond the Politics of Federalism: An Alternative Model', *Yale Journal on Regulation* 1 (1984), 217. None of these authors, however, suggests the use of an abstract allocation of power formula similar to the principle of subsidiarity contained in the Treaty on European Union.

[25] See Weschler, 'The Political Safeguards of Federalism' at 558. The view that the

this position is that courts should not get involved in deciding whether a particular federal action is within or beyond the authority of the central government. Such questions should be seen as non-justiciable and should therefore be left to the political branches.[26]

Given the prevalence of this position in US Constitutional law, it is no surprise that courts have traditionally shown much reluctance to limit the legislative freedom of Congress in order to protect the regulatory autonomy of the states.[27] Perhaps the most serious modern attempt by the Supreme Court to limit the exercise of Congressional legislative powers occurred in 1976 when, in *National League of Cities* v. *Usery*, the Supreme Court held unconstitutional an attempt by Congress to apply the Fair Labor Standards Act (FLSA) to most state and municipal employees.[28] The court based its decision on the ground that 'there are attributes of sovereignty attaching to every state government which may not be impaired by Congress, not because Congress may lack an affirmative grant of legislative authority to reach the matter, but because the Constitution prohibits it from exercising the authority in that manner'.[29] Although recognizing that the enactment of the FLSA falls within Congress' broad commerce power, the court therefore ruled that such a power does not extend so far as to displace the states' authority to structure employment relations in areas of 'traditional governmental functions'.[30] Cases immediately following *National League of Cities* indicated, however, that the area sheltered from Congressional governance by this ruling was a 'narrow one',[31] limited to matters which are inextricably related to the concept of state sovereignty.[32] On the other hand, Congress' power to

---

political process is sufficient to safeguard federalism has been criticized by several authors. See, e.g., L. Kramer, 'Understanding Federalism', *Vanderbilt Law Review* 47 (1994), 1,485, 1,503; D. Merrit, 'The Guarantee Clause and State Autonomy: Federalism for a Third Century', *Columbia Law Review* 88 (1988), 1, 15.

[26] See, in particular, Choper, 'The Scope of National Power' at 1,557.

[27] See Bermann, 'Taking Subsidiarity Seriously' at 416ff.

[28] 426 US 833 (1976). Generally on this case, see L. Tribe, 'Unraveling *National League of Cities*: The New Federalism and Affirmative Rights to Essential Governmental Services', *Harvard Law Review* 90 (1977), 1,065; F. Michelman, 'States' Rights and States' Roles: Permutations of "Sovereignty" in *National League of Cities* v. *Usery*, *Yale Law Journal* 86 (1977), 1,165; S. Barber, '*National League of Cities* v. *Usery*: New Meaning for the Tenth Amendment?' *Supreme Court Review* (1976), 161.

[29] 426 US 833 (1976) at 845.

[30] *Ibid.* at 852.

[31] See Bermann, 'Taking Subsidiarity Seriously' at 418.

[32] See, e.g., *Equal Employment Opportunity Commission* v. *Wyoming*, 460 US 226 (1983) (applicability of the Age Discrimination in Employment Act to state and local governments); *Federal Energy Regulatory Commission* v. *Mississippi*, 456 US 742 (1982)

allocate regulatory control over individuals and businesses (i.e., the traditional targets of environmental-protection laws and socio-economic regulations in general) was not limited to any meaningful degree.[33]

Any doubt regarding Congressional legislative freedom in the areas of shared competence was, however, removed when, nine years later, *National League of Cities* was overruled by *Garcia v. San Antonio Metropolitan Transit Authority*.[34] In that case, which concerned the application of the FSLA to public mass-transit authority, the court recognized that its attempt in *National League of Cities* to draw the borders of state regulatory immunity in terms of 'traditional governmental function' was 'not only unworkable but inconsistent with established principles of federalism'.[35] Refusing to limit in any way the sphere of application of the FLSA, the court declared that:

the Framers chose to rely on a federal system in which special restraints on federal power over the States inhered principally in the workings of the National Government itself rather than in discrete limitations on the objects of federal authority. States' sovereign interests, then, *are more properly protected by procedural safeguards* inherent in the structure of the federal system than by judicially created limitations on federal power.[36]

As this language clearly indicates, *Garcia* strongly reaffirms the traditional view expressed by Weschler that it is the political process rather than judicially enforceable limits that should structure the allocation of powers between the federal government and the states.[37]

(constitutionality of certain provisions of the 1978 Public Utility Regulatory Policies Act); *United Transportation Union* v. *Long Island RR Co.*, 455 US 678 (1982) (application of the Railway Labor Act to a dispute between a state-owned railway company and its unions); *Hodel* v. *Virginia Surface Mining Control and Reclamation Association*, 452 US 264 (1981) (constitutionality of certain provisions of the 1977 Surface Mining Control and Reclamation Act).

[33] See Pierce, 'Regulation, Deregulation' at 642.

[34] 469 US 528 (1985). For discussions on this case, see M. Field, '*Garcia* v. *San Antonio Metropolitan Authority*: The Demise of a Misguided Doctrine', *Harvard Law Review* 99 (1985), 84; D. Howard, 'Garcia and the Values of Federalism: On the Need for a Recurrence to Fundamental Principles', *Georgia Law Review* 19 (1985), 789; A. Rapaczynski, 'From Sovereignty to Process: The Jurisprudence of Federalism after *Garcia*', *Supreme Court Review* (1985), 341.

[35] 469 US 528 (1985) at 531.

[36] *Ibid.* at 552 (emphasis added).

[37] But see Haas, 'States Bounce Back', *National Law* 23 (1991), 10 August, who argues that the *Garcia* court was dominated by liberal judges who were deferential to Congress and that the current conservative majority in the Supreme Court is likely to review federal legislation more critically. An illustration of this stricter approach towards federal legislation can be found, for example, in *United States* v. *Lopez*, 115 S. Ct 1,624 (1995)

In the absence of any judicially enforceable mechanism designed to limit the exercise of Congressional powers in the areas of shared competences, it is interesting to examine to what extent the federal government has used its broad legislative powers to intervene in the environmental field. Until the end of the 1960s, the federal government's role in environmental policy-making was sharply limited.[38] Although Congress adopted some environmental legislation in the period following the Second World War, federal involvement was generally limited to encouraging states to adopt environmental-protection measures.[39] The federal programmes enacted in the 1950s and in the beginning of the 1960s were based on the assumption that environmental problems were the responsibility of states and local governments. By the end of the 1960s, however, Congress started to appreciate the national dimension of most environmental problems. It also realized the failure of non-regulatory approaches where the federal role was limited to assisting states with research grants while letting them be responsible for the adoption of pollution-control measures.[40] All that changed dramatically when President Nixon signed the National Environmental Policy Act (NEPA) on 1 January 1970, the first major federal statute in the environmental field.[41]

Following the enactment of NEPA, Congress launched a succession of far-reaching regulatory programmes to control pollution and protect threatened environmental resources.[42] Examples of such programmes include the Clean Air Act which provides the basic framework for modern

where the Supreme Court placed some limits on the use of the interstate Commerce Clause as a basis for federal action. See discussion at p. 146 above.

[38] See generally R. Percival *et al.*, *Environmental Regulation – Law, Science and Policy* (Boston: Little Brown, 1992) at 105.

[39] See, e.g., Federal Water Pollution Control Act of 1948, Pub. L. No. 80-245, 62 Stat. 1,155 (supporting research on water pollution and providing grants to support water-pollution-control programmes); Air Pollution Control Act, Ch. 360, Pub. L. No. 84-159, 69 Stat. 322 (setting up a federal programme to undertake research and to provide technical assistance to the states); Motor Vehicle Act of 1960, Pub. L. No. 86-493, 74 Stat. 162 (1960) (authorizing research into the effects of air pollution from cars); Clean Air Act of 1963, Pub. L. No. 88-206, 77 Stat. 392 (1963) (establishing federal research and technical-assistance programmes and giving the Department of Health, Education and Welfare authority to adopt advisory air-quality criteria).

[40] See M. Kraft and N. Vig, 'Environmental Policy from the Seventies to the Nineties: Continuity and Change' in Vig and Kraft (eds.), *Environmental Policy in the 1990s* (Washington, DC: CQ Press, 1990) at 11.

[41] 42 USC paras. 4,321–70(b) (1978 and Supp. 1994).

[42] For a good summary of these programmes, see D. Burtraw and P. Portney, 'Environmental Policy in the United States' in Helm (ed.), *Economic Policy towards the Environment* (Oxford: Blackwell, 1993).

air-pollution control.[43] Another comprehensive federal statute is the Clean Water Act whose ambitious objective is 'to restore and maintain the chemical, physical and biological integrity of the nation's waters'.[44] A series of federal statutes also attempt to regulate the release of hazardous substances in all environmental media. Among the most important of them are the Federal Insecticide, Fungicide and Rodenticide Act (FIFRA),[45] the Toxic Substance Control Act (TSCA),[46] the Resource Conservation and Recovery Act (RCRA)[47] and the Comprehensive Environmental Response, Compensation, and Liability Act (CERCLA or 'Superfund').[48] Also worthy of mention is the Endangered Species Act of 1973 which constructs a comprehensive regime for protecting wildlife.[49]

It should be noted that, when it decides to intervene in the environmental field, nothing prevents Congress from deferring to state autonomy. For example, Congress may choose to legislate only on certain aspects of a particular environmental problem and leave other aspects of this problem to state regulation. Congress may also set standards that are general in nature or that are expressly non-pre-emptive in order to allow states to provide for local needs and to ensure a higher level of environmental protection. More generally, Congress may attempt to establish a 'partnership' between state and federal authorities.[50] It is indeed often possible to divide specific regulatory powers and responsibilities between these authorities based on an evaluation of their respective comparative advantages in exercising these powers and fulfilling these obligations.

This form of 'creative' or 'cooperative' federalism can be observed, for example, in federal statutes designed to regulate industrial processes,[51]

---

[43] 42 USC paras. 7,401–671(q) (1983 and Supp. 1995).

[44] 33 USC paras. 1,251–387 (1995).

[45] 7 USC para. 136–136(y) (1995).

[46] 15 USC paras. 2,601–92 (1982 and Supp. 1995).

[47] 42 USC paras. 6,901–92(k) (1983 and Supp. 1995).

[48] 42 USC paras. 9,601–75 (1983 and Supp. 1995).

[49] 16 USC paras. 1,531–44 (1985 and Supp. 1995).

[50] See R. Mott, 'Federal–State Relations in US Environmental Law: Implications for the European Community', European University Institute Working Paper EPU No. 90/2; R. Manley, 'Federalism and Management of the Environment', *Urban Lawyer* 19 (1987), 661, 663. See also Conference Report, 'Federal versus State Environmental Protection Standards: Can a National Policy Be Implemented Locally?' *Environmental Law Reporter* 22 (1992), 10,009.

[51] By way of contrast, federal statutes regulating products involve federal standards, implemented and enforced at federal level. Such a degree of centralization can be explained by the need for uniformity in product regulation. For a survey of the different degrees of federal–state control in environmental legislation, see E. Strohbehn, 'The Bases for Federal/State Relationships in Environmental Law',

such as the Clean Air Act,[52] the Clean Water Act[53] and the Surface Mining Control and Reclamation Act.[54] In these statutes, Congress tends to favour standard-setting at a federal level.[55] This reflects the fact that the federal government is usually seen as best placed to carry out the scientific research on which most standards are based. By setting up standards common to all states Congress can also guarantee to all citizens fundamental levels of environmental quality and prevent states from competing for industry by adopting lax environmental standards. On the other hand, licensing of industrial installations is an activity traditionally left to the states.[56] State authorities have a better knowledge of local conditions and, thus, are usually seen as best situated to carry out the practical implementation of environmental regulation. Finally, enforcement is a function traditionally shared between federal and state authorities.[57] Congress will generally allow states to carry out the enforcement process in the first place.[58] This reflects Congress' desire to involve state authorities in its environmental action, but also the need to save federal administrative resources.[59] Nevertheless, given that state authorities may be subject to strong pressures from local industries,[60] the federal govern-

---

Environmental Law Reporter 12 (1982), 15,074. See also Rehbinder and Stewart, 'Environmental Protection Policy', at 46.

[52] 42 USC paras. 7,401–671(q) (1983 and Supp. 1995).

[53] 33 USC paras. 1,251–387 (1995).

[54] 30 USC (1995). For a discussion on the federal–state partnership established by the Surface Mining Control and Reclamation Act, see J. Edgcomb, 'Cooperative Federalism and Environmental Protection: The Surface Mining Control Act of 1977', *Tulane Law Review* 58 (1983), 299.

[55] See Mott, 'Federal–State Relations' at 4.

[56] *Ibid.*

[57] *Ibid.*

[58] Whether or not Congress has the authority to require, rather than encourage, state authorities to undertake enforcement of federal standards against private actors is a question that has raised much controversy. See R. Walston, 'State Control of Federal Pollution: Taking the Stick Away from the States', *Ecology Law Quarterly* 6 (1977), 429. This question seems, however, to have been settled in *New York* v. *United States*, 112 S. Ct 2,408 (1992), where the Supreme Court ruled that Congress does not have the right, as a general matter, to compel the states to enact and enforce federal regulatory programmes. See also *Board of Natural Resources* v. *Brown*, 992 F. 2d 937 (9th Cir. 1993).

[59] See Stewart, 'Pyramids of Sacrifice?' at 1,200–1.

[60] The same economic factors that may induce states to lower environmental standards to retain industry or increase investment opportunities also exert a compromising effect on state enforcement. See D. Hodas, 'Enforcement of Environmental Law in a Triangular Federal System: Can Three Not be a Crowd when Enforcement is Shared by the United States, the States and their Citizens?' *Maryland Law Review* 54 (1995), 1,552, 1,574.

ment will usually retain some residual enforcement authority to supplement state enforcement when it proves to be insufficient.[61]

Over the last fifteen years, enthusiasm for environmental causes has been tempered in governmental circles by concerns about the competitiveness of American industry.[62] But environmental advocates have retained a strong position in Congress and the political importance of environmental concerns has remained high. As a result, no significant reversals of federal legislation have occurred and, on some occasions, federal environmental legislation has even been strengthened.[63] Basic changes have, however, been undertaken at the executive level. In order to increase the competitiveness of American business and to reduce governmental presence across all sectors of industry, President Reagan attempted to reduce the stringency of federal environmental requirements.[64] In order to do so, he cut the federal budget for environmental action programmes,[65] appointed several administrators who were less favourable to environmental goals than their predecessors,[66] imposed an extensive system of cost–benefit analysis and review to control the environmental regulatory proposals made by federal agencies,[67] and

---

[61] See, e.g., section 309 of the Clean Water Act which provides that, after a state has adopted a qualified state implementation programme of federal standards, the EPA shall, on the basis of the information available to it, notify state authorities of discharge permit or effluent limit violations. If state authorities fail to institute an enforcement action within thirty days after notice, the EPA shall either issue a compliance order or begin civil action. 33 USC para. 1,319(a) (1995). For a similar provision, see also section 133 of the Clean Air Act, 42 USC para. 7,413 (1983 and Supp. 1995).

[62] This paragraph draws heavily on R. Stewart, 'Environmental Regulation and International Competitiveness', Yale Law Journal 102 (1993), 2,039 and Rehbinder and Stewart, 'Environmental Protection Policy' in Cappelletti et al. (eds.), Integration through Law (Walter de Gruyter, 1985), vol. I, at 110.

[63] See, e.g., the respective amendments of the Resource Conservation and Recovery Act (1984), Comprehensive Environmental Response, Compensation and Liability Act (1986), Safe Drinking Water Act (1987), Clean Water Act (1987), and Clean Air Act (1990).

[64] See Vig, 'Presidential Leadership: From the Reagan to the Bush Administration' in Kraft and Vig (eds.), Environmental Policy in the 1990s (Washington, DC: CQ Press, 1990) at 33.

[65] Ibid. at 38.

[66] See U. Wasserman, 'United States: Environmental Deregulation', Journal of World Trade Law 17 (1983), 365, 366.

[67] See President Reagan's Executive Order 12,291 (3 CFR 127 (1981)) which directed federal agencies, before proposing significant regulations, to perform detailed cost–benefit analyses and not to regulate unless benefits outweighed costs. To enforce these directives, agencies were required to submit all proposed and final rules to the Office of Management and Budget for review prior to publication. It is usually admitted that Executive 12,291 had an important deregulatory effect. See Olson, 'The Quiet Shift of

sought to delegate further implementation and enforcement responsibilities to the states.[68] The Reagan administration, however, gained little success in its attempts to convince Congress to reduce the level of stringency of the basic provisions of federal environmental laws. Although he attempted to pursue the regulatory relief effort undertaken by President Reagan,[69] President Bush adopted a more positive stance towards federal intervention in the environmental field and was instrumental in the amendments to the Clean Air Act in 1990.[70] Finally, it is important to note that, although the Clinton administration has shown no particular hostility to federal environmental laws, the New Republican majority in Congress present a serious threat to such laws.[71] Republican leaders in Congress are largely 'pro-business' and have announced their intention to scale back federal environmental laws in order to re-establish the competitiveness of American industry and create new jobs.[72] It remains to been seen how far they are ready to go.

The question posed at the beginning of this section can therefore be answered as follows. US constitutional law contains no judicially enforceable provisions designed to limit the exercise of Congressional powers in the areas of shared competence, including environmental protection. There are therefore no general safeguard clauses equivalent to the

Power: Office of Management and Budget Supervision of Environmental Protection Agency Rulemaking under Executive Order 12,291', *Virginia Journal of Natural Resources* 4 (1984), 1. Executive Order 12,291 was repealed in September 1993 by President Clinton and replaced by Executive Order 12,866 on Regulatory Planning and Review (58 Fed. Reg. 51,735 (1993)).

[68] See President Reagan's Executive Order 12,612 (3 CFR 252 (1987)) which, according to its preamble, is designed 'to restore the division of governmental responsibilities between the national government and the States . . . and to ensure that the principles of federalism established by the Framers guide the Executive departments and agencies in the formulation and implementation of policies'. According to Bermann, this Order, whose provisions echo in many ways the Community law principles of subsidiarity and proportionality, has not had a very important impact on agency rulemaking. See Bermann, 'Taking Subsidiarity Seriously' at 447. More generally, on President Reagan's policy of increased reliance on states for environmental policymaking, see Lester, 'A New Federalism? Environmental Policy in the States' in Kraft and Vig (eds.), *Environmental Policy in the 1990s* (Washington, DC: CQ Press, 1990) at 39.

[69] President Bush continued President Reagan's regulatory relief programme, notably through the creation of the Council on Competitiveness chaired by Vice-President Dan Quayle. On the impact of the Council on Competitiveness on environmental policymaking, see Percival *et al.*, *Environmental Regulation* at 700.

[70] *Ibid.* at 765 and 823.

[71] See 'Assault on Green Laws Endangers Newt Brigade', *Independent on Sunday*, 23 April 1995, at 15.

[72] See R. Percival, 'Environmental Federalism: Historical Roots and Contemporary Models', *Maryland Law Review* 54 (1995), 1,141, 1,167.

principles of subsidiarity and proportionality as these principles have been developed and interpreted in European Community law. The residual powers of the states are to be protected through the political process in Congress rather than judicial intervention. Congressional intervention in the environmental field has been extensive even though concerns have been expressed about the impact of federal environmental requirements on the competitiveness of US industry. A process of deregulation initiated by the Reagan and Bush administrations at the agency level has not affected federal environmental laws in themselves. A more serious threat is the new 'pro-business' Republican majority in Congress. When adopting legislation in the environmental field, Congress has generally attempted to involve state authorities in its action. State involvement has, however, usually been limited to the implementation and enforcement process.

Harmonization of state environmental standards

Having discussed the power of the federal government to regulate the environment and having noted the absence of judicial limits on the exercise of such a power out of respect for the states' regulatory autonomy, it is now important to examine how, in the areas of product standards, process standards and waste, the federal government has concretely attempted to deal with the various kinds of tension that may occur between the competing interests of trade and environmental protection.

Product standards

As has been seen, the adoption by states of inconsistent environmental product standards may impede interstate trade and create market fragmentation. The logical answer to this problem is the adoption of federal standards applicable in all states. In the area of product regulation, the adoption of federal standards may also be necessary to correct inadequate state regulatory policies and therefore ensure a higher level of environmental protection throughout the federation. The difficulty, however, is that economic and environmental objectives may not always be coincidental. This can be illustrated by the competing positions usually adopted by industrialists and environmentalists over the nature and content of federal regulation of environmental product standards.[73] The main pre-

---

[73] The reference here to the broad categories of industrialists and environmentalists is not accidental. Industrialists and environmentalists represent very important actors in the context of the elaboration of federal product regulation. This is particularly clear

occupation of industrialists, such as large automobile or chemical manufacturers, is that federal standards ensure a high level of uniformity by
pre-empting more stringent or inconsistent state regulations. As to the
federal standards themselves, industrialists will seek the level of regulation that has the minimum impact on their patterns of production and
distribution. Environmentalists, on the other hand, want to make sure
that federal standards ensure a high level of environmental protection
irrespective of the costs they impose on manufacturers. They may not
necessarily be opposed to pre-emption provisions provided that federal
standards provide for a high level of protection. The difficulty for the
federal legislature is to reconcile these competing positions.

Although the tension between economic and environmental objectives
is present in all areas of product regulation, again it can be illustrated by
a brief survey of federal legislation in the area of motor-vehicle-exhaust
emissions.[74] As has been noted in the European Community context, the
regulation of motor-vehicle-exhaust emissions is an area where the
economic and environmental interests at stake are enormous.[75] It is also
an area where the federal government's intervention has been extremely
controversial. The roots of the first federal statute regulating motor-
vehicle-exhaust emissions, the Motor Vehicle Air Pollution Control Act
of 1965, were to be found in the development in the beginning of the
1960s of inconsistent state regulations governing motor-vehicle-exhaust

in the context of federal regulation of motor-vehicle-exhaust emissions. Since a large
share of the car production is concentrated in the state of Michigan, automobile
manufacturers cannot rely on the political influence of that state, which is only one of
the fifty American states, to veto or delay federal regulation. Manufacturers therefore
attempt to influence directly the regulatory process in Washington, DC and
environmentalists will attempt to counterbalance the industry's influence. In this
regard, the situation is different in the European Community where car production in
particular, and industrial production in general, is less geographically concentrated.
Automobile manufacturers can therefore usually rely on a number of member states
such as France, Germany, Italy or the United Kingdom to protect their interests against
excessively stringent Community regulation. This is not to say that lobbyists play no
role in Brussels. But due to the greater influence of member states on the political
process, their impact on regulation will usually be less important than in the United
States.

[74] Generally on the regulation of motor-vehicle-exhaust emissions, see R. Crandall et al.,
Regulating the Automobile (Washington, DC: Brookings Institution, 1986); F. Grad et al.,
The Automobile and the Regulation of its Impact on the Environment (Springfield, Va.:
National Technical Information Service, 1975).

[75] See Judge Leventhal's observation in *International Harvester* v. *Ruckleshaus*, 478 F. 2d 615
(DC Cir. 1973) ('The automobile is an essential pillar of the American Economy . . .
[that] has had a devastating impact on the environment.').

emissions.[76] In order to deal with its severe air-pollution problems, California had adopted a regulatory programme requiring the installation of emission controls on all new cars in the state.[77] Moreover, a vehicle emissions bill was pending in Pennsylvania and New York was considering an emissions bill even stricter than the one adopted in California.[78] State air-pollution legislation was therefore posing a serious threat to automobile manufacturers. What these manufacturers particularly feared was a kind of 'political domino' effect, whereby states would adopt, one after another, increasingly stringent emission standards without regard to the costs and the technical difficulties involved.[79] The adoption of such standards would in turn fragment the American car market and increase car prices, with resulting losses in sale opportunities. Although automobile manufacturers would have preferred to remain free of any government regulation of vehicle emissions, to the extent they should be regulated, federal regulation was to be preferred, particularly if those federal standards took due account of costs and technical difficulties and pre-empted further state regulations.[80]

It was therefore with the automobile industry's backing that Congress enacted the 1965 Motor Vehicle Air Pollution Control Act, which authorized the Secretary of the Department of Health, Education and Welfare to establish motor-vehicle-exhaust-emission standards after considering their costs and technological feasibility.[81] The first federal controls on motor-vehicle-exhaust emissions of carbon monoxide and hydrocarbons were enacted in 1965. Two years later, Congress passed the 1967 Air Quality Act which retained the regulatory provisions of the 1965 Act while

[76] See generally D. Elliott et al., 'Toward a Theory of Statutory Evolution: The Federalization of Environmental Law', Journal of Law, Economics and Organization 1 (1985), 313, 330.

[77] See generally J. Krier and E. Ursin, Pollution and Policy: A Case Essay on California and Federal Experience with Motor Vehicle Air Pollution 1940–1975 (Berkeley: University of California Press, 1977), 41–177. See also H. Kennedy and M. Weekes, 'Control of Automobile Emissions – California Experience and the Federal Legislation', Law and Contemporary Problems 33 (1968), 297.

[78] See Elliott et al., 'Toward a Theory' at 330.

[79] Ibid. at 331.

[80] Ibid.

[81] The entire Act was enacted as para. 101(8) of the Clean Air Act Amendments of 1965, Pub. L. No. 89-272, 79 Stat. 992. Although industry wanted to see state standards pre-empted by federal legislation, the 1965 Act did not contain any pre-emption provision. Legislative history appeared, however, to indicate that more stringent state standards were to be pre-empted by federal legislation. See D. Currie, 'Motor Vehicle Air Pollution: State Authority and Federal Pre-emption', Michigan Law Review 68 (1970), 1,083, 1,087–9.

adding a specific provision pre-empting state regulation of emission standards except for California, which was authorized to retain its more stringent standards.[82] The Senate report explained this provision as a compromise between California's interest in setting 'more stringent standards to meet peculiar conditions' and the automobile industry's desire for 'a single national standard in order to eliminate undue economic strain on the industry'.[83] According to the report, this compromise was beneficial because it would allow California to address its severe pollution problems, but also to serve as a laboratory for new regulations without subjecting industry to more than two regulations.[84]

In 1970, however, Congress stunned automobile manufacturers by ordering them to curtail new vehicle emissions of carbon monoxide and hydrocarbon by 90 per cent within five years and nitrogen oxide within six years.[85] The mandated reductions would be implemented through a programme of testing and certification of new model prototypes by the newly created Environmental Protection Agency (EPA). The 1970 Clean Air Act, which reflected the increased popular concerns for environmental issues, represented a major shift in policy: instead of stressing improvements in available technology, the new standards forced the development of new technologies capable of meeting the strict requirements contained in its provisions. To enforce this strategy of 'technology forcing', the Act included sanctions that prohibited all vehicles not certified as meeting the standards and provided a \$10,000 penalty for the sale of each non-complying vehicle. Even though the automobile industry employed 800,000 people and generated 10 per cent of all tax revenues, it was to cease manufacture of vehicles which could not meet the prescribed standards.[86] The original function of federal intervention in the area of

---

[82] Clean Air Act Amendments of 1967, Pub. L. No. 90-184, para. 2, 81 Stat. 501 (amending Clean Air Act para. 208). It should be noted that, in fact, the 1967 Air Quality Act had also been prompted by the concerns of another major industry over the development of stringent state and local air-pollution regulations. In 1967, the threat of strict state legislation which would eliminate markets for high-sulphur coals in most metropolitan areas induced coal producers to push for federal legislation that would pre-empt state legislation. They therefore strongly supported and influenced the Congressional bill that became the 1967 Air Quality Act. See Elliott *et al.*, 'Toward a Theory' at 332.

[83] S. Rep. No. 403, 90th Congress, 1st Sess. 81 (1967).   [84] *Ibid.* at 33.

[85] Clean Air Act Amendments of 1970, Pub. L. No. 91-604, para. 6(a), 84 Stat. 1,690 (amending Clean Air Act, para. 202(b)(1)). Generally on these provisions, see Ditlow, 'Federal Regulation of Motor Vehicle Emissions under the Clean Air Act Amendments of 1970', *Ecology Law Quarterly* 4 (1975), 495; J. O'Connor, 'The Automobile Controversy – Federal Control of Vehicle Emissions', *Ecology Law Quarterly* 4 (1975), 661.

[86] 116 Cong. Rec. 33,080-1 (1970) (remarks of Senator Griffin).

motor-vehicle-exhaust emissions was to facilitate interstate trade in cars and to avoid a market fragmentation of the car market, but the centre of gravity of that intervention had suddenly shifted onto the side of environmental protection.

In the years following the adoption of the 1970 Clean Air Act, the automobile industry successfully delayed through numerous lawsuits and administrative challenges the implementation of the strict standards contained in the Amendments.[87] Congress amended the Clean Air Act in 1977 to grant the automobile industry further extensions.[88] The 1977 Amendments, however, relaxed the pre-emption provision contained in the Act in order to allow states with serious air-quality problems to adopt the California standards.[89] The result is a two-tier system of pollution controls, with one level of control on cars sold in most states and stricter controls in the states applying the stricter California standards.[90] According to Stewart, this two-tier system of controls has apparently not impaired the achievement of economies of scale in production and distribution.[91] On the other hand, it has permitted states with serious air-quality problems to protect better their atmosphere without imposing unnecessary costs on states which do not suffer from such problems.[92] The 1990 Amendments of the Clean Air Act, which tighten emission controls for certain pollutants,[93] confirmed this strategy of a two-tier system of controls.[94]

---

[87] See, e.g., Anderson et al., Environmental Protection – Law and Policy (Boston: Little Brown Co., 1990) at 205.

[88] As a result of these extensions, the original hydrocarbon and carbon dioxide standards did not take effect until 1980 and 1981 respectively. The final nitrogen oxide standard was substantially relaxed and the deadline extended to 1981. For a discussion on the 1977 Amendments, see D. Currie, 'The Mobile-Source Provisions of the Clean Air Act', University of Chicago Law Review 46 (1979), 811, 830.

[89] Clean Air Act Amendments of 1977, Pub. L. No. 91-95, para. 129(b), 91 Stat. 750 (amending Clean Air Act, para. 177).

[90] A number of northeastern states have indeed taken advantage of this provision. See Percival et al., Environmental Regulation at 844.

[91] Stewart, 'Environmental Law in the United States and the European Community: Spillovers, Cooperation, Rivalry, Institutions', University of Chicago Legal Forum (1992), 39, 60. On the contrary, it seems that such an approach could only mean economies of scale (and thus lower costs) for the alternative type of vehicle (i.e., the type of vehicle complying with the more stringent California standards). See Krier and Ursin, Pollution and Policy at 342.

[92] It should be noted that, contrary to the policy of optional harmonization adopted by the European Community, Congress has never authorized the states to adopt motor-vehicle-emissions standards that are less stringent than federal standards.

[93] 42 USC 7,521(b)(1)(A) (1983 and Supp. 1995).

[94] Clean Air Act Amendments of 1990, section 177, 42 USC para. 7,507 (1983 and Supp. 1995).

For the same reasons it has regulated motor-vehicle-exhaust emissions (avoiding market fragmentation and protecting the environment), the federal government has also adopted federal statutes to regulate the environmental characteristics of other products, such as motor-vehicle fuel additives,[95] noise-generating equipment,[96] pesticides[97] and toxic chemicals.[98] These federal statutes usually follow regulatory patterns that had already been used in the case of the federal regulation of motor-vehicle-exhaust emissions: standards are set at federal level and the EPA is charged with implementing and enforcing these standards. State intervention in the regulatory process is therefore virtually non-existent. As pointed out by Rehbinder and Stewart, such a high degree of centralization can be explained by the need for uniformity in product regulation.[99] For the same reason, federal statutes regulating products often, but not invariably, pre-empt more stringent or inconsistent state regulations.[100]

Finally, it should be noted that contrary to the approach which is currently being pursued by the European Community in several areas of regulation, the federal government has not had recourse to private standardization bodies to regulate the technical characteristics of products. While Congress generally adopts the broad policy options, the setting of technical standards is left to the administrative agencies, the most important of which in the environmental field being the EPA.[101] Although it is sometimes argued that these agencies are dominated or 'captured' by industry,[102] they nevertheless present some advantages. First, contrary to private standardization bodies, these agencies are

---

[95] 42 USC para. 7,545 (1983 and Supp. 1995).
[96] See the Noise Control Act, 42 USC paras. 4,901–18 (1984 and Supp. 1995).
[97] See the Federal Insecticide, Fungicide and Rodenticide Act, 7 USC para. 1,364 (1995).
[98] See the Toxic Substances Control Act, 15 USC paras. 2,601–71 (1982 and Supp. 1995).
[99] See Rehbinder and Stewart, 'Environmental Protection Policy' at 46.
[100] See pp. 175–80 below.
[101] For a brief account of the regulatory powers of the EPA, see S. Breyer and R. Stewart, *Administrative Law and Regulatory Policy* (Boston: Little Brown Co., 2nd edn, 1985) at 6. For a list of the other agencies bearing responsibilities in the environmental field, see Rehbinder and Stewart, 'Environmental Protection Policy' at 185.
[102] On the capture theory, see G. Stigler, 'The Theory of Economic Regulation', *Bell Journal of Economics and Management Science* 2 (1971), 3 and S. Peltzman, 'Toward a More General Theory of Regulation', *Journal of Law and Economics* 19 (1976), 211. To resist this 'agency capture' model of the regulatory process, 'action-forcing' provisions such as citizen-suit provisions and provisions for judicial review of agency actions were incorporated by Congress in most modern environmental statutes. See generally R. Stewart, 'The Reformation of Administrative Law', *Harvard Law Review* 88 (1975), 1,667.

publicly accountable.[103] Moreover, they carry on their regulatory activities pursuant to well-defined procedures where all interested parties (including environmental groups and industry) have a right to be heard.[104] On the other hand, it must be acknowledged that the excessive formalism of these procedures, compliance with which is enforceable in the courts, has generated a form of 'regulatory legalism' as a result of which the regulatory process is often paralysed by extensive litigation initiated by interest groups.[105]

Process standards

In the United States, federal intervention in the area of environmental process standards has traditionally been justified mainly under two rationales. First, federal intervention has often been seen as necessary to ensure that fundamental levels of environmental protection are respected throughout the nation and that transboundary pollution does not occur.[106] Second, the adoption of federal standards has also been seen as necessary to remove the distortions of competition and incentives for industrial relocation that may arise when states adopt inconsistent environmental process standards.[107] From a political standpoint, this latter rationale for federal intervention has been traditionally supported by the highly industrialized, but also heavily polluted, northeastern states for which unilateral adoption of strict pollution controls could not be achieved without significant competitiveness costs. At the same time, these states feared that the less developed southern states would engage in strategies of competitive deregulation in order to give a boost to their local economies and to attract new investment opportunities.[108] In this context, the rational strategy for the northeastern states, usually sup-

---

[103] See G. Majone, 'Controlling Regulatory Bureaucracies: Lessons from the American Experience', European University Institute Working Paper SPS No. 93/3.

[104] These procedures are encapsulated in the Administrative Procedure Act, 5 USC paras. 551–703 (1978 and Supp. 1995).

[105] For a discussion on this problem, see R. Stewart, 'Antidotes for the "American Disease"', Ecology Law Quarterly 20 (1993), 85.

[106] See, e.g., section 126 of the Clean Air Act, 42 USC para. 7,426 (1983 and Supp. 1995) (placing limits on the amount of pollution from upwind states that is permitted to affect air quality in downwind states).

[107] See R. Revesz, 'Rehabilitating Interstate Competition: Rethinking the "Race-To-The-Bottom" Rationale for Federal Environmental Regulation', New York University Law Review 67 (1992), 1,210.

[108] See Z. Plater et al., Environmental Law and Policy: Nature, Law, and Policy (St Paul, Minn.: West Publishing Co., 1992) at 776 ('Calls for more stringent pollution control in the nation's heavily industrialized areas were met with threats of industrial relocation by the polluters who, simultaneously, were being wooed to relocate by less developed

ported by environmentalists and the labour unions, has been to use their superior political power in Congress to ensure the adoption of federal legislation harmonizing environmental process standards.[109]

Against this background, it should be no surprise that the adoption of uniform process standards is the central strategy of the Clean Water Act and the Clean Air Act, the principal federal environmental statutes controlling water and air pollution respectively.[110] The focus of the Clean Water Act is a system of geographically uniform technologically based requirements established by the EPA for major pollution sources, including steel and chemical plants, food-processing plants, paper mills, leather tanneries, etc.[111] Pursuant to such a system, all pollution sources belonging to the same category of industry must respect the same effluent or emission limits regardless of their location or the quality of the water into which the discharge is made.[112] The economic rationale for the adoption of uniform effluent limits is expressed in *Natural Resources Defense Council Inc.* v. *Costle*, where the court of Appeals of the District of Columbia circuit noted that:

the primary purpose of the effluent limitations . . . was to provide uniformity . . . and prevent the 'Tragedy of the Commons' that might result if jurisdictions can compete for industry and development by providing more liberal limitations than their neighboring states.[113]

areas willing to trade environmental amenity values for increased benefits of economic development.').

[109] On this strategy and its implications, see P. Pashigian, 'Environmental Regulation: Whose Self-Interests Are Being Protected?' *Economic Inquiry* 23 (1985), 551; Pashigian, *The Political Economy of the Clean Air Act: Regional Self-Interest in Environmental Legislation* (Center for the Study of American Business, 1982).

[110] A similar strategy has also been pursued in other areas of environmental regulation; usually to prevent regulatory competition between states. See, e.g., *Hodel* v. *Virginia Surface Mining and Reclamation Association*, 452 US 264, 282 (1981) ('surface mining and reclamation standards are essential in order to insure that competition in interstate commerce among sellers of coal produced in different states will not be used to undermine the ability of the several States to improve and maintain adequate standards on coal mining operations within their borders').

[111] See Federal Water Pollution Control Act, section 301, 33 USC para. 1,311 (1995). For a strong critique of such a system, see W. Pedersen, 'Turning the Tide on Water Quality', *Ecology Law Quarterly* 15 (1988), 69 (arguing that a system of effluent standards is highly inefficient).

[112] See, e.g., *Weyerhauser Co.* v. *Costle*, 590 F. 2d 1,011, 1,041–2 (DC Cir. 1978) (holding that the condition of the receiving waters should not be taken in establishing emission limits). See also *Association of Pacific Fisheries* v. *EPA*, 615 F. 2d 794, 805 (9th Circ. 1980); *Appalachian Power Co.* v. *Train*, 545 F. 2d 1,351, 1,378 (4th Cir. 1976).

[113] 568 F. 2d 1,369, 1,378 (1977). See also *Natural Resources Defence Council Inc.* v. *Train*, 510 F. 2d 692, 711–12 (DC Cir. 1975).

The central objective of this system of effluent limitations is clear: it is to prevent environmentally damaging strategies of competitive deregulation by which states relax pollution-control requirements in order to attract investment opportunities (the 'race to the bottom').[114] Because it fully equalizes the conditions of competition, such a system also prevents states from exploiting their natural locational advantages independently of any strategy of environmental deregulation.

The basic strategy of the Clean Air Act is to rely on a system of national ambient air-quality standards for widespread pollutants to be established by the EPA.[115] Following adoption of the air-quality standards by the EPA, each state must submit a state implementation plan that contains the emission limitations and other implementation measures necessary to attain and maintain the federal standards.[116] The system of national air-quality standards adopted by the Clean Air Act provides for less uniformity than the national effluent limits system adopted by the Clean Water Act since, contrary to the latter, the former does not ensure that all pollution sources belonging to the same category of industry must respect the same emission limitations in practice. Because of their natural locational advantages, the states whose atmosphere is relatively un-polluted are able to attain the national air quality standards by imposing more generous emission limitations than the states whose atmosphere is more polluted. Although national air quality standards guarantee the respect of certain levels of environmental quality throughout the United States, they may not prevent certain categories of industry from flying from states imposing strict emission limits on their installations in order to attain the national air quality standards to states that are able to meet such standards by imposing more generous emission limitations.

However, the Clean Air Act relies on two mechanisms in order to lessen the comparative attractiveness of locating polluting sources in a clean air area. First, Congress required the EPA to adopt uniform technology-based pollution controls on all *new* major industrial sources wherever they are located through the New Source Preference Standards (NSPS) requirements.[117] Like the effluent limitations contained in the Clean Water Act, the NSPS apply irrespective of the quality of the air of the particular area

---

[114] For a discussion on the concept of 'race to the bottom', see Revesz, 'Rehabilitating Interstate Competition'.

[115] Clean Air Act, sections 108–9, 42 USC paras. 7,408–9 (1983 and Supp. 1995).

[116] Ibid., section 110, 42 USC para. 7,410 (1983 and Supp. 1995).

[117] Ibid., section 111, 42 USC para. 7,411 (1983 and Supp. 1995). See also *Portland Cement Association* v. *Rucklehaus*, 486 F. 2d 375, 391 (DC Cir. 1973).

in which the source is operated.[118] They are set for all new sources at the emission rate that can be achieved by using the 'Best Adequately Demonstrated Technology' (BADT). By requiring the application of a uniform technology nationwide, the NSPS reduce the incentive for industry to seek out less polluted areas for the location of new polluting sources.[119]

Second, despite the strong opposition of southern states, the 1977 Amendments to the Clean Air Act established three classes of clean-air regions and specified graduated amounts of permitted 'increments' that limit the cumulative increase in air pollution levels in the different classes (the 'Prevention of Significant Deterioration' programme, or PSD).[120] Although a clean-air area could, for example, increase pollution emissions by 1,000 per cent and still meet the national air-quality standards, the PSD increments will, however, limit the maximum increase in emissions for such an area to a much smaller percentage. By capping growth in emissions in clean-air areas to a level well short of the level that would be allowed by the national air-quality standards, the PSD programme therefore decreases the incentive for industry to locate in clean-air rather than in dirty-air areas.[121]

---

[118] It should be noted that the NSPS set by the EPA were criticized because, in certain circumstances, their main effect (and arguably their purpose) was not to equalize the conditions of competition between clean- and dirty-air areas but to favour the economic interests of certain regions. For example, in 1979, the EPA required for coal-fired plants the installation of expensive desulphurization equipment (so-called 'scrubbers'), a measure which had the effect of encouraging the eastern and midwest coal-fired plants to continue to burn the high-sulphur coal available in their regions rather than to burn the less environmentally damaging low-sulphur coal produced in the west. This measure protected the high sulphur deposits and mining jobs in the eastern and midwest regions at the expense of the western coal-producing regions (west of the Mississippi and the Rocky Mountains). See generally B. Ackerman and W. Hassler, *Clean Coal/Dirty Air or How the Clean Air Act Became a Multi-Billion Dollar Bail for High-Sulfur Coal Producers and What Should be Done About It* (New Haven: Yale University Press, 1981) and their article 'Beyond the New Deal: Coal and the Clean Air Act', *Yale Law Journal* 89 (1980), 1,466.

[119] The legislative history of section 111 clearly indicates that a central objective of the NSPS programme was to ensure that clean air regions would not be able to use their natural locational advantages in order to compete for industry. See HR 1,146, 91st US Cong., 2nd Sess. (1970) ('The promulgation of Federal emission standards for new sources . . . will preclude efforts on the part of the States to compete with each other in trying to attract new plants and industries.').

[120] Clean Air Act, section 165(a), 42 USC para. 7,475(a) (1983 and Supp. 1995). See generally C. Oren, 'Prevention of Significant Deterioration: Control-Compelling versus Site-Shifting', *Iowa Law Review* 74 (1988), 1; S. Melnick, *Regulation and the Courts – The Case of the Clean Air Act* (Washington, DC: Brookings Institution, 1983) at 71.

[121] The legislative history of the 1977 Amendments indicates that one of the central objectives of the PSD programme was to prevent industry located in dirty-air areas

The above analysis illustrates that Congress has usually attempted to provide for uniform solutions when it has regulated environmental process standards. Although uniform standards may be partly justified for reasons of administrative efficiency, we have seen that the main rationale for such standards was to prevent states from adopting strategies of competitive deregulation, as well as to prevent southern states from exploiting their natural locational advantages in order to attract investment opportunities. In this regard, it is important to emphasize here that, because it operates on the basis of majority voting procedures,[122] the federal legislative system tends to favour, or at least to facilitate, the adoption of uniform over non-uniform solutions.[123] Contrary to the system that operated during the first thirty years of the history of the European Community, states or, more exactly, their elected representatives (House representatives and senators) cannot threaten to veto legislative proposals that are unfavourable to their interests in order to extract concessions.[124]

Finally, it should be noted that there is increasing concern among environmental experts over the effectiveness of uniform process standards as a pollution-control strategy. First, uniform standards are thought to be inefficient.[125] Because the same requirements are applied in all

from moving into clean-air areas. It was indeed argued that it was necessary to prevent 'flight of industry – and jobs – from areas where pollution levels were approaching or exceed the minimum Federal standards' and to 'shield the developed and polluted states from the natural advantages which otherwise may be enjoyed by less developed and clean states'. See HR 294, at 133 and 504, 95th Cong. 1st Sess. (1977).

[122] For a good description of the federal legislative process, see J. Frank, 'Le Congrès' in Orban (ed.), Le Système Politique des Etats-Unis (Montréal: Presses Universitaires de Montréal, 1987) at 153.

[123] This is not to say, of course, that the federal legislative process is fluid. Because they have to go through a number of committees and have to be adopted in both House and Senate, most legislative proposals will not be adopted or will be adopted only after considerable amendments. However, as will be seen below in the text, a central characteristic of the process is that no state or small group of states can veto a legislative proposal because it is contrary to its interests.

[124] See Pashigian, 'Environmental Regulation' at 559 (showing how representatives from southern states, who were strongly opposed to the PSD programme, were outvoted by representatives of the northern and midwest states who were generally in favour of this programme).

[125] See, e.g., C. Sunstein, After the Rights Revolution – Reconceiving the Regulatory State (Cambridge, Mass.: Harvard University Press, 1990) at 90 ('Congressional insensitivity to regional and industrial variations is reflected in the many environmental statutes that impose uniform standards. Because the costs and benefits of anti-pollution strategies will vary in the different parts of the nation uniform strategies are likely to cause serious inefficiencies.').

states, uniform standards can lead to overregulation in some states and underregulation in others.[126] Moreover, technology-based, uniform standards may impose unnecessary costs on industry and may tend to stifle innovation.[127] As an answer to these problems, leading commentators, such as Ackerman and Stewart, have suggested that federal environmental laws be modified in order to incorporate economic incentives (also known as market-based systems).[128] According to these commentators, market-based systems would generally decrease the costs of pollution control and would give incentives to develop cleaner and less expensive technologies.[129] Because they are more flexible, they could also lessen regional conflicts and allow for more diversity in pollution controls.[130] Despite the advantages they seem to present, market-based schemes have so far remained a relatively marginal pollution-control strategy.[131]

---

[126] As will be seen below, the problem created by underregulation can be solved by allowing states to adopt stricter standards than federal standards. Since it can only be solved by allowing some states to apply laxer standards than federal standards (a solution generally unacceptable for competitiveness reasons), the problem created by overregulation is more complicated and has so far received no solution. On these problems, see generally J. Krier, 'The Irrational National Air Quality Standards: Macro- and Micro-Mistakes', *UCLA Law Review* 22 (1974), 323.

[127] Technology-based uniform standards may be unnecessarily costly because they impose the same requirements on producers independently of the nature and quality of the receiving environment. They may also stifle innovation because they give no incentive to producers to develop new technologies in order to reduce their level of emissions.

[128] See R. Stewart, 'Controlling Environmental Risks through Economic Incentives', *Columbia Journal of Environmental Law* 17 (1988), 1; B. Ackerman and R. Stewart, 'Reforming Environmental Law', *Stanford Law Review* 37 (1985), 1,333. But see H. Latin, 'Ideal versus Real Regulatory Efficiency: Implementation of Uniform Standards and "Fine-Tuning" Regulatory Reforms', *Stanford Law Review* 37 (1985), 1,267 (arguing strongly in favour of the current system of technology-based uniform controls). For a general discussion on this debate, see J. Mintz, 'Economic Reform of Environmental Protection: A Brief Comment on a Recent Debate', *Harvard Environmental Law Review* 15 (1991), 149.

[129] See Ackerman and Stewart, 'Reforming Environmental Law' at 1,341ff.

[130] For example, according to Stewart, the legislative logjam on acid rain, which was caused by regional conflicts over the economic effects of the various legislative proposals that were made to deal with this problem, was broken by the adoption of a Bush administration proposal to use a system of marketable pollution permits to reduce sulphur emissions. Clean Air, section 404, 42 USC para. 7,561(c) (1983 and Supp. 1995). See R. Stewart, 'International Trade and the Environment: Lessons from the Federal Experience', *Washington and Lee Law Review* 49 (1992), 1,329.

[131] For an excellent account of the various federal initiatives involving the use of market-based schemes see, however, R. Hahn and R. Stavins, 'Incentive-Based Environmental Regulation: A New Era from an Old Idea?' *Ecology Law Quarterly* 18 (1991), 1.

Waste

As we have seen in the context of European Community law, one central reason for interstate shipments of waste is economic: in order to reduce production costs, manufacturers have a strong incentive to dispose of their waste where it costs the least, usually in states where the legal requirements regarding waste disposal are the least stringent.[132] As it tends to reduce costs disparities in waste disposal between states, harmonization of waste-disposal standards on a nationwide basis appears therefore a useful means to decrease incentives for producers to transfer their waste out-of-state. Against this background, I will first examine to what extent waste-disposal standards have been harmonized in US federal law and evaluate the impact such a harmonization has had on interstate movements of waste. Next, I will discuss to what extent Congress has permitted or plans to permit states to restrict interstate movements of waste.

Harmonization of waste-disposal standards

In the United States, the principal federal statute harmonizing waste-disposal standards is the Resource Conservation and Recovery Act (RCRA).[133] Enacted in 1976, the RCRA establishes a two-tier pollution-control scheme: Subtitle C provides a comprehensive regulatory programme to ensure proper treatment and disposal of 'hazardous' waste,[134] while Subtitle D provides a largely non-regulatory programme designed to

---

[132] See also K. Florini, 'Issues of Federalism in Hazardous Waste Control: Cooperation or Confusion?' *Harvard Environmental Law Review* 6, 307, 311 (explaining that when, in the beginning of the 1980s, New Jersey and Rhode Island tightened their waste-disposal standards, dumping increased in Pennsylvania which had considerably weaker standards).

[133] 42 USC paras. 6,901–92(k) (1983 and Supp. 1995). In 1980, Congress also adopted the Comprehensive Environmental Response, Compensation and Recovery Act (CERCLA or Superfund) which imposes a strict regime of liability for remediation of sites where hazardous waste was disposed in the past. 42 USC paras. 9,601–75 (1983 and Supp. 1995). Although this statute has no direct impact on interstate transfers of hazardous waste, it may nevertheless have an influence on such transfers since, by imposing a strict federal liability scheme, it decreases the incentives that producers may have to transfer their hazardous waste to other states in order to escape liability. On the other hand, large national corporations may seek to limit CERCLA liability by selecting a limited number of disposal facilities for their hazardous waste. This may in turn encourage interstate transfers of waste to such facilities. Generally on CERCLA, see 'Developments in the Law – Toxic Waste Litigation', *Harvard Law Review* 99 (1986), 1,458.

[134] Resource Conservation and Recovery Act, sections 3,001–20; 42 USC paras. 6,921–39(b) (1983 and Supp. 1995).

encourage states to improve their management of 'non-hazardous' solid waste.[135] In order to correct market failures and replace inadequate state regulations, Subtitle C requires the EPA to promulgate regulations governing the identification of waste as hazardous, set standards applicable to generators and transporters of such waste, and establish standards and permit procedures for owners and operators of treatment, storage and disposal facilities that handle hazardous waste.[136] Although Subtitle C institutes a broad federal programme, it authorizes the individual states to develop a hazardous-waste-disposal programme so that hazardous-waste-management activities can be regulated at state level.[137] Once approved by the EPA, a particular regulatory scheme replaces the RCRA regime and the state's environmental agency carries out the EPA's record-keeping, licensing and enforcement role. In order to ensure the respect of minimum waste-management standards throughout the nation, state programmes must incorporate standards that are at least as stringent as the federal standards.

Although it is generally admitted that the RCRA has had a substantial impact on waste-management practices throughout the nation, it is difficult to evaluate the practical impact of this statute on interstate transfers of waste. On the one hand, by harmonizing standards applicable to generators, transporters and hazardous-waste-disposal facilities, the RCRA has removed the risk that some states transform themselves into 'pollution havens' by failing to enforce minimum waste-disposal standards.[138] For the same reason, the RCRA has reduced cost disparities in hazardous-waste disposal between states and therefore has decreased the incentive for producers to ship their waste to other states. On the other

[135] *Ibid.* at sections 4,001–10, 42 USC 6,941–9(a) (1983 and Supp. 1995). Congress has been criticized for what has been perceived as a failure to control non-hazardous solid waste adequately. RCRA, sections 4,002–10 provide guidelines for the development of state plans for treatment and disposal of such waste. Compliance with these guidelines is, however, voluntary. Initially, the federal government provided financial and technical assistance as an incentive for states to comply with the RCRA guidelines; but, at the end of the 1980s, federal grant money ran out, thereby removing the only incentive for states to comply with the federal guidelines. See J. Meyers, 'Confronting the Garbage Crisis: Increased Federal Involvement as a Means of Addressing Municipal Solid Waste Disposal', *Georgetown Law Journal* 79 (1991), 567, 569.

[136] For an overview of the RCRA and its implementing regulations, see R. Hill, 'An Overview of RCRA: The "Mind Numbing" Provisions of the Most Complicated Environmental Statute', *Environmental Law Reporter* 21 (1991), 10,254.

[137] RCRA, sections 3,006–9, 42 USC paras. 6,926 and 6,929 (1983 and Supp. 1995).

[138] Avoiding race-to-the-bottom scenarios was one of the main rationales for adopting the RCRA. See HR 1,491, 94th Cong., 2nd Sess., 30 (1976).

hand, the effectiveness of the RCRA as a means to decrease interstate transfers of waste is reduced by its limited scope. As noted above, the RCRA concentrates on regulating hazardous waste, leaving the regulation of non-hazardous waste to the states. As a result, instead of there being a uniform system of state regulation of non-hazardous waste, a 'patchwork of conflicting state requirements' has developed, with the resultant effect of waste being shipped to the least regulated territories.[139] But even with regard to hazardous waste, the RCRA-harmonized provisions appear to have largely failed to stop huge amounts of hazardous waste being transferred between states.[140] In a great number of cases, such shipments have been made necessary by opposition by local communities to the siting of hazardous-waste-disposal facilities on their territory (the 'NIMBY' syndrome).[141] The reaction of the federal government to this problem is discussed below.

Regulation of interstate movements of waste

In the United States, Congress has so far failed to restrict, or at least control, interstate movements of waste. The dominant wish has been to ensure the unimpeded operation of a 'common market' for waste in which shipments of waste can move, under the supervision of uniform rules, to the most adequate disposal installations, wherever such installations are located in the nation.[142] The shortcoming of this is that it provides a fertile ground for the development of NIMBY behaviour.[143] As we have seen in the context of European Community law, in a market where waste circulates freely, it is tempting for state and local authorities to avoid the political cost of creating 'loathsome' waste-disposal facilities by sending their waste to jurisdictions where such facilities already exist.[144] As a result, the few

---

[139] See Meyers, 'Confronting the Garbage Crisis' at 569.

[140] For some alarming figures on the amounts of hazardous waste in interstate commerce, see J. Pancoast and L. Payne, 'Hazardous Waste in Interstate Commerce: The Triumph of Law over Logic', *Ecology Law Quarterly* 20 (1993), 817, 825.

[141] As will be seen below, local communities have often used the absence of pre-emption provisions in the RCRA to impose total disposal bans on certain waste-disposal activities. See pp. 178–9 below.

[142] As we have seen, the Supreme Court has supported this view, striking down all state attempts to restrict interstate movements of waste.

[143] The 'NIMBY' syndrome is a classic 'prisoner's dilemma'. Overall, total welfare is highest when neither party cheats. However, each party has an incentive to cheat, because if one cheats while the other is honest, the cheater is far better off than if they are both honest. However, if both cheat, they are both far worse off.

[144] See Florini, 'Issues of Federalism' at 327 ('Unfortunately, a reverse commons problem exists at the state as well as at the local level. The costs of a new facility, including the financial and political costs of dealing with local opposition, fall primarily on the

states which possess adequate waste-disposal facilities become dumping grounds for the rest of the nation.[145]

In the Superfund Amendments and Reauthorization Act (SARA) of 1986, Congress attempted to address this problem, which is particularly severe with regard to hazardous waste, by stimulating self-sufficiency in waste disposal on a state or regional basis.[146] Specifically, section 104(c)(9) of SARA authorized the EPA to require each state to come up with a Capacity Assurance Plan that assures:

the availability of hazardous-waste treatment or disposal facilities which . . .
(a) have adequate capacity for the destruction, treatment, or secure disposition of all hazardous waste that are reasonably expected to be generated within the state [during the next twenty years] . . .
(b) are within the State or outside the State in accordance with an interstate agreement or regional agreement or authority . . .[147]

While section 104(c)(9) represents a positive step toward addressing the growing problems associated with hazardous waste and the interstate transfers of such waste, it has failed to ensure a more equitable distribution of hazardous-waste disposal between the states.[148] The sanction for non-compliance with this provision, which is the withdrawal of federal assistance for the clean-up of dangerous waste sites, has indeed generally

host state, whereas the benefits of the facility accrue in part to the several surrounding states. Conversely, the costs of a state's failure to ensure that new facilities are built fall primarily on surrounding states whose facilities receive the excess wastes, whereas the benefits of such a decision accrue to the state which, in effect, decides to export its hazardous wastes. Thus, states that have too few hazardous-waste facilities lack incentives to participate in the siting process and thereby to ensure that new facilities are built within their borders.'). On the NIMBY syndrome, see generally M. Gerrard, 'The Victims of NIMBY?' *Fordham Urban Law Journal* 21 (1994), 495; O. Delogu, '"NIMBY" is a National Environmental Problem', *South Dakota Law Review* 35 (1990), 198.

[145] For example, during 1987, Alabama, which possesses the largest commercial hazardous-waste facility, imported approximately 500,000 tons of hazardous waste for treatment and disposal, while Alabama industries exported only 57,000 tons of hazardous waste out of state for disposal. See *National Solid Wastes Management Association and Chemical Waste Management Inc.* v. *Alabama Department of Environmental Management*, 910 F. 2d 713, 717 note 6 (11th Cir. 1990).

[146] Superfund Amendments and Reauthorization Act of 1986, Pub. L. No. 99-499, para. 104, 100 Stat. 1,613, 1,782. SARA aimed at reauthorizing CERCLA, discussed at note 133, p. 168 above.

[147] 42 USC para. 9,604(c)(9) (1983 and Supp. 1995). On this provision, see generally C. Fixl, 'Hazardous Waste and Partial Import Bans: An Environmentally Sound Exception to the Commerce Clause', *Villanova Environmental Law Journal* 3 (1992), 149. See also Note, 'Constitutionally Mandated Southern Hospitality', *North Carolina Law Review* 69 (1991), 1,001, 1,030–40.

[148] See Pancoast and Payne, 'Hazardous Waste in Interstate Commerce' at 822.

provided an insufficient deterrent for the states opposed to the siting of hazardous-waste-disposal facilities within their borders.

On the other hand, a number of state legislatures have specifically referred to section 104(c)(9) as the basis for aggressive legislation affecting the flow of hazardous waste within state borders. In *National Solid Waste Management Association* v. *Alabama Department of Environmental Management*, the court of Appeals for the Eleventh Circuit found one such Act to be constitutionally invalid.[149] The legislation in question, Alabama's 'Holley Bill', forbade waste-disposal facilities located in Alabama from receiving hazardous waste from states that were not yet in compliance with the capacity assurance obligation of section 104(c)(9) and prohibited Alabama facilities from contracting with a state other than Alabama to satisfy the other state's capacity-assurance obligation.[150] Applying the principles developed by the Supreme Court in *Philadelphia* v. *New Jersey*,[151] the court held that hazardous waste is an object of commerce and that, because it is a protectionist measure not based adequately on a legitimate state concern, the Holley Bill represented an unconstitutional barrier to interstate commerce.[152]

The court then addressed Alabama's contention that section 104(c)(9) constituted Congressional authorization to restrict the flow of hazardous waste within state borders. Specifically, Alabama contended that this provision 'effected a redistribution of power over interstate commerce', authorizing states to restrict the flow of hazardous waste into their borders in order to encourage other states to develop adequate disposal facilities within their borders.[153] The court agreed with Alabama that 'a state statute that erects a barrier to interstate commerce may nonetheless be upheld where Congress authorizes the state to regulate in such a manner',[154] but it insisted that, in order for such Congressional authoriza-

---

[149] 910 F. 2d 713 (1990), opinion modified, 924 F. 2d 1,001 (1991), and cert. denied, *Alabama Department of Environmental Management* v. *National Solid Waste Management Association*, 111 S. Ct 2,800 (1990). For discussions on this case, see R. Levy, 'Federalism and the Environment: *National Solid Waste Management* v. *Alabama Department of Environmental Management*', *Whittier Law Review* 12 (1991), 635; Note, '*National Solid Waste Management Association* v. *Alabama Department of Environmental Management*: Environmental Protection and the Commerce Clause – Is Environmental Protection a Legitimate Local Concern?' *Loyola Law Review* 37 (1991), 189.

[150] ALA Code, para. 22-30-11 (1989).

[151] 437 US 617 (1978).

[152] 910 F. 2d. 713 (1990) at 720.

[153] *Ibid.* at 721.

[154] *Ibid.* (citing *South-Central Timber Development Inc.* v. *Wunnicke*, 467 US 82, 87–8 (1984) and *White* v. *Massachusetts Council of Construction Employers Inc.*, 460 US 204 (1983)).

tion to affect commerce, it must be 'expressly stated' and 'unmistakably clear'.[155] According to the court these conditions were not present in the case in point.[156] Although section 104(c)(9) gave the states more responsibility for hazardous-waste management, nothing in that provision 'evidences Congressional authorization for each state to close its borders to waste generated in other states to force other states to meet federally mandated hazardous-waste requirements'.[157] Section 104(c)(9) offered therefore no justification for discriminatory out-of-state hazardous-waste bans.[158]

The decision reached by the Eleventh Circuit was later applied in *Hazardous Waste Treatment Council* v. *State of South Carolina* where a district court was confronted with a South Carolina legislation imposing discriminatory quotas and other restrictions on the management of out-of-state hazardous waste.[159] Like Alabama, South Carolina argued that, although they restricted interstate commerce, such restrictions were effectively authorized under section 104(c)(9) of SARA. Expressly referring to the Eleventh Circuit's decision in *National Solid Waste Management*, the district court rejected this argument and primarily enjoined South Carolina from enforcing its legislation on the basis that it may violate the Commerce Clause.[160]

---

[155] *Ibid*. As an example of express Congressional authorization of environmental state measures impeding interstate trade, the Supreme Court referred to the Low-Level Radioactive Waste Policy Act, 42 USC paras. 2,021(b)–(j) (1983 and Supp. 1995) which encourages states to form interstate compacts in order to provide for the establishment and operation of regional disposal facilities for low-level radioactive waste: *ibid*. at para. 2,021(d). In this Act, Congress expressly authorizes the states which form these compacts to prohibit the importation of low-level radioactive waste generated in non-compact states: *ibid*. at para. 2,021(e). On these provisions and their implications, see generally J. Conrad, 'Glowing their Own Way: State Embargoes and Exclusive Waste-Disposal Sites under the Low-Level Radioactive Waste Policy Act of 1980', *George Washington Law Review* 53 (1985), 654.

[156] See, *mutatis mutandis*, Justice O'Connor's dissenting opinion in *C&A Carbone Inc*. v. *Town of Clarckstown*, 114 S. Ct 1,677 (1994), 1994 US Lexis 3,477, at *42 (arguing that the RCRA could not be interpreted as expressly authorizing the states to restrict the export of waste).

[157] 910 F. 2d. 713 (1990) at 721.

[158] One should note that Alabama persisted in its efforts to control the flow of out-of-state waste into its own facilities. In April 1990, it enacted new legislation imposing a fee on hazardous waste disposed at in-state commercial facilities and an additional fee if hazardous waste were generated outside the state. As we have seen, this new legislation was again struck down by the Supreme Court in *Chemical Waste Management Inc*. v. *Hunt*, 112 S. Ct 2,009 (1992).

[159] 766 F. Supp. 431 (1991), affirmed in part, remanded in part, 945 F. 2d 781 (4th Cir. 1991).

[160] *Ibid*. at 440.

Frustrated by the courts' invalidation of their efforts to restrict or ban out-of-state hazardous, as well as non-hazardous waste, states at the receiving end of these interstate movements of waste are now seeking explicit authorization from Congress for such restrictions.[161] In the wake of the RCRA's reauthorization legislation, a large number of bills that would authorize the states to restrict out-of-state waste have been proposed by Congress.[162] Although Congress is still trying to find a workable compromise,[163] it is unlikely, however, that it will authorize the states to adopt unilateral restrictions on the movements of hazardous waste. According to an attentive observer, there seems to be a consensus in Congress that, because of the costs of setting up new hazardous-waste-disposal facilities and the need to make them profitable, such facilities should not operate on a state basis.[164] Most environmental experts, however, call for the establishment and the operation of such facilities on a regional basis through the establishment of interstate compacts.[165] In order to stimulate the establishment of such compacts, they also urge Congress to authorize the states which form interstate compacts to

[161] See J. T. Smith and J. Sarnoff, 'Free Commerce and Sound Waste Management: Some International Comparative Perspectives', *International Environment Reporter* (1992), 207, 210.

[162] See, e.g., S. 439, 103rd Cong., 1st Sess. (1993) (permitting governors to limit disposal of out-of-state municipal and industrial waste); HR 1,076, 103rd Cong., 1st Sess. (1993) (same); HR 2,848, 103rd Cong., 1st Sess. (1993) (same); S. 1,873, 103rd Cong., 2nd Sess. (1993) (same); HR 963, 103rd Cong., 1st Sess. (1993) (same); S. 2,877, 102nd Cong., 2nd Sess. (1992) (authorizing state import bans); HR 3,865, 102nd Cong., 1st Sess. (1992) (same); HR 2,380, 102nd Cong., 1st Sess. (1992) (authorizing discriminatory fees upon out-of-state waste); S. 2,384, 102nd Cong., 2nd Sess. (1992) (prohibiting out-of-state waste disposal without local government authorization). Following the Supreme Court judgment in *C&A Carbone* v. *Town of Clarckstown*, bills have also been proposed which would authorize states to adopt restrictions on the exports of waste. See, e.g., HR 1,357, 103rd Cong., 2nd Sess. (1994) (authorizing flow-control laws); HR 4,643, 103rd Cong., 2nd Sess. (1994) (same); S. 1,634, 103rd Cong., 2nd Sess. (1994) (same); S. 2,227, 103rd Cong., 2nd Sess. (1994) (same); HR 4,662, 103rd Cong., 2nd Sess. (1994) (same). See generally J. Satterfield, 'High Hopes and Failed Expectations: The Environmental Record of the 103rd Congress', *Environmental Law Reporter* 25 (1995), 10,089; J. Satterfield, 'A Tale of Sound and Fury: The Environmental Record of the 102nd Congress', *Environmental Law Reporter* 23 (1993), 10,015.

[163] So far, these bills have been blocked by representatives of states which are net exporters of waste.

[164] See J. T. Smith, 'The Challenge of Environmentally Sound and Efficient Regulation of Waste – The Need for an Enhanced International Understanding', *Journal of Environmental Law* 5 (1993), 91, 103.

[165] See, e.g., Pancoast and Payne, 'Hazardous Waste in Interstate Commerce' at 852; Florini, 'Issues of Federalism' at 334.

restrict the imports of waste from non-compact states.[166] Although the Low-Level Radioactive Waste Policy Act offers a useful precedent,[167] it is not clear at this stage whether Congress is prepared to adopt such provisions. On the other hand, there is now a strong prospect that Congress will adopt legislation allowing states and local authorities greater control on the flows of non-hazardous waste.[168] Contrary to hazardous waste, the disposal of non-hazardous waste is generally seen as a matter of state and local interest which should be regulated at state and local level.[169]

The question of pre-emption

The question examined in this section is whether, once the federal government has legislated, states remain free to adopt stricter standards than federal standards or if federal standards pre-empt more protective state actions. As already noted in the context of European Community law, pre-emption questions are difficult to answer from a policy stand-point.[170] On the one hand, allowing states to adopt stricter standards

---

[166] See, e.g., S. Brietzke, 'Hazardous Waste in Interstate Commerce: Minimizing the Problem after *Philadelphia* v. *New Jersey*', *Valparaiso University Law Review* 24 (1989), 77, 108.

[167] See note 155, p. 173 above.

[168] See D. Hosansky, 'Backers May Push Garbage Bill in Session after Election', *Congressional Quarterly*, 2,949 (15 October 1994). See also R. Roddewig and G. Sechen, 'Recent Developments with RCRA Subtitle D and Commerce Clause Cases After *Hunt* and *Fort Gratiot* Decisions', *Urban Lawyer* 35 (1993), 797, 811.

[169] See note 135, p. 169 above.

[170] Generally on the concept of pre-emption, see S. Gardbaum, 'The Nature of Pre-emption', *Cornell Law Review* 79 (1994), 767; Project: 'The Role of Pre-emption in Administrative Law', *Administrative Law Review* 45 (1993), 107 (hereafter the 'Pre-emption Project'); C. Hoke, 'Pre-emption Pathologies and Civil Republican Values', *Boston University Law Review* 71 (1991), 685; W. Cohen, 'Congressional Power to Define State Power to Regulate Commerce: Consent and Pre-emption' in Sandalow and Stein (eds.), *Courts and Free Markets* (Oxford University Press, 1982) at 523; Note, 'Pre-emption as a Preferential Ground: A New Canon of Construction', *Stanford Law Review* 12 (1959), 208. On the issue of pre-emption in the specific context of environmental protection, see J. Fernandez, 'The Purpose Test: Shielding Environmental Statutes from the Sword of Pre-emption', *Syracuse Law Journal* 41 (1990), 1,201, J. Newman, 'A Consideration of Federal Pre-emption in the Context of State and Local Environmental Regulation', *UCLA Journal of Environmental Law and Policy* 9 (1990), 97; Comment, 'Environmental Law: A Reevaluation of Federal Preemption and the Commerce Clause', *Fordham Urban Law Journal* 7 (1979), 649; Comment, 'Pre-emption Doctrine in the Environmental Context: A Unified Method of Analysis', *University of Pennsylvania Law Review* 127 (1978), 197; S. Kilbourn, 'Environmental Control: Higher State Standards and the Question of Pre-emption', *Cornell Law Review* 55 (1970), 846.

than federal standards appears to be advantageous since it allows states to provide for particular local needs and to ensure a higher level of environmental protection on their territory. On the other hand, stricter state standards may disrupt the harmony of the federal regulatory scheme and reintroduce the kind of trade distortions that motivated the adoption of uniform federal standards in the first place. Pre-emption questions therefore require the striking of a delicate balance between the federal interest in uniform regulations and the state interest in local autonomy and environmental diversity.

In a number of cases, Congress has attempted to solve pre-emption questions in advance by indicating in federal environmental statutes whether the provisions they contain pre-empt stricter state standards or if they only impose minimum standards. As in the European Community context, the degree of uniformity required by federal legislation has usually varied depending on the area of regulation involved. In this regard, a first distinction can be established between product and process regulations. In the area of product regulation, Congress has traditionally pre-empted more rigorous state regulations on the ground that a high degree of uniformity is needed to facilitate the free movement of goods throughout the nation.[171] For example, section 2,617(a) of the Toxic Substances Control Act (TSCA) indicates in its relevant part that, with the exception of disposal rules, states may not regulate a chemical once the EPA has acted to regulate the substance under section 2,603 (testing), section 2,604 (notice) or section 2,605 (other regulations) of the Act, unless the state requirement is either identical to the EPA's rule, adopted under another federal law, or prohibits the use of such substance in the state.[172] Similarly, section 7,617 of the Clean Air Act specifies that 'no State or local government may enforce any requirement concerning the design of any new or recalled appliance for the purpose of protecting the strato-spheric ozone layer'.[173] It is clear from these pre-emption clauses that the opportunity for states to adopt stricter product standards than federal standards has been circumscribed.

By way of contrast, when it has regulated processes, Congress has generally opted for minimum harmonization schemes.[174] For example,

---

[171] See Rehbinder and Stewart, 'Environmental Protection Policy' at 46.

[172] 15 USC para. 2,617(a)(1)(2)(A) (1982 and Supp. 1995). On the pre-emptive effect of the TSCA, see J. Florio, 'Federalism Issues Related to the Probable Emergence of the Toxic Substances Control Act', *Maryland Law Review* 54 (1995), 1,354.

[173] 42 USC para. 7,671(m) (1983 and Supp. 1995).

[174] It is interesting to note that, despite the existence of such regimes, several states have

section 1,370 of the Clean Water Act allows states to adopt and enforce more stringent limits on discharges than those required by the federal government.[175] Similarly, with regard to the regulation of stationary source polluters, the Clean Air Act provides for minimum standards that must be met by the states although they are free to impose higher standards.[176] The differences in the approaches taken by Congress in the areas of product and process regulations can be explained by their different economic objectives. As has been seen, what matters in the context of product regulation is the adoption of an upper regulatory limit which guarantees that all products which comply with such a limit will circulate freely throughout the nation. On the other hand, what matters in the context of process regulation is the adoption of a lower regulatory limit that will prevent states from competing for industry by relaxing environmental standards.

It should be noted, however, that, even if Congress tends to prefer uniform solutions in the context of product regulation, various mechanisms are used to enable within strictly defined limits more extensive measures to be taken by states. An illustration of this can be observed in the Toxic Substances Control Act where, pursuant to a procedure which recalls Article 100A(4) of the EC Treaty,[177] states may apply to the EPA for an exemption from the pre-emption provision contained in section 2,617(a), which the EPA may grant if the exemption would not lead to a violation of the Act and provides a significantly higher degree of protection from the risk than the federal regulation without unduly burdening commerce.[178] Mechanisms allowing for state diversity in product regulation can also be found in other major federal statutes. First, as already observed, the Clean Air Act provides for a two-tier control system of motor-vehicle-exhaust emissions whereby it establishes compulsory uniform limits but nevertheless authorizes states with serious air quality problems to apply the stricter California standards.[179] Second, in an attempt to balance the needs of commerce with local environmental protection, section 163v of the Federal Insecticide, Fungicide, and Rodenti-

---

prohibited their state agencies from adopting stricter standards than federal environmental standards. See J. Organ, 'Limitations on State Agency Authority to Adopt Environmental Standards More Stringent than Federal Standards: Policy Considerations and Environmental Problems', *Maryland Law Review* 54 (1995), 1,373.

[175] 33 USC para. 1,370 (1995).
[176] 42 USC para. 7,416 (1983 and Supp. 1995).
[177] For a discussion on this provision, see pp. 135–9 above.
[178] 15 USC para. 2,617(b) (1982 and Supp. 1995).
[179] See p. 160 above.

cide Act (FIFRA) provides for a dual regime whereby states are prohibited from imposing any labelling or packaging requirements in addition to or different from those required under the Act,[180] but remain free to regulate the sale and use of federally registered pesticides.[181]

In the area of waste, the principal federal statute regulating disposal standards explicitly allows states to adopt stricter standards than federal standards. The RCRA's section 6,929 indicates that:

> nothing in this chapter shall be construed to prohibit any state or political subdivision thereof from imposing any requirement including those for site election, which are more stringent than those imposed by [federal] regulations.[182]

Although this provision appears relatively straightforward, its interpretation has created difficulties since, because of local public pressure, a number of states and local communities have relied on its language to adopt aggressive hazardous-waste legislation.[183] A particularly controversial issue has been whether section 6,929 permits states to impose a complete hazardous-waste-disposal ban.[184] In *Ensco Inc.* v. *Dumas*,[185] the

---

[180] 7 USC para. 136(v)(b) (1995).

[181] *Ibid.* at 136(a) (1980 and Supp. 1995). Generally on the pre-emptive effect of FIFRA, see M. Rosso Grossman, 'Environmental Federalism in Agriculture: The Case of Pesticides Regulation in the United States' in Braden, Folmer and Ulen (eds.), *Environmental Policy with Political and Economic Integration* (Cheltenham, UK, Brookfield, US: Edward Elgar, 1996), 276.

[182] 42 USC para. 6,929 (1983 and Supp. 1995). Similarly, in the Superfund Amendments and Reauthorization Act of 1986 (SARA), Congress made clear that the Superfund legislation did not pre-empt a state from 'imposing any additional liability or requirements with respect to the release of hazardous substances within such state'. See 42 USC para. 9,614(a) (1983 and Supp. 1995).

[183] See 'Pre-emption Project' at 215. See also J. Stone, 'Supremacy and Commerce Clause Issues Regarding State Hazardous Waste Bans', *Columbia Journal of Environmental Law* 15 (1990), 1, 9.

[184] One should note that a state measure prohibiting disposal of all hazardous waste regardless of its origin would probably not violate the Commerce Clause. In *City of Philadelphia* v. *New Jersey*, the Supreme Court ruled that, although New Jersey could not validly discriminate between domestic and out-of-state waste in order to protect the environment, it could pursue this aim 'by slowing down the flow of all waste into the state's remaining landfills, even though interstate commerce may be incidentally affected': 437 US 617, 626 (1978). The Supreme Court seems therefore to recognize implicitly the compatibility with the Commerce Clause of total waste-disposal bans. See 'Pre-emption Project' at 215.

[185] 807 F. 2d 743 (8th Cir. 1986). See also *Ogden Environmental Services* v. *City of San Diego*, 687 F. Supp. 1,436 (SD Cal. 1988) (holding that a total ban on certain hazardous-waste-disposal activities was pre-empted by the RCRA). It should also be noted that in *Rollins Environmental Services (FS) Inc.* v. *Parish of St James*, 775 F. 2d 627 (5th Circ. 1985), the Court of Appeals of the Fifth Circuit ruled that a local ordinance totally banning the

Court of Appeals for the Eighth Circuit invalidated an ordinance from the County Union, Arkansas that prohibited the storage, treatment or disposal of 'acute hazardous waste' within its boundaries. The court strongly rejected the county's reliance on section 6,929 holding that although this provision 'acknowledges the authority of state and local governmental entities to make good-faith adaptations of federal policy to local conditions',[186] the county could not:

by attaching the label 'more stringent requirements' or 'site selection' to an ordinance that in language and history defies such description, arrogate to itself the power to enact a measure that as a practical matter cannot function other than to subvert federal policies concerning the safe handling of hazardous waste.[187]

By rejecting the County Union's measure, the Eighth Circuit placed a 'common sense' limitation on the scope of the RCRA's 'anti-pre-emption' provision. Although section 6,929 authorizes states and local communities to adopt stricter standards than federal standards in order to provide for particular local conditions, this provision offers no justification for state restrictions that, because they are driven by isolationist purposes, would frustrate the RCRA's essential objective of ensuring the development of a network of safe hazardous-waste-disposal facilities throughout the nation.

In the absence of a clear legislative guidance on the issue of pre-emption, federal courts may be asked to determine whether, by enacting a regulatory scheme with regard to a specific cause of concern, Congress has 'occupied the field' or if it has left room for stricter state regulations.[188] If Congress has decided to 'occupy the field', stricter state

---

disposal of PCB was pre-empted under the TSCA's pre-emption provisions. Generally on the specific problem of PCB disposal bans, see W. Andreen, 'Defining the "Not in my Backyard Syndrome": An Approach to Federal Pre-emption of State and Local Impediments to the Siting of PCB Disposal Facilities', *North Carolina Law Review* 63 (1985), 811.

[186] 807 F. 2d 743 (8th Cir. 1986) at 745.

[187] *Ibid.*

[188] It is important to note that, even when Congress has not chosen to 'occupy a field', pre-emption may occur to the extent that state and federal law 'actually conflict'. Such a conflict arises when 'compliance with both federal and state regulations is a physical impossibility': *Florida Lime & Avocado Grocers Inc. v. Paul*, 373 US 132, 142–3 (1963); or when a state law 'stands as an obstacle to the accomplishment and execution of the full purposes and objectives of Congress': *Hines v. Davidovitz*, 312 US 52 (1941). Contrary to 'occupation of the field' pre-emption, 'actual conflict' pre-emption does not, however, generally prevent states from adopting stricter standards than federal standards. It only pre-empts stricter state standards when they conflict with federal legislation. See, e.g., *Ensco Inc. v. Dumas* 807 F. 2d 743 (8th Cir. 1986) (holding that, even though the RCRA authorizes states to adopt stricter hazardous-

regulations will be invalidated since federal legislation is exhaustive. But federal occupation of the field will not be lightly inferred. Courts will invalidate state laws only if it is 'the clear and manifest purpose of Congress' that an area be exclusively federally regulated.[189] Pursuant to the Supreme Court's pre-emption case law, this purpose may be evidenced in three principal ways. First, '[t]he scheme of federal regulation may be so pervasive as to make reasonable the inference that Congress left no room for the states to supplement it'.[190] Second, 'Congress may regulate a field of such dominant federal interest that similar state laws are presumed pre-empted'.[191] Third, an intention to pre-empt may be inferred when 'the state policy may produce a result inconsistent with the objective of a federal statute'.[192]

In a number of cases, courts have applied these principles to infer federal pre-emption of stricter state environmental legislation. For example, in *Burbank* v. *Lockheed Air Terminal*,[193] a city ordinance which, in order to protect local citizens against excessive noise during normal sleeping hours, prohibited any pure jet aircraft from taking off from the privately owned city airport between 11 p.m. and 7 a.m. was found to be pre-empted by exhaustive federal legislation. After an examination of the federal legislation dealing with aircraft noise, the Supreme Court concluded that federal intervention had so much 'pervaded' that field that it had effectively pre-empted it.[194] Similarly, in *Northern States Power Company* v. *State of Minnesota*,[195] the court of Appeals for the Eighth Circuit found that a Minnesota statute regulating radioactive waste releases by nuclear power plants was pre-empted by federal legislation. The court indicated that both the language and the legislative history of the Atomic Energy

waste-disposal standards than federal standards, a total ban on hazardous-waste-disposal is nevertheless pre-empted by the RCRA because it violates its essential objectives).

[189] See *Rice* v. *Santa Fe Elevator Corp.*, 331 US 218, 230 (1946).

[190] *Ibid.*

[191] *Ibid.*

[192] *Ibid.*

[193] 411 US 624 (1973). But see *British Airways Board* v. *Port Authority of New York*, 558 F. 2d 75 (2nd Cir. 1977); *National Aviation* v. *City of Hayward*, 418 F. Supp. 417 (1975) (both courts holding that city ordinances which prohibited aircraft exceeding a certain noise level from landing or taking-off from an airport of which the city was proprietor were not pre-empted).

[194] 411 US 624 (1973). See also *Ray* v. *Atlantic Richfield Co.*, 435 US 151 (1978) (holding that in so far as it required all tankers in Puget Sound to comply with certain safety design standards, a Washington state law was pre-empted by the 1972 Ports and Waterways Safety Act).

[195] 447 F. 2d 1,143 (1971).

Act demonstrated that 'Congress intended federal occupancy of regulations over all radiation hazards except where jurisdiction was expressly transferred to the states'.[196] The Supreme Court affirmed this holding without issuing an opinion.[197]

It seems, however, that, in recent years, the Supreme Court has grown increasingly reluctant to infer that federal statutes and attendant regulations pre-empt more stringent state statutes aimed at the same activity.[198] For example, in *Pacific Gas & Electric Co.* v. *Energy Resources Commission*,[199] the Supreme Court found that the Atomic Energy Act did not pre-empt a California statute imposing a moratorium on the construction of nuclear power plants until a state agency determined that the federal government had resolved the problem of nuclear waste disposal. Similarly, in *Silkwood* v. *Kerr McGee*,[200] the Supreme Court upheld a state-authorized award of punitive damages arising out of the escape of plutonium from a plant whose safety measures were in compliance with federal regulations. In *California Coastal Commission* v. *Granite Rock*,[201] the Supreme Court also upheld a California statute that required a mining company to apply for a state permit, even though the company was operating on national forest land pursuant to a valid federal permit. The court concluded that the California statute was not pre-empted by the federal Forest Service regulations, federal land-use statutes, or the federal Coastal Management Zone Act of 1972. Finally, in *Wisconsin Public Intervenor* v. *Mortier*,[202] the court decided that FIFRA did not pre-empt the regulation of pesticides by local governments. The court found that FIFRA 'nowhere expressly supersedes local regulation of pesticide use'[203] and also 'fails to provide any clear and manifest indication that Congress sought to supplant local authority over pesticide regulation implicitly'.[204]

---

[196] *Ibid.* at 1,150.
[197] See Minnesota v. Northern States Power Co., 405 US 1,035 (1972) (*per curiam*).
[198] See R. Stewart, 'Interstate Commerce, Environmental Protection, and US Federal Law' in Cameron, Demaret and Geradin (eds.), *Trade and the Environment – The Search for Balance* (London: Cameron & May, 1994) at 351; D. Geradin, 'Free Trade and Environmental Protection in an Integrated Market: A Survey of the Case Law of the United States Supreme Court and of the European Court of Justice', *Florida State University Journal of Transnational Law and Policy* 2 (1993), 141, 149. See also Pierce, 'Regulation, Deregulation' at 635.
[199] 461 US 190 (1983).
[200] 464 US 238 (1984).
[201] 480 US 572 (1987).
[202] 111 S. Ct 2,476 (1991).
[203] *Ibid.* at 543.
[204] *Ibid.* at 547.

This recent case law indicates a general readiness on the part of the court to uphold state environmental-protection measures against preemption challenges. In the absence of serious disruption to interstate trade, it is submitted that the position currently adopted by the Supreme Court presents a number of advantages. First, since when it adopts uniform standards the federal government cannot take into account all local human and geographical circumstances, federal legislation may lead to a degree of underregulation in a number of states.[205] Allowing states to adopt stricter standards than federal standards therefore gives them a guarantee that no regulatory gap will occur when primary regulatory authority over certain environmental matters is transferred from the state to the federal level. Second, it is generally recognized that allowing some states to go beyond what has been decided at federal level provides the federal government and the other states with a useful source of experimentation and innovation.[206] Some states, such as California, have traditionally played a very active role in environmental policy and it has not been uncommon that, when successful, solutions first adopted at state level were then applied to the entire nation.[207] Finally and perhaps more fundamentally, it seems that at a time when, due to a broad construction of the Commerce Clause, there has been a considerable growth of Congressional powers over environmental matters, it is important that federal courts protect the residual regulatory authority of the states over such matters by refusing to interpret ambiguous federal environmental statutes expansively.[208]

---

[205] Uniform federal regulation may also lead to overregulation in other states. See, e.g., Krier, 'The Irrational National Air Quality Standards' at 328. Some techniques may be envisaged to deal with this problem, including adoption of exceptions to uniform standards or more flexible attainment deadlines for a number of states, as well as technical and financial assistance.

[206] See Justice Brandeis' famous *dictum* in *New Ice Co.* v. *Liebmann*, 285 US 262, 311 (1932): 'It is one of the happy incidents of the federal system that a single courageous State may, if its citizens choose to, serve as a laboratory; and try novel social and economic experiments without risk to the rest of the country.' But see A. Rapaczynski, 'From Sovereignty to Process: The Jurisprudence of Federalism after *Garcia*', *Supreme Court Review* (1985), 341, 408 (dismissing Justice Brandeis' call to state legislatures as 'one of the least examined verities of constitutional theory').

[207] See, e.g., Lester, 'A New Federalism?' at 62; Percival *et al.*, *Environmental Regulation* at 117.

[208] See L. Tribe, 'California Declines the Nuclear Gamble: Is Such a State Choice Preempted?' *Ecology Law Quarterly* 7 (1979), 679, 690.

7 Comparative analysis

In this chapter, I first discuss and compare the powers of the Community and the US federal government to take action in the environmental field, as well as the potential limits that may be placed on the exercise of such powers out of respect for the states' residual sphere of competence over this field. Then, I compare how in the areas of product standards, process standards and waste, the Community and the US federal government have concretely attempted to balance trade and environmental protection through or in the context of their legislative action. Finally, I compare the extent to which the Community and the US federal government have allowed the states to adopt stricter measures than Community/federal harmonized measures.

The principle of attributed powers

Since both the European Community and the US federal systems are based on the principle of attributed powers, the first question examined in this Part was to what extent the Community and the US federal government have the power to legislate in the environmental field. While there is no specific provision in the US Constitution providing authority for federal regulation of the environment, the federal government has, however, legislated in this area, relying on the Supreme Court's broad interpretation of its power to regulate interstate commerce.[1] Similarly, in the period prior to the adoption of the SEA, the European Community compensated for the absence in the EC Treaty of an explicit source of authority for environmental action by using two provisions originally created for economic purposes, Articles 100 and 235, as legal bases for

---

[1] See pp. 144–6 above.

Community environmental legislation.[2] However, unlike the US government which has always employed a form of majority rule for environmental action, Articles 100 and 235 require unanimity on the part of the Council members and not a simple or qualified majority. This had the detrimental effect of complicating the decision-making process and hence reducing the effectiveness of Community environmental policy. Adoption of Community environmental legislation has, however, been facilitated by the SEA which introduced explicit legal bases for Community action in the environmental field: Articles 100A and 130S.[3] Article 100A has had a particularly significant impact on Community environmental-protection policy, since, unlike Article 130S (in its SEA version), proposals brought under Article 100A may be adopted by a qualified majority of the Council.

The SEA, however, gave birth to a new problem (of a kind unknown in US law) since it requires a dividing line to be drawn between Article 100A and Article 130S.[4] From the point of view of the relationship between trade and environmental protection, the choice of the proper legal basis for a particular Community environmental action is significant for two reasons. First, it determines which of the safeguard clauses contained in Articles 100A(4) and 130T the member states may have recourse to. This in turn may have important trade implications since Article 130T seems to offer more leeway to the member states than Article 100A(4). Second, the test used by the court to determine whether a particular Community environmental measure should be based on Article 100A or 130S relies on finding whether the principal objective of the measure in question is to further the accomplishment of the internal market or to protect the environment.

Whatever its merits may be, this test is difficult to apply in practice and has led to much confusion. In this regard, the amendments brought about by the TEU came as a disappointment. If the TEU has generally reinforced the powers of the Community in the environmental field, it has failed to articulate a dividing line between Articles 100A and 130S and in some respects has complicated the situation by creating no less than four procedures for environmental action. Against this background, it seems that one of the tasks for the 1996–7 Intergovernmental Conference[5] will

---

[2] See pp. 76–7 above.
[3] See pp. 77–80 above.
[4] See pp. 80–90 above.
[5] Pursuant to Article N of the TEU '[a] Conference of representatives of the governments of the member states shall be convened in 1996 to examine those provisions of this TEU for which revision is provided'. Generally on the challenges facing this Conference, see

be to simplify the present haphazard combination of several voting rules and varying institutional procedures for environmental action. It is suggested that the qualified-majority-voting system and the co-decision procedure currently contained in Article 100A should be extended in a unified procedure to all forms of environmental action.[6]

Need for and intensity of Community or federal environmental action

Another important institutional question is to what extent the broad regulatory authority of the Community and the US federal government over environmental matters is limited out of respect for the states' residual sphere of competence over these matters.[7] As we have seen, US constitutional law does not contain any judicially enforceable mechanism designed to protect the residual powers of the states against excessive federal intervention in areas of shared competence, such as environmental protection.[8] The working assumption is that influence through the political process, rather than judicially imposed limits, is to be the primary means by which the states should protect themselves against excessive federal intervention. In this regard, the American example has been used as a reference by those opposed to the justiciability of the principle of subsidiarity and for whom this principle should be seen as a mere guideline for the political institutions of the Community.[9] The prevalent view, however, is that subsidiarity *is* justiciable, but that the

---

Justius Lipsius, 'The 1996 Intergovernmental Conference', *European Law Review* 20 (1995), 235.

[6] See *ibid.* at 262 (arguing for a decrease in the number of legislative procedures and a simplification of the decision-making process).

[7] Few studies have examined this question from a comparative perspective. See, however, J. Pfander, 'Environmental Federalism in Europe and the United States: A Comparative Assessment of Regulation through the Agency of Member States' in Braden, Folmer and Ulen (eds.), *Environmental Policy with Political and Economic Integration* (Cheltenham, UK, Brookfield, US: Edward Elgar, 1996), 59; C. Kimber, 'A Comparison of Environmental Federalism in the United States and in the European Union', *Maryland Law Review* 54 (1995), 1,658; G. Vause, 'The Subsidiarity Principle in European Union Law – American Federalism Compared', *Case Western Reserve Journal of International Law* 27 (1995), 61; G. Bermann, 'Taking Subsidiarity Seriously: Federalism in the European Community and the United States', *Columbia Law Review* 94 (1994), 331; T. Fischer, '"Federalism" in the European Community and the United States: A Rose by Any Other Name', *Fordham International Law Journal* 17 (1994), 390.

[8] See pp. 148–9 above.

[9] See, e.g., R. Dehousse, 'Does Subsidiarity Really Matter?' European University Institute Working Paper Law No. 92/32.

Court of Justice would be well advised to confine itself to procedural grounds and to check whether the Community legislative authorities have sufficiently considered why there is a need for Community action. Justiciable or not, we have seen that the principle of subsidiarity imposes an extremely low threshold with regard to the assessment of the need for Community environmental action. The guidelines developed by the Edinburgh European Council seem indeed broad enough to uphold most possible forms of Community environmental action.[10]

In this context, I have argued that, as understood by the Edinburgh European Council, the requirement of proportionality contained in Article 3B(3) of the Treaty will have a more lasting effect on the development of Community environmental law than the principle of subsidiarity itself.[11] This principle has always been present in some form in Community environmental action. Traces of the idea of proportionality can also be found in US environmental law, particularly in the area of process regulation where Congress has usually tried to establish a 'partnership' between the states and the federal government.[12] It should be noted, however, that federal intervention in the environmental field has been very extensive and, by the standards set by the Edinburgh European Council, disproportionate.[13] Federal regulatory excesses, combined with the conservative ideology of two successive Republican Presidents, have in turn generated a wave of deregulation, which, although it had an important impact on administrative practices, has left federal environmental statutes largely unaffected. The integrity of such statutes is, however, endangered by the post-1994 pro-business, anti-regulation Republican majority in Congress.[14]

In the European Community, the principle of proportionality is to play an essential role in the future as a general guideline in favour of less regulatory density in Community legislation and, as far as possible, the adoption of non-uniform rather than uniform solutions. In a Community whose heterogeneity has been and is likely to be increased by successive enlargements, this principle presents the advantage of giving to the member states increased flexibility in the attainment of Community environmental goals. On the other hand, the danger is that pro-develop-

---

[10] See pp. 93–5 above.
[11] See pp. 95–8 above.
[12] See pp. 153–4 above.
[13] See, e.g., R. Stewart, 'Antidotes for the "American Disease"', *Ecology Law Quarterly* 20 (1993), 85, 88.
[14] See pp. 154–5 above.

ment member states may use this concept as a pretext for regulatory competition and environmental deregulation. As already noted, the task of the Community will be to find an appropriate balance between the member states' interest in regulatory autonomy and environmental diversity and the Community interest in uniform regulation.

Against this institutional background, I have attempted to examine how, in the areas of product standards, process standards and waste, the Community and the US federal government have attempted to deal with the various kinds of tension that may arise between trade and environmental protection.

Harmonization of environmental standards

Product standards

In the area of environmental product standards, I have concentrated my analysis on the evolution of the Community and US federal legislation on motor-vehicle-exhaust emissions. Setting aside its economic and environmental significance, this legislation contains a number of important features that can generally be extended to other areas of product regulation. First, it was stimulated by the threat that inconsistent state regulations governing motor-vehicle-exhaust emissions would impede interstate trade in cars and create market fragmentation. In order to avoid such negative trade consequences, the Community and the US federal government decided to adopt harmonized motor-vehicle-exhaust-emission limits applicable throughout the Community and the United States respectively.[15] A similar rationale induced them to adopt uniform standards for a wide range of environmentally sensitive products, such as toxic chemicals, pesticides, fuels and noise-generating equipment.

Second, in order to avoid the states reintroducing trade restrictions, the two legislatures pre-empted the states from adopting stricter limits than

---

[15] It is interesting to note that for similar reasons the Community and the US federal government are now trying to harmonize their motor-vehicle-emission limits. For example, two US government agencies have recently proposed the creation of an international forum to harmonize environmental and safety regulations for automobile engines. This would be done by extending the existing UN Economic Commission for Europe (UNECE) working party on vehicle construction. See 'US Proposes Harmonization of Auto Regulations through UN Forum', *Environment Watch*, 19 July 1996 at 6. Similarly, the EC Commission has recently proposed that the Community aligns its emission limits for non-road motor vehicles to US standards, so as to create a large transatlantic market. See 'Transatlantic Norms Agreed on for Mobile Machinery Emissions', *Environment Watch*, 3 July 1996, at 14.

the harmonized motor-vehicle-exhaust-emission limits. In the United States, however, Congress made an exception to this rule, allowing California to maintain its stricter standards. In order to gain further flexibility, Congress subsequently authorized the other states to opt for the stricter California standards, thereby creating a two-tier pollution-control scheme.[16] The Community has not provided for similar exceptions. It initially adopted a system of optional harmonization, whereby member states must ensure market access to vehicles complying with Community standards but were free to allow on their territory the operation of vehicles that do not meet such standards. It then opted for a system of total harmonization, whereby regulations must be uniform throughout the member states.[17] As we have seen, an example of integration at different speeds can, however, be found in the context of the regulation of lead content in petrol where the Community set a harmonized minimum level of 0.40 g/l for lead in petrol but authorized member states to establish a stricter level as low as 0.15 g/l.[18]

Third, an important characteristic of the Community and US federal legislation on motor-vehicle-exhaust emissions is that, although this legislation was primarily adopted for economic reasons (i.e., to facilitate interstate trade and avoid market fragmentation), it has become a strong environmental policy instrument.[19] In the United States, the stringency of federal motor-vehicle-exhaust-emission regulations strongly increased with the adoption of the Clean Air Act of 1970, a statute which was influenced by the wave of environmentalism that took place in the United States in the beginning of the 1970s.[20] For institutional reasons, it took more time for the Community to strengthen the environmental content of its motor-vehicle-exhaust-emission legislation. However, by removing

---

[16] See pp. 158–60 above.

[17] See pp. 102–3 above.

[18] For another example of integration at different speeds, see Article 6 of Directive 94/62 on packaging and packaging waste, OJ 1994, L 365/10 (establishing minimum and maximum packaging standards but allowing some member states (i.e., Greece, Ireland and Portugal) to adopt less stringent standards than Community minimum standards and all member states to adopt stricter standards than Community maximum standards after obtaining approval from the Commission).

[19] A similar evolution has also occurred in the areas of chemicals. While the initial objective of EC and US chemical regulations was to promote free trade, the focus of more recent chemical regulations is to protect the environment. Compare, e.g., R. Percival, 'Environmental Federalism: Historical Roots and Contemporary Models', *Maryland Law Review* 54 (1995), 1,141, 1,149 with S. Johnson and G. Corcelle, *The Environmental Policy of the European Communities* (London: Graham & Trotman) at 187.

[20] See pp. 159–60 above.

the veto power possessed by member states having strong car-manufacturing interests and by increasing the role of a usually pro-environment Parliament in the legislative process through a procedure of co-operation, the introduction of Article 100A in the Treaty by the SEA allowed the Community to make rapid progress towards the adoption of emission limits equivalent to those adopted earlier in the United States. By further increasing the role of the Parliament in the legislative process, the new procedure of co-decision introduced by the TEU in Article 100A should generally favour the adoption of even stricter product regulations.[21]

Process standards

As in the case of product standards, the Community and US federal government have adopted legislation harmonizing environmental process standards for a large number of industrial activities. Contrary to product standards, however, the objective of this legislation is not to facilitate interstate trade but to ensure that such trade takes place under fair conditions of competition. As has been seen, adoption by one state of more stringent process standards increases the costs of producers located in that state, thereby creating a competitive advantage for producers located in states applying less stringent standards. When it is significant, this advantage may give an incentive to producers to locate new facilities in states applying less stringent standards or even to relocate existing facilities to such states.[22] Harmonization of environmental process standards has been the solution adopted in the Community and the United States to deal with such distortions.

Harmonization of process standards is generally rendered difficult by conflicting state interests. First, states may disagree over the necessity of harmonization itself. In order to preserve their competitive position,

---

[21] See pp. 105–6 above.

[22] From a general standpoint, it seems that Community member states applying strict process standards have been less concerned than American states applying strict process standards about the threat created by industrial relocation. Because of the existence of a less perfectly unified market, the transaction costs for producers of moving from one state to another are higher in the Community than in the United States, hence rendering industrial relocation less attractive for producers. The recent progress in economic integration realized by the 1992 programme could, however, reduce such transaction costs in the European Community and stimulate scenarios of industrial relocation between member states. See R. Stewart, 'Environmental Law in the United States and the European Community: Spillovers, Cooperation, Rivalry, Institutions', *University of Chicago Legal Forum* (1992), 39, 43, 64 (arguing that the completion of the internal market will increase the importance of economic spillovers).

states applying stringent standards will generally attempt to ensure that standards equivalent to their standards are applied everywhere. However, in so far as they are able to market their products (manufactured under laxer process standards) in other states, states applying less stringent process standards will generally oppose such harmonization. Second, even if they agree on some form of harmonization, states may disagree over the level of stringency and the appropriate structure of process standards. As we have seen, environmental quality standards give a competitive advantage to those states where air or water is relatively unpolluted because they can accommodate new industry and additional pollution without violating the standards. By contrast, uniform technology-based effluent standards deny such a competitive advantage to less polluted states since all polluters belonging to a particular category of industry will have to apply the same standards. While the less polluted states will generally favour the former regulatory strategy, the more polluted states will generally favour the latter.

In this context, the adoption but also the shape and content of harmonized process standards will depend heavily on the respective bargaining powers of the states. In the United States, the majority voting procedure applied in Congress has favoured the politically powerful northeastern states.[23] With the support of environmentalists and the labour unions, these states have generally imposed on southern states the adoption of strict uniform technologically based standards. In the European Community, the member states opposed to the adoption of uniform standards were until recently protected by the rule of unanimity. As we have seen, pro-development member states such as the less-developed southern member states and the United Kingdom[24] have generally managed to force pro-environment member states such as Denmark, Germany or the Netherlands to compromise on asymmetrical regimes[25] or regimes of alternative harmonization.[26] With the entry into force of

---

[23] See pp. 162–3 above.

[24] For a good discussion on the ability of the United Kingdom to extract concessions from its European partners, see J. Golub, 'The Pivotal Role of British Sovereignty in EC Environmental Policy', European University Institute Working Paper RSC No. 94/17.

[25] See, e.g., Directive 88/609 of 24 November 1988 on the limitation of emissions of certain pollutants into the air from large combustion plants, OJ 1988, L 336/1 (providing for different emission-reduction targets for each member state and authorizing some member states to increase their emissions).

[26] See, e.g., Directive 76/464 of 4 May 1976 on pollution caused by certain dangerous substances discharged into the aquatic environment, OJ 1976, L 129/23 (allowing member states to choose between a strategy of water-quality standards and a strategy of effluent standards).

the TEU, the bargaining power of pro-development member states has been considerably reduced by the extension of the qualified majority to Article 130S(1). Since these member states have lost their ability to veto Community environmental legislation contrary to their interests, one can expect the adoption in the future of stricter and more uniform process-standards regulations.

The abandonment of the rule of unanimity for process-standards harmonization does not mean, however, that the standards applied in the member states will be completely uniform. First, as illustrated by the negotiations on the draft directive on integrated pollution prevention and control, there will be instances where member states will be equally divided over the regulatory strategy to be pursued and compromises will have to be made.[27] Second, although its full significance is not entirely clear, the principle of proportionality contained in Article 3B(3) of the Treaty seems to recommend the use of flexible approaches. In a Community which is becoming increasingly heterogeneous, this principle could be used by some member states as an argument for the adoption of non-uniform solutions. Third, even if member states manage to agree on uniform standards, there is no guarantee that such standards will be uniformly applied at member state level. The same political and economic factors that conspire to create 'pollution havens' through lax regulation may indeed also exert a compromising effect on member state enforcement.[28] Finally, to the extent process standards are adopted

---

[27] See pp. 115–17 above.

[28] In the United States, most major environmental statutes provide for direct federal enforcement against the regulated enterprises when state enforcement is deficient. See, e.g., section 309 of the Clean Water Act, 33 USC para. 1,319(a) (1995); section 113 of the Clean Air Act, 42 USC para. 7,604(a)(2) (1983 and Supp. 1995); and section 3,008 of the Resource Conservation and Recovery Act, 33 USC 1,365(a)(2) (1983 and Supp. 1995). In addition to direct federal enforcement, major environmental statutes contain citizen-suit provisions allowing direct citizen enforcement of federal regulation through action in federal district courts against regulated enterprises. See, e.g., section 505(a)(1) of the Clean Water Act, 33 USC 1,365(a)(1) (1995); section 304(a)(1) of the Clean Air Act, 42 USC 7,604(a)(1) (1983 and Supp. 1995); and section 7,001(a)(1) of the Resource Conservation and Recovery Act, 42 USC 6,972(a)(1) (1983 and Supp. 1995). In the European Community, the enforcement process is much weaker since it essentially relies on the supervision of the Commission through the procedure contained in Article 169 of the Treaty. On the weaknesses of the Community enforcement system and the potential consequences on the conditions of competition in the internal market, see Geradin, 'Trade and Environmental Protection: Community Harmonization and National Environmental Standards', *Yearbook of European Law* 13 (1994), 151, 187.

under Article 130S, Article 130T authorizes member states to adopt stricter standards than Community standards.

Waste

In the area of waste, I have concentrated my analysis on two essential issues: (i) to what extent the Community and US federal legislatures have harmonized waste-disposal standards and the impact of such a harmonization on the interstate movements of waste; and (ii) to what extent the legislatures have attempted to restrict, or at least control, the movements of waste between states.

Although to a different degree,[29] the Community and the US federal government have adopted legislation harmonizing waste-disposal standards applied by the states. The main objective of this legislation is to ensure a minimum level of environmental protection in all states. Harmonization of waste-disposal standards may, however, also have an effect on the interstate movements of waste. Since the cost of waste-disposal activities is influenced by the standards applicable to these activities, such harmonization should reduce cost disparities in waste disposal between states and, hence, the incentives for producers to transfer their waste to other states. Harmonization of waste-disposal standards may not, however, entirely prevent interstate movements of waste. As we have seen, the cost of waste disposal is also influenced by non-regulatory factors, such as the cost of land and labour. Even assuming that waste-disposal standards were perfectly harmonized at Community/ federal level,[30] waste would nevertheless continue to move to certain regions or states. Moreover, independently of the cost of waste disposal, there may be circumstances where interstate transfers of waste are rendered necessary by the shortage of waste-disposal facilities in some states. As we have seen, this shortage usually comes from the fact that, in a market where waste circulates freely, it is economically and politically convenient for states to export their waste to other states rather than to develop waste-disposal facilities on their territory (the NIMBY syndrome).

---

[29] The harmonization of waste-disposal standards in the Community is broad in scope (because it covers both hazardous and non-hazardous waste), but low in intensity (because Community standards are relatively lax). On the other hand, harmonization of waste-disposal standards by the US federal government is narrower in scope (because only hazardous wastes are subject to binding standards), but more intense (because harmonized hazardous-waste-disposal standards are extremely strict).

[30] As we have seen, this is not the case since Community and US federal waste legislation only provides for minimum harmonization. Nothing therefore prevents the states from adopting stricter standards than Community/federal harmonized standards.

In order to stimulate the creation of waste-disposal facilities in all states, there may be a need for some form of control on the interstate movements of waste.

As far as the control of the interstate movements of waste is concerned, the Community and the US federal government have relied on different options. In the Community, Regulation 259/93 on the transfrontier shipments of waste provides for a system of control on intra-Community shipments of waste through prior notification and consent of the relevant member state authorities.[31] Article 4.3.a.1 of Regulation 259/93 also authorizes member states to object systematically to certain categories of shipments of waste in order to implement the principles of proximity and self-sufficiency. The transfrontier shipment of waste is an issue of extreme political sensitivity in the Community and this provision reflects the anxiety of a number of member states to retain or regain some degree of sovereignty over that issue.[32] The product of many political compromises, Article 4.3.a.1 has been criticized by industry commentators who claim that this provision will allow member states to adopt protectionist measures, disrupt the integrated waste-management schemes developed by certain companies and generally lead to a high degree of inefficiency in waste disposal. On the other hand, as we have seen, one advantage of Article 4.3.a.1 is that, by preventing member states becoming free riders on the waste-disposal efforts of other member states, this provision could stimulate the development of adequate disposal capacity in all member states.

In the United States, Congress has so far refused to allow states to adopt restrictions on the interstate movements of waste. The prevalent view in Congress has been in favour of a free market in waste in which shipments can move freely to the most adequate waste-disposal facilities wherever located.[33] For reasons expressed above, the principal inconvenience of a free market in waste is that it gives an incentive to states to export their waste to other states rather than to develop sufficient disposal capacity within their borders. Frustrated by the courts' invalidation of their efforts

---

[31] See pp. 123–7 above.

[32] As we have seen, in the *Belgian Waste* case, the Court of Justice ruled that, as far as they concerned hazardous waste, the Walloon import restrictions were pre-empted by Directive 84/361 of 6 December 1984 on the supervision and control of the transfrontier shipments of hazardous waste. See pp. 17–18 above. Thanks to the presence of Article 4.3.a.1 in Regulation 259/93, member states will therefore regain the power to adopt restrictions on the movement of hazardous waste and retain the power to adopt such restrictions with regard to non-hazardous waste.

[33] See pp. 170–1 above.

to restrict imports of out-of-state waste, the receiving states have been seeking express authorization from Congress for such restrictions and there is now a strong prospect that Congress will pass legislation to this effect. To the extent such legislation is adopted, it is likely, however, to apply only to non-hazardous waste. There is recognition in Congress that the efficient management of hazardous waste can be better realized through economies of scale achievable by large, technically advanced, facilities located on a regional basis as opposed to a state basis.[34]

Legislation on the movements of waste in the Community and the United States may therefore eventually converge.[35] Increasingly, states, regions and local authorities will be responsible for the disposal of their non-hazardous waste and, to preserve their disposal resources, will be free to restrict the imports of such waste. A difference between the Community and the United States will, however, remain with regard to hazardous waste. While the Community is prepared to allow member states to adopt restrictions on the movements of hazardous waste,[36] the US Congress seems keen to preserve a national market for the management of such waste.[37]

The question of pre-emption

A central question with regard to the relationship between trade and environmental policies is whether, once the Community or the US federal government have legislated, states remain free to adopt stricter measures or are pre-empted from taking further action.[38] In Community law, it is necessary in order to address that question to distinguish between Community legislation adopted in the period prior to and that adopted following the SEA. In the period prior to the SEA, questions of pre-emption were sometimes solved in advance by the Community legislature when it expressly indicated whether a particular directive was exhaustive

---

[34] See J. T. Smith, 'The Challenge of Environmentally Sound and Efficient Regulation of Waste – The Need for Enhanced International Understanding', *Journal of Environmental Law* 5 (1993) at 103.

[35] *Ibid.* at 104.

[36] See, however, Article 4.3.2 of Regulation 259/93.

[37] See Smith, 'The Challenge of Environmentally Sound and Efficient Regulation of Waste' at 104.

[38] There does not seem to exist at present any detailed comparative study on the question of pre-emption in Community and United States law. For some general points of comparison see, however, K. Lenaerts, 'Constitutionalism and the Many Faces of Federalism', *American Journal of Comparative Law* 38 (1990), 205.

or if it permitted further member state action. In the absence of such guidance, the Court of Justice can be asked to interpret Community legislation to determine whether it occupies the field or leaves space for further member state action.[39] Since the adoption of the SEA, the answer to pre-emption questions is to be found in Articles 130T and 100A(4) of the Treaty which, under certain conditions, allow member states to apply environmental measures that are more stringent than Community measures. In the United States, determining the pre-emptive effect of US federal environmental legislation requires a very similar exercise to that required to determine the pre-emptive effect of pre-SEA Community environmental legislation. In the absence of provisions comparable to Articles 100A(4) or 130T in the US Constitution, pre-emption questions are solved either expressly by Congress or, in the absence of express Congressional guidance, by federal courts through an analysis of Congressional intent.[40] Given this conceptual affinity, I will first discuss and compare the pre-emptive effect of pre-SEA Community and US federal environmental legislation. I will then briefly discuss the implications of the introduction of Articles 100A(4) and 130T in the Treaty.

In the United States and in the Community in the period prior to the SEA, the US federal government and the Community legislature have sometimes expressly solved pre-emption questions by indicating whether harmonization legislation is exhaustive or allows further state action. In both systems, the degree of uniformity required by harmonization legislation has usually varied depending on the areas regulated. In the area of product standards, US federal and pre-SEA Community legislation has usually expressly pre-empted stricter state regulation on the ground that a high degree of uniformity is needed to facilitate interstate trade and avoid market fragmentation.[41] In a number of circumstances, techniques have, however, been used to allow states to adopt more exacting regulations than Community/federal harmonized regulations.[42] By contrast, in

---

[39] See pp. 132–3 above.

[40] See pp. 175–82 above.

[41] Compare, e.g., Article 9 of Directive 78/631 of 26 June 1978 on the approximation of the laws of the member states relating to the classification, packaging and labelling of dangerous preparations (pesticides), OJ 1978, L 206/13, with section 7,617 of the Clean Air Act, 42 USC para. 7,671(m) (1983 and Supp. 1995) (product regulations expressly pre-empting states from adopting stricter standards than harmonized standards).

[42] Compare, e.g., Article 2 of Directive 78/611 of 29 June 1978 on the approximation of the laws of the member states concerning the lead content of petrol, OJ 1978, L 197/19, with section 177 of the Clean Air Act, 42 USC para. 7,507 (1983 and Supp. 1995) (product regulations allowing states to adopt stricter standards than harmonized standards within certain limits).

the area of process standards, US federal and pre-SEA Community legislation has usually expressly provided for minimum harmonization.[43] The rationale is that what is needed in the area of process standards is the adoption of a lower regulatory limit to prevent states giving a competitive advantage to their industry by relaxing environmental regulations. On the other hand, there is no federal or Community interest in preventing stricter state regulations.

As in the case of process standards, US federal and pre-SEA Community waste-management legislation usually contains provisions allowing the states to adopt stricter regulations.[44] Contrary to the area of process standards, however, such provisions may create difficulties. On the one hand, it may seem desirable to authorize states to adopt stricter waste-disposal standards than Community/federal harmonized standards in order to take into account local conditions and generally improve the level of environmental safety of the waste-disposal facilities located on their territory. On the other hand, there may be circumstances where the main reason why states decide to adopt stricter standards is not to improve the level of environmental safety of their waste-disposal facilities but rather to drive these facilities outside their borders. By allowing states unilaterally to increase the stringency of their waste-disposal standards, anti-pre-emption may provide a fertile ground for NIMBY behaviour.[45] To avoid such behaviour, US federal courts have been asked in a number of cases to place limitations on the RCRA's anti-pre-emption provision. For example, in *Ensco Inc. v. Dumas*,[46] the court of Appeals for the Eighth Circuit ruled that, because it was motivated by NIMBY purposes rather

---

[43] Compare, e.g., Article 10 of Directive 76/464 of 4 May 1976 on pollution caused by certain dangerous substances discharged into the aquatic environment of the Community, OJ 1976, L 129/23, with section 1,370 of the Clean Water Act, 34 USC 1,370 (1995) (process-standards regulations expressly authorizing states to adopt stricter standards than harmonized standards).

[44] Compare Article 8 of Directive 78/319 of 20 March 1978 on toxic and dangerous waste, OJ 1978, L 84/43, with section 6,929 of the Resource Conservation and Recovery Act, 42 USC para. 6,929 (1995) (waste regulations expressly authorizing states to adopt stricter standards than harmonized standards).

[45] From that standpoint, waste-disposal standards and process standards raise diametrically opposed problems. While states may have an incentive to increase their waste-disposal standards in order to drive outside their borders certain waste-disposal activities whose environmental consequences outweigh their economic benefits, they may have an incentive to reduce their process standards in order to attract certain industrial activities whose economic benefits outweigh their environmental consequences. The NIMBY syndrome is therefore the mirror image of the race to the bottom.

[46] 807 F. 2d 743 (8th Cir. 1986).

than legitimate environmental concerns, a local regulation banning the disposal of hazardous waste could not be justified as a stricter measure under the RCRA's anti-pre-emption provision. So far, the Court of Justice has not been confronted with this question.[47]

In the absence of legislative guidance, the Supreme Court and the Court of Justice may be asked to infer whether a particular US federal or pre-SEA Community legislation is exhaustive or whether it leaves room for stricter state regulation. As we have seen, the Supreme Court has imposed clear limits on its doctrine of pre-emption. It has established a general presumption in favour of the preservation of state law: a state law may be pre-empted only if it is 'the clear and manifest purpose of Congress' that an area be exclusively federally regulated. It has also established a series of standards to determine when Congressional purpose to occupy a field may be inferred. In the specific area of environmental protection, the Supreme Court has been particularly reluctant to infer that federal statutes pre-empt more stringent state regulations. *Pacific Gas*, *Silkwood* v. *McGee*, *Granite Rock* and *Mortier* are recent cases where the Supreme Court has decided to uphold state environmental statutes against pre-emption challenges.[48] So far, the Court of Justice has not adopted similar restraints on its use of the doctrine of pre-emption. Unlike the Supreme Court, it has not instituted a general presumption in favour of the survival of member state law, and has been criticized for lacking direction in its pre-emption case law.[49] In the specific area of environmental protection, it is also difficult to find any particular trend in the court's pre-emption case law. There are only a few court decisions in this area and these are inconsistent.[50] Given the absence of well-defined criteria indicating in which circumstances Community legislation is considered as exhaustive,

---

[47] This could soon changed. Since all waste directives adopted since the entry into force of the SEA are based on Article 130S, member states retain the freedom to adopt stricter standards than Community standards on the basis of Article 130T. In order to protect their environment against the pollution created by certain waste-disposal activities, some member states may be tempted to use Article 130T in order to justify total bans on these activities. If member states were to adopt such bans, the question to be solved by the court would be whether such measures can be considered as stricter measures than Community measures compatible with Article 130T or as measures of an entirely different nature incompatible with Article 130T.

[48] See pp. 181–2 above.

[49] See E. Cross, 'Pre-emption of Member State Law in the European Community: A Framework for Analysis', *Common Market Law Review* 28 (1992), 447.

[50] Compare, e.g., Case 148/78, *Ratti* [1979] ECR 1,629, 1,643 and Case 278/85, *Commission* v. *Denmark* [1987] ECR 4,069, 4,087 (stricter national standards pre-empted by Community measures of harmonization) with Case 125/88, *Nijman* [1989] ECR 3,533, 3,546 (stricter national standards not pre-empted by a Community measure of harmonization).

it is difficult to predict how much latitude is left to the member states by pre-SEA Community environmental legislation.

With regard to the legislation adopted after the SEA, pre-emption questions have to be answered with reference to the safeguard clauses contained in Articles 130T and 100A(4) of the Treaty.[51] Article 130T allows member states to adopt more protective measures than Community measures adopted under Article 130S, i.e., most Community instruments regulating waste, as well as directives harmonizing process standards that principally aim at protecting the environment. Since pre-SEA Community legislation covering these matters generally provided for schemes of minimum harmonization, Article 130T essentially confirms pre-SEA Community practice regarding pre-emption. Article 100A(4) authorizes member states under certain conditions to apply stricter measures than the Community harmonization measures adopted under Article 100A. Article 100A(4) has generated criticism since, contrary to traditional pre-SEA practice, it authorizes member states to apply stricter product standards than Community harmonized standards, thus threatening the accomplishment of the single market. Since the adoption of the SEA, Article 100A(4) has, however, only been used once by Germany in order to maintain its stricter limits on the use of PCP in products. As with their pre-SEA counterpart, post-SEA product-standards harmonization directives have in practice retained a high degree of uniformity.

[51] See pp. 134–42 above.

Conclusion

In this study, I have identified three areas of regulation where conflicts may arise between trade and environmental protection. I have examined how the Court of Justice and the Supreme Court (Part 1) and the Community and the US federal legislatures (Part 2) have attempted to deal with such conflicts. The objective of this conclusion is (i) to highlight the main findings made in Parts 1 and 2; and (ii) to place the question of the relationship between trade and environmental protection in the broader context of the world trading system.

One of the central findings of this study is that the relationship between trade and environmental protection varies considerably depending on the area of environmental regulation in question. Even if equally designed to protect the environment, state regulations governing product standards, process standards and the movement and disposal of waste raise trade issues that are conceptually distinct. There is no one conflict between trade and environmental protection, but several kinds of conflict depending on which of these areas of environmental regulation is involved. Only the instruments to solve such conflicts (i.e., judicial and legislative intervention) remain constant. But, again, the usefulness of these instruments varies considerably depending on the area of environmental regulation in question.

In the area of product standards, the conflicts between trade and environmental protection have traditionally been solved through a mix of negative and positive harmonization. The Court of Justice and the Supreme Court have respectively used Articles 30ff of the Treaty and the dormant Commerce Clause doctrine to invalidate state standards which burden trade in an unacceptable manner. However, judicial intervention has mainly a corrective effect: it can only remove particular obstacles to trade. As a result, when the obstacles created by inconsistent product standards are widespread, the Community and US federal legislatures have been called on to harmonize such standards. Due to the combination of such judicial and legislative interventions, the Community and the United States systems have generally managed to ensure a high degree of unity in their respective markets in products.

This does not mean that there has been no place for regulatory diversity. The Court of Justice and the Supreme Court have ruled that it is only when they are disproportionate that non-discriminatory state product standards are invalid. State product standards imposing a 'reasonable' burden on interstate trade will therefore withstand judicial scrutiny.[1] Moreover, even though product-standards legislation has traditionally provided for total harmonization regimes, the Community and US federal legislatures have usually allowed some degree of regulatory flexibility in such regimes by authorizing states, under strictly defined limits, to apply stricter standards than Community/federal harmonized standards.[2] In the area of product standards a fair balance has therefore generally been struck between the Community/federal interest in regulatory uniformity and the state interest in environmental diversity.

If negative harmonization has played an important role in the area of product standards, it has played virtually no role in the area of process standards. Variations in the level of stringency of state environmental process standards may create distortions of competition between states. However, the traditional free-movement-of-goods case law of the Court of Justice and the Supreme Court appears to offer little protection to states whose industrial competitiveness is harmed by other states' lax process standards. Although the adoption by one state of lax process standards may distort trade, it does not as such generate barriers to trade susceptible of falling within the scope of Article 30 of the Treaty or of the dormant Commerce Clause doctrine. By contrast, it seems that if a state enforcing strict process standards attempted to equalize the conditions of competition by imposing restrictions on the imports of products manufactured under lax process standards, it would probably violate Article 30 or the Commerce Clause.

Against this background, states applying strict process standards have usually attempted to influence the Community/federal legislative process

[1] We have seen, however, that it may not be easy for the courts to determine what is a 'reasonable' burden on interstate trade.

[2] In the Community context, the right of the member states to apply stricter standards than Community standards has now been institutionalized in Article 100A(4) of the Treaty.

to ensure the adoption of equivalent standards on a Community/national basis. In the United States, the industrialized northeastern states have used their superior political power in Congress to impose on southern states strict uniform technologically based standards. In the Community, Germany, usually supported by other pro-environment member states and the Commission, has often managed to export its strict domestic standards through Community harmonization. From that standpoint, it seems that environmental protection has benefited from economic integration. Rather than leading to a lowering of environmental process standards, economic integration has led to a 'levelling up', whereby states applying strict process standards have generally managed to ensure that states applying lax process standards realign their standards on their own stricter standards.

In the area of waste, environmental protection does not necessarily benefit from economic integration. In a market where waste circulates freely, it is tempting for states to avoid the political and economic costs of creating waste-disposal facilities on their territory by sending their waste to other states. The result of such NIMBY behaviour may be to create a shortage of waste-disposal facilities in the free-trade area, as well as serious environmental damage in the receiving states. In the *Belgian Waste* case, the Court of Justice acknowledged this problem by authorizing the Belgian Region of Wallonia to impose restrictions on the shipments of non-domestic solid waste. The court justified these restrictions on the grounds that 'waste should be disposed as close as possible to the place where it is produced' (proximity) and that 'it is up to each region, commune or other local entity to take appropriate measures to receive, process and dispose its own waste' (self-sufficiency). This restrictive approach to the movements of waste was confirmed in Regulation 259/93 on the transfrontier movements of waste, which authorizes member states to object systematically to certain categories of shipments of waste in order to enforce the principles of proximity and self-sufficiency. Taken together, these developments seem to indicate that, in the area of waste, the Community has developed a *ius singulare* based on the principle that free movement should be the exception rather than the rule.[3]

In the United States, the Supreme Court has taken a very tough line on state measures designed to restrict interstate shipments of waste. In a number of decisions, the court has considered these restrictions as

---

[3] See opinion of Advocate-General Tesauro in Case C-155/91, *Commission* v. *Council* [1993] ECR I-939 at para. 9.

protectionist measures rather than legitimate state environmental measures. Moreover, unlike the Community legislature, Congress has so far failed to regulate the movements of waste between states. American waste law is, however, in evolution. The strict application of the dormant Commerce Clause doctrine to the movement of waste has had the effect that a number of states have become dumping grounds for the rest of the nation. Frustrated by the courts' invalidation of their efforts to restrict imports of out-of-state waste, these states have been seeking for a number of years express authorization from Congress for such restrictions, and there is now a strong prospect that Congress will grant such an authorization.[4] As in Community law, some degree of self-sufficiency in waste disposal may soon be required in United States federal law.

One limitation of this study is that, largely for reasons of space, it has exclusively focused on the *internal* aspects of the relationship between trade and environmental protection in the Community and United States systems. But this relationship has also important *external* or *global* aspects. Because of the increasing globalization of trade, Community and United States environmental policies will be increasingly influenced by the trade and environmental policies of other nations or trading blocs, as well as by the policies developed within the framework of the World Trade Organization (WTO).[5] As will be seen below, this external influence will be particularly significant in the area of product and process standards.

Global aspects will have a growing impact on the regulation of product standards in the Community and United States. Inconsistent product standards impede interstate trade and create market fragmentation. This is true in the context of integrated markets such as the Community and United States. But it is also true in the context of the world market where inconsistent product standards may deny manufacturers the ability to realize economies of scale in production and distribution. The Community and United States experiences suggest two solutions to this problem. A first solution is for a judicial body to invalidate state standards that impose undue burdens on trade. In the international context, this form of negative harmonization could be realized through the disciplines imposed by GATT[6] as well as the Technical Barriers to Trade Agreement

---

[4] As we have seen, such an authorization is likely, however, to be limited to non-hazardous waste. See pp. 174–5 above.

[5] Generally on the WTO, see Dillon, 'The World Trade Organization: A New Legal Order for World Trade', *Michigan Journal of International Law* 16 (1995), 349.

[6] General Agreement on Tariffs and Trade, 30 October 1947, 51 Stat. A11, 55 UNTS 187.

(TBT)[7] and Sanitary and Phytosanitary Agreement (SPS),[8] which are both a part of the Uruguay Round package. Another solution to the problem is to adopt international standards and ensure market access to products complying with such standards.[9]

This is not the place to discuss the extent to which product standards have been negatively or positively harmonized at international level.[10] However, to the extent that such a negative or positive harmonization takes place, it can have important effects on Community and United States product standards. As far as negative harmonization is concerned, strict GATT disciplines could place limits on the ability of the Community and the United States to enact product standards pursuing a high level of environmental protection. To the extent these standards impose an important burden on external trade, they could be found incompatible with international trade law.[11] As far as positive harmonization is concerned, international harmonization of product standards could also have the effect of lowering the level of protection imposed by product standards in the Community and United States. Because of the rule of unanimity which prevails at the international level, there is a danger that international standards will reflect a lowest common denominator.[12] If

---

[7] Agreement on Technical Barriers to Trade, GATT Doc. MTN/FA II-A1A-6 (15 December 1993) in 'Final Act Embodying the Results of the Uruguay Round of Multilateral Trade Negotiations' (hereinafter 'Uruguay Round'), reprinted in ILM 33 (1994), 9. Generally on the TBT Agreement and its impact on domestic product standards, see J. Cameron and A. Ward, 'The Uruguay Round's Technical Barriers to Trade Agreement' (WWF Research Report, 1993).

[8] Agreement on the Application of Sanitary and Phytosanitary Measures, GATT Doc. MTN/FA II-A1A-4 (15 December 1993) in 'Uruguay Round'. Generally on the SPS Agreement and its implications on domestic product standards, see J. Barcello III, 'Product Standards to Protect the Local Environment – The GATT and the Uruguay Round Sanitary and Phytosanitary Agreement', *Cornell International Law Journal* 27 (1994), 755.

[9] In this regard, it should be noted that the TBT and SPS Agreements encourage their members to take a full part in the harmonization process, as well as to base their domestic standards on international standards when such standards exist. See Articles 2.4 and 2.6 of the TBT Agreement and para. 12 of the SPS Agreement.

[10] On this aspect, see S. Charnovitz, 'Environmental Harmonization and Trade Policy' in Zaelke D. et al. (eds.), *Trade and the Environment – Law, Economics and Policy* (Washington, DC: Island Press, 1993) at 267.

[11] See P. Goldman, 'The Legal Effects of Trade Agreements on Domestic Health and Environmental Regulation', *Journal of Environmental Law and Litigation* 7 (1992), 11.

[12] Environmentalists have also criticized the international organizations setting certain kinds of product standards, such as, for example, the Codex Alimentarius Commission, for operating largely in secret, with extensive industry input, but without the participation of environmental-protection or consumer interests. See, e.g., P. Goldman, 'Resolving the Trade and Environment Debate: In Search of a Neutral Forum and Neutral Principles', *Washington and Lee Law Review* 49 (1992), 1,279, 1,287.

compliance with such standards ensures access to the Community and United States markets, environmentally unsafe products could find their way to these markets.[13]

Global aspects will also be important in the area of process standards. Inconsistent process standards may create distortions of competition and incentives for industrial relocation. These distortions are significant in the context of integrated markets such as the Community and the United States. But they are even more significant in the context of the world market where, with greater heterogeneity, bigger differences can be found in the level of stringency of process standards between states. The Community and the United States experiences suggest that the solution to such distortions is the adoption of compulsory minimum process standards applicable to all states.[14] Again, this is not the place to discuss the extent to which process standards have been harmonized at international level.[15] But if such a minimum harmonization were not to take place, competitiveness concerns may well have a depressing effect on process standards regulation in the Community and the United States.[16] In the future, the level of stringency of environmental process standards in the Community and the United States may therefore be as much influenced by external factors as by internal factors.[17]

---

[13] *Ibid.*

[14] Another possible solution is to allow states applying strict standards to impose trade restrictions on products that have been manufactured under lax process standards. At the present time, process-related trade restrictions do not, however, appear to be a valid option. First, as we have seen above, GATT panels found in the *Mexican Tuna* cases such restrictions to be incompatible with GATT. Moreover, even if process-related trade restrictions were compatible with GATT, they would still not be effective to create a level playing field since the industries of the state imposing such restrictions would be protected on their domestic market but not on the international market.

[15] On this aspect, see R. Stewart, 'Environmental Regulation and International Competitiveness', *Yale Law Journal* 102 (1993), 2,039, 2,100.

[16] See, e.g., A. Aman, 'A Global Perspective on Current Regulatory Reform: Rejection, Relocation, or Reinvention?' *Indiana Journal of Global and Legal Studies* 2 (1995), 429 (arguing that the existence of global competition in general contributes to an overall political context that encourages domestic deregulatory reform proposals).

[17] As a matter of fact, internal factors have already considerably influenced the regulatory process in these legal orders. As we have seen above, the deregulatory ideology of the Reagan and Bush administrations was partly motivated by concerns over the competitiveness of American industry. See pp. 154–5 above. Competitiveness concerns have also influenced the Community regulatory process. They were, for example, clearly responsible for the Community's failure to adopt a carbon tax. More recently, such concerns have also induced the European Commission to agree on a partial deregulation of the biotechnology sector. See 'EU Commission Agrees to Deregulate Biotechnology', *Environment Watch*, 3 June 1994, at 1.

The preceding remarks suggest that the relationship between trade and environmental protection will increasingly take the form of a three-level game, involving not only member states and the Community/US federation, but also other nations and trading entities.[18] By focusing on the internal aspects of the relationship between trade and environmental protection in the Community and United States systems, this study has attempted to contribute to the understanding of the first two levels. Further studies will have to concentrate on the relationship between these first two levels and the third, international, level.

[18] See, *mutatis mutandis*, R. Putnam, 'Diplomacy and Domestic Politics: The Logic of Two-Level Games', *International Organization* 42 (1988), 427.

Bibliography

EUROPEAN COMMUNITY LAW

Books

Abraham, F., Deketelaere, K. and Stuyck, J. (eds.), *Recent Economic and Legal Developments in European Environmental Policy* (Leuven University Press, 1995)

Burrows, F., *Free Movement in European Community Law* (Oxford: Clarendon Press, 1987)

de Sadeleer, N., *Le Droit Communautaire et les Déchets* (Paris, Brussels: LGDJ, Bruylant, 1995)

Farr, S., *Harmonization of Technical Standards in the European Community* (London: Chancery, 1992)

Faure, M., Vervaele, J. and Weale, A., *Environmental Standards in the European Union in an Interdisciplinary Framework* (Maklu, Nomos, Blackstone, Bruylant, Schultes, 1994)

Gormley, L., *Prohibiting Restrictions on Trade within the EEC* (Amsterdam, New York, Oxford: North-Holland, 1985)

Hannequart, J. P., *Le Droit Européen des Déchets* (Brussels: IBGE, 1993)

Johnson, S. and Corcelle, G., *L'Autre Europe 'Verte': La Politique Communautaire de l'Environnement* (Paris: Nathan – Labor/RTL, 1987)

   The Environmental Policy of the European Communities (London: Graham & Trotman, 1989)

Kapteyn, P. and Verloren van Themaat, P., *Introduction to the Law of the European Communities* (Deventer, Boston: Kluwer, 2nd edn, by Gormley, 1990)

Kramer, L., *EEC Treaty and Environmental Protection* (London: Sweet & Maxwell, 1990)

   Focus on European Environmental Law (London: Sweet & Maxwell, 1992)

   European Environmental Law Casebook (London: Sweet & Maxwell, 1994)

   EC Treaty and Environmental Law (London: Sweet & Maxwell, 1995)

Oliver, P., *Free Movements of Goods in the EEC* (London: European Law Centre, 2nd edn, 1988)

Slot, P. J., *Technical and Administrative Obstacles to Trade* (Leyden: Sijthoff, 1975)
Von Wilmowsky, P., *Abfallwirtschaft im Binnenmarkt* (Dusseldorf: Werner Verlag, 1990)
Weatherill, S. and Beaumont, P., *EC Law* (London: Penguin, 1993)
  Law and Integration in the European Union (Oxford: Clarendon Press, 1995)
Wyatt, D. and Dashwood, A., *European Community Law* (London: Sweet & Maxwell, 3rd edn, 1993)

Articles
Barents, R., 'The Internal Market Unlimited: Some Observations on the Legal Basis of Community Legislation', *Common Market Law Review* 30 (1993), 85
Béraud, R. C., 'Fondements Juridiques de la Protection de l'Environnement dans le Traité de Rome', *Revue du Marché Commun* (1979), 35
Bradley, K., 'The European Court and the Legal Basis of Community Legislation', *European Law Review* 13 (1988), 379
  'L'Arrêt Dioxide de Titane – Un Jugement de Salomon?' *Revue Trimestrielle de Droit Européen* (1992), 609
Bribosia, H., 'Subsidiarité et Répartition des Compétences entre la Communauté et les Etats Membres', *Revue du Marché Unique Européen* (1992), 165
Brinkhorst, L., 'Subsidiarity and EC Environment Policy', *European Environmental Law Review* (1993), 3
Cass, D., 'The Word that Saves Maastricht? The Principle of Subsidiarity and the Division of Powers within the Community', *Common Market Law Review* 29 (1992), 1,107
Chalmers, D., 'Free Movement of Goods within the European Community: An Unhealthy Addiction to Scotch Whisky?' *International and Comparative Law Quarterly* 42 (1993), 269
  'Repackaging the Internal Market – The Ramifications of the Keck Judgment', *European Law Review* 19 (1994), 585
  'Community Policy on Waste Management – Managing Environmental Decline Gently', *Yearbook of European Law* 14 (1994), 257
Clarck, J. and Arnold, M., 'The Danish Bottles Case' in *The Greening of World Trade* (US Environmental Protection Agency, 1993)
Close, G., 'Harmonization of Laws: Use and Abuse of Powers under the EC Treaty?' *European Law Review* 6 (1978), 461
Collins, K., 'Plans and Prospects for the European Parliament in Shaping Future Environmental Policy', *European Environmental Law Review* (1995), 74
Constantinesco, V., 'La Subsidiarité Comme Principe Constitutionel de l'Union Européenne', *Aussenwirtschaft* (1991), 439
Crosby, S., 'The Single Market and the Rule of Law', *European Law Review* 16 (1991), 451
Cross, E., 'Pre-emption of Member State Law in the European Community: A Framework for Analysis', *Common Market Law Review* 28 (1992), 447
Currall, J., 'Some Aspects of the Relation between Articles 30–36 and Article 100

of the EEC Treaty, with a Closer Look to Optional Harmonization', *Yearbook of European Law* 3 (1984), 187

Dashwood, A., 'Hastening Slowly: The Community's Path Towards Harmonization' in Wallace, Wallace and Webb (eds.), *Policy-Making in the European Community* (London: Wiley, 1983), 177

'Community Legislative Procedures in the Era of the European Union', *European Law Review* 19 (1994), 343

de Bruycker, P. and Morrens, P., 'Qu'est ce qu'un Déchet dans l'Union Européenne?' *Aménagement – Environnement* (1993/3), 154

de Burca, G., 'The Principle of Proportionality and its Application in EC Law', *Yearbook of European Law* 13 (1994), 105

Dehousse, R., 'Does Subsidiarity Really Matter?' European University Institute Working Paper Law No. 92/32

'Completing the Internal Market: Institutional Constraints and Challenges' in Bieber *et al.* (eds.), *1992: One European Market* (Baden-Baden: Nomos, 1988), 311

'Integration v. Regulation? On the Dynamics of Regulation in the European Community', *Journal of Common Market Studies* 30 (1992), 383

Demaret, P., 'Environmental Policy and Commercial Policy: The Emergence of Trade-Related Measures (TREMs) in the External Relations of the European Community' in Maresceau (ed.), *The European Community's Commercial Policy After 1992: The Legal Dimension* (Martinus Nijhoff, 1993), 315

Demaret, P. and Stewardson, R., 'Border Tax Adjusments under GATT and EC Law and General Implications for Environmental Taxes', *Journal of World Trade* 28 (1994), 5

Demiray, D., 'The Movement of Goods in a Green Market', *Legal Issues of European Integration* (1994/1), 73

de Sadeleer, N., 'La Reconnaissance du Principe de Proximité comme Autorisant les Etats Membres à Interdire l'Importation des Déchets dont les Transfers n'ont pas Eté Harmonisés par une Règle de Droit Communautaire Dérivé: Une Victoire à la Pyrrhus?' *Aménagement – Environnement* (1993/2), 166

'Observations – Les Limites Posées à la Libre Circulation des Déchets et Exigences de Protection de l'Environnement', *Cahiers de Droit Européen* (1993), 693

'L'Agrément des Collectes de Déchets au Regard des Règles du Droit Communautaire', *Aménagement – Environnement* (1993/4), 238

'La Libre Circulation des Déchets et le Marché Unique Européen', *Revue du Marché Unique Européen* (1994), 71

'Les Emballages, l'Environnement et le Marché Intérieur: Une Singulière Trilogie', *Revue du Marché Unique Européen* (1995/2), 87

de Villeneuve, C., 'Les Mouvements Transfrontier des Déchets Dangereux (Convention de Bâle et Droit Communautaire)', *Revue du Marché Commun* (1990), 568

Dwyer, S., 'EC Directive 91/173 Pertaining to Dangerous Substances: When May a Member State Impose Environmental Restrictions which are Stricter than those Mandated by the European Community?', *Boston College International and Comparative Law Review* 17 (1994), 127

Ehlermann, C. D., 'How Flexible is Community Law? An Unusual Approach to the Concept of "Two Speeds"', *Michigan Law Review* 82 (1984), 1,274

'The Internal Market Following the Single European Act', *Common Market Law Review* 24 (1987), 361

Emerson, M., 'The Appropriate Level of Regulation in Europe: Local, National or Community Wide?' *Economic Policy* (1989), 467

Emiliou, N., 'Subsidiarity: An Effective Barrier against "the Enterprises of Ambition"?' *European Law Review* 17 (1992), 383

'Opening the Pandora's Box: The Legal Basis of Community Measures before the Court of Justice', *European Law Review* 19 (1994), 488

Farquhar, J. T., 'The Policies of the European Community Towards the Environment – The "Dangerous Substance" Directive', *Journal of Planning and Environmental Law* (1983), 145

Fluck, J., 'The Term "Waste" in EU Law', *European Environmental Law Review* (1994), 79

Flynn, J., 'How Will Article 100A(4) Work? A Comparison with Article 93', *Common Market Law Review* 24 (1987), 689

Folmer, H. and Howe, C., 'Environmental Problems and Policy in the Single European Market', *Environmental Resources and Economics* 1 (1991), 17

Freestone, D., 'European Community Environmental Policy and Law', *Journal of Law and Society* 18 (1991), 135

Gaudissart, M. A., 'La Subsidiarité: Facteur de (Dés)intégration Européenne?' *Journal des Tribunaux* (1993), 173

Geradin, D., 'Trade and Environmental Protection: Community Harmonization and National Environmental Standards', *Yearbook of European Law* 13 (1994), 151

'Balancing Free Trade and Environmental Protection – The Interplay between the European Court of Justice and the Community Legislator' in Cameron, Demaret and Geradin (eds.), *Trade and Environmental Protection – The Search for Balance* (London: Cameron & May, 1994), 204

Geradin, D. and Stewardson, R., 'Trade and Environment: Some Lessons from *Castlemaine Tooheys* (Australia) and *Danish Bottles* (European Community)', *International and Comparative Law Quarterly* 44 (1995), 41

Gérard, A., 'Les Limites et les Moyens Juridiques de l'Intervention des Communautés Européennes en Matière de Protection de l'Environnement', *Cahiers de Droit Européen* (1975), 14

Golub, J., 'The Pivotal Role of British Sovereignty in EC Environmental Policy', European University Institute Working Paper RSC No. 94/17

Gormley, L., 'Recent Case Law on the Free Movement of Goods: Some Hot Potatoes', *Common Market Law Review* 27 (1990), 825

Grabitz, E. and Langenheine, B., 'Legal Problems Related to a Proposed "Two-Tier" System of Integration within the Community', *Common Market Law Review* 18 (1981), 33

Grabitz, E. and Zacker, C., 'Scope for Action by the EC Member States under EEC Law: The Example of Environmental Taxes and Subsidies', *Common Market Law Review* 26 (1989), 423

Gulman, C., 'The Single European Act – Some Remarks from a Danish Perspective', *Common Market Law Review* 24 (1987), 31

Guruswamy *et al.*, 'The Development and Impact of an EEC Directive: The Control of Discharge of Mercury to the Aquatic Environment', *Journal of Common Market Studies* 22 (1983), 71

Haagsma, A., 'The European Community's Environmental Policy: A Case Study in Federalism', *Fordham International Law Journal* 12 (1989), 311

Hannequart, J. P., 'Le Règlement Européen sur les Mouvements de Déchets', *Aménagement – Environnement* (1993/2), 67

Hession, M. and Macrory, R., 'Maastricht and the Environmental Policy of the European Community: Legal Issues for a New Environmental Policy' in O'Keeffe and Twomey (eds.), *Legal Issues of the Maastricht Treaty* (London: Wiley, 1993), 151

Hunter, R., 'Standardization and the Environment', *International Environmental Reporter*, 10 March 1993, 185

Jadot, B., 'Observations – Mesures Nationales de Police de l'Environnement, Libre Circulation des Marchandises et Proportionalité', *Cahiers de Droit Européen* (1990), 408

Jans, J., 'Envenredigheid: Ja, Maar Wartussen?' *Sociale-Economische Wetgeuing* (1992), 751

'Waste Policy and European Community Law: Does the EEC Treaty Provide a Suitable Framework for Regulating Waste?' *Ecology Law Quarterly* 20 (1993), 165

'Self-Sufficiency in European Waste Law', *European Environmental Law Review* (1994), 223

Joseph, T., 'Preaching Heresy: Permitting Member States to Enforce Stricter Environmental Laws than the European Community', *Yale Journal of International Law* 20 (1995), 277

Kelly, M., 'International Regulation of Transfrontier Hazardous Waste Shipments: A New EEC Environmental Directive', *Texas International Law Journal* 21 (1985), 85

Koppen, I., 'The European Community's Environment Policy: From the Summit in Paris, 1972 to the Single European Act', European University Institute Working Paper No. 88/328

'The Role of the European Court of Justice in the Development of the European Community Environmental Policy', European University Institute Working Paper EPU No. 92/18

Kramer, L., 'The Single European Act and Environment Protection: Reflections on Several New Provisions in Community Law', *Common Market Law Review* 24 (1987), 659

'Community Environmental Law – Towards a Systematic Approach', *Yearbook of European Law* 11 (1991), 151

'Environmental Protection and Article 30 of the Treaty', *Common Market Law Review* 30 (1993), 111

'Community Environmental Law under the Maastricht Treaty on European Union and the Fifth Environmental Action Programme' in Abraham, F., Deketelaere, K. and Stuyck, J. (eds.), *Recent Economic and Legal Developments in European Environmental Policy* (Leuven University Press, 1995), 75

Langeheine, B., 'Le Rapprochement des Législations Nationales selon l'Article 100A du Traité: L'Harmonisation Communautaire face aux Exigences de Protection Nationale', *Revue du Marché Commun* (1989), 347

Lecrenier, S., 'Les Articles 30 et Suivants CEE et les Procédures de Contrôle Prévues par la Directive 83/189/CEE', *Revue du Marché Commun* (1985), 6

Lenaerts, K., 'The Principle of Subsidiarity and the Environment in the European Union: Keeping the Balance of Federalism', *Fordham International Law Journal* 17 (1994), 846

Lenaerts, K. and van Ypersele, P., 'Le Principe de Subsidiarité et son Contexte: Etude de l'Article 3B du Traité CE', *Cahiers de Droit Européen* (1994), 3

Lipsius, J., 'The 1996 Intergovernmental Conference', *European Law Review* 20 (1995), 235

Lomas, O., 'Environmental Protection, Economic Conflict and the European Community', *McGill Law Journal* 33 (1988), 506

London, C., 'Droit Communautaire de l'Environnement', *Revue Trimestrielle de Droit Européen* (1994), 291

London, C. and Llamas, M., 'Packaging Laws in France and in Germany', *Journal of Environmental Law* 6 (1994), 1

Macrory, R., 'The Enforcement of Community Environmental Laws: Some Critical Issues', *Common Market Law Review* 29 (1992), 347

'European Community Water Law', *Ecology Law Quarterly* 20 (1993), 119

Marenco, G., 'Pour une Interprétation Traditionelle de la Notion de Mesure d'Effet Equivalent à une Restriction Quantitative', *Cahiers de Droit Européen* (1984), 291

Mattera, A., 'Protectionism inside the EC', *Journal of World Trade Law* 18 (1984), 283

'L'Article du Traité CEE, la Jurisprudence "Cassis de Dijon" et le Principe de Reconnaissance Mutuelle', *Revue du Marché Unique Européen* (1992), 13

'De l'Arrêt "Dassonville" à l'Arrêt "Keck": L'Obscure Clarté d'une Jurisprudence Riche en Principes Novateurs et en Contradictions', *Revue du Marché Unique Européen* (1994/1), 117

McGee, A. and Weatherill, S., 'The Evolution of the Single Market – Harmonization or Liberalization', *Modern Law Review* 53 (1990), 578

Morgan de Rivery, E. and Note-Pinte, F., 'La Gestion des Déchets Industriels – Action Passée, Présente et Future de la Communauté', *Revue du Marché Commun* (1992), 414

Pelkmans, J., 'The New Approach to Technical Harmonization and Standardization', *Journal of Common Market Studies* 25 (1986), 249

'Regulation and the Single Market: An Economic Perspective' in Siebert (ed.), *The Completion of the Internal Market* (Tübingen: Mohr, 1989), 388

Pescatore, P., 'Some Critical Remarks on the Single European Act', *Common Market Law Review* 24 (1987), 9

Pinder, J., 'Positive Integration and Negative Integration: Some Problems of Economic Union in the EEC', *World Today* 24 (1968), 88

Rehbinder, E., 'Environmental Regulation through Fiscal and Economic Incentives in a Federalist System', *Ecology Law Quarterly* 20 (1993), 57

Reich, N., 'Competition between Legal Orders: A New Paradigm for EC Law', *Common Market Law Review* 29 (1992), 861

Renaudière, P., 'Le Droit Communautaire de l'Environnement après Maastricht', *Aménagement – Environnement* (1992), 70

Roelants du Vivier, F. and Hannequart, J. P., 'Une Nouvelle Stratégie Européenne pour l'Environnement dans le Cadre de l'Acte Unique', *Revue du Marché Commun* (1988), 225

Salter, J., 'Environmental Standards and Testing', *European Environmental Law Review* (1993), 276

Sands, P., 'Environment, Community and International Law', *Harvard International Law Journal* 30 (1989), 393

   'EC Environmental Legislation Law: The ECJ and Common-Interest Groups', *Modern Law Review* 53 (1990), 685

   'European Community Environmental Law: The Evolution of a Regional Regime of International Environmental Protection', *Yale Law Journal* 100 (1991), 2,511

Schemmel, M. and de Regt, B., 'The European Court of Justice and the Environmental Protection Policy of the European Community', *Boston College International and Comparative Law Review* 17 (1994), 53

Scheuer, H., 'Aspects Juridiques de la Protection de l'Environnement dans le Marché Commun', *Revue du Marché Commun* (1975), 441

Schmidt, A., 'Transboundary Movements of Waste under EC Law: The Emerging Regulatory Framework', *Journal of Environmental Law* 4 (1992), 57

   'Trade in Waste Under Community Law' in Cameron, Demaret and Geradin (eds.), *Trade and the Environment – The Search for Balance* (Cameron & May, 1994) at 184

Schnutenhaus, J., 'Integrated Pollution Prevention and Control: New German Initiatives in the European Environment Council', *European Environmental Law Review* (1994), 323

Schultz, T. and Crockett, C., 'Developing a Unified European Environmental Law and Policy', *Boston College International and Comparative Law Review* 14 (1991), 301

Sexton, T., 'Enacting National Environmental Laws More Stringent than Other States' Laws in the European Community: *Re Disposal Beer Cans: Commission v. Denmark*', *Cornell International Law Journal* 24 (1991), 563

Skroback, A., 'Even a Sacred Cow Must Live in a Green Pasture: The Proximity Principle, Free Movement of Goods, and Regulation 259/93 on the Transfrontier Waste Shipments within the EC', *Boston College International and Comparative Law Review* 17 (1994), 85

Sloan, R. and Carbonnel, P., 'Exemptions from Harmonization Measures under Article 100A(4): The Second Authorization of the German Ban on PCP', *European Environmental Law Review* (1995), 45

Slotboom, M., 'State Aid in Community Law: A Broad or Narrow Definition?' *European Law Review* 20 (1995), 289

Slynn of Hadley, Lord, 'The European Community and the Environment', *Journal of Environmental Law* (1993), 261

Smith, H., 'Recent Development in EC Environmental Law, with a Particular Emphasis on the Conflict between Free Movement and the Environment and the Recent Wallonia Decision of the European Court of Justice', *Elsa Law Review* (1993), 1

Smith, T. and Hunter, R., 'The European Community Environmental Legal System', *Environmental Law Reporter* (1992), 10,116

Sommer, J., 'Les Déchets, de l'Autosuffisance et de la Libre Circulation des Marchandises', *Revue du Marché Commun* (1994), 246

Soumastre, S., 'Les Leçons d'une Expérience pour une Politique de Gestion des Déchets Industriels en France: La Récupération des Huiles Usagées' in *Les Déchets Industriels et l'Environnement* (Paris: PUF, 1984), 29

Steiner, J., 'Drawing Lines: Uses and Abuses of Article 30 EEC', *Common Market Law Review* 29 (1992), 749

Strozzi, G., 'Le Principe de Subsidiarité dans la Perspective de l'Union Européenne: Une Enigme et Beaucoup d'Attentes', *Revue Trimestrielle de Droit Européen* (1994), 374

Stuyck, J., 'Le Traitement des Déchets dans la (Non-)Réalisation du Marché Intérieur', *Journal des Tribunaux Européen* (1994), 10

Sun, J. M. and Pelkmans, J., 'Regulatory Competition in the Single Market', *Journal of Common Market Studies* 33 (1995), 67

Taylor, D., Diprose, G. and Duffy, M., 'EC Environmental Policy and the Control of Water Pollution: The Implementation of Directive 76/464 in Perspective', *Journal of Common Market Studies* 24 (1986), 225

Thieffry, P., 'Politique de l'Environnement et Subsidiarité: L'Exemple des Comportements Environnementaux de l'Entreprise', *Revue du Marché Unique Européen* (1994/3), 177

Tiebout, C.,'A Pure Theory of Local Expenditures', *Journal of Political Economy* 64 (1956), 416

Toth, A., 'The Principle of Subsidiarity in the Maastricht Treaty', *Common Market Law Review* 29 (1992), 1,079

'Is Subsidiarity Justiciable?' *European Law Review* 19 (1994), 268

van den Bergh R., 'The Subsidiarity Principle in European Community Law: Some Insights from Law and Economics', *Maastricht Journal of European and Comparative Law* 1 (1994), 337

van den Bergh, R., Faure, M. and Lefevere, J., 'The Subsidiarity Principle in European Environmental Law: An Economic Analysis', paper prepared for the Conference on the Law and Economics of the Environment, Oslo, 8–9 June 1995

Vandermeersch, D., 'The Single European Act and the Environmental Policy of the European Community', *European Law Review* 12 (1987), 407

'Het Vrije Verkeer van Alfvalstoffen binen de Europese Gemeenschap', *Tijdschrift Voor Milieurecht* (1992), 84

van Empel, M., 'The 1992 Programme: Interaction between the Legislator and the Judiciary', *Legal Issues of European Integration* (1992/1), 1

van Gerven, W., 'Principe de Proportionalité, Abus de Droit et Droits Fondamentaux', *Journal des Tribunaux* (1992), 305

Veldkamp, A., 'Community Waste Policy and the Internal Market: Conflicting Interests?' in Faure, M., Vervaele, J. and Weale, A. (eds.), *The European Union in an Interdisciplinary Framework* (Maklu, Nomos, Blackstone, Schultess, 1994), 219

Vogel, D., 'Environmental Protection and the Creation of the Single Market', paper prepared for delivery at the 1992 Annual Meeting of the American Political Science Association, 3–6 September 1992

von Wilmowsky, P., 'Waste Disposal in the Internal Market: The State of Play after the ECJ's Ruling on the Walloon Import Ban', *Common Market Law Review* 30 (1993), 541

Waelbroeck, D., 'L'Harmonisation des Règles et des Normes Techniques dans la CEE', *Cahiers de Droit Européen* (1988), 243

Waelbroeck, M., 'The Emergent Doctrine of Community Preemption – Consent and Redelegation' in Sandalow and Stein (eds.), *Courts and Free Markets* (Oxford University Press, 1982), 548

Wasserman, U., 'The Seveso Affair', *Journal of World Trade Law* 17 (1983), 371

Weale, A., 'Environmental Protection, The Four Freedoms and Competition Among Rules' in Faure, M., Vervaele, J. and Weale, A. (eds.), *The European Union in an Interdisciplinary Framework* (Maklu, Nomos, Blackstone, Schultess, 1994), 219

Weatherill, S., 'Regulating the Internal Market: Result Orientation in the House of Lords', *European Law Review* 16 (1992), 299

'Beyond Pre-emption? Shared Competence and Constitutional Change in the European Community' in O'Keeffe and Twomey (eds.), *Legal Issues of the Maastricht Treaty* (London: Wiley, 1993)

White, E., 'In Search of the Limits to Article 30 of the EEC Treaty', *Common Market Law Review* 26 (1989), 235

Wilke, M. and Wallace, H., 'Subsidiarity: Approaches to Power-Sharing in the European Community', Royal Institute for International Affairs Discussion Papers No. 27 (1990)

Wilkinson, D., 'Maastricht and the Environment: Implications for the EC's Environment Policy of the Treaty on European Union', *Journal of Environmental Law* 4 (1992), 221

'Using the European Union's Structural and Cohesion Funds for the Protection of the Environment', *Review of European Community and International Environmental Law* 3 (1994), 119

Wils, W., 'The Search for the Rule in Article 30 EEC: Much Ado About Nothing?'
    European Law Review 19 (1993), 475
    'Subsidiarity and EC Environmental Policy: Taking People's Concerns
    Seriously', *Journal of Environmental Law* 6 (1994), 85
Zacker, C., 'Environmental Law of the European Economic Community: New
    Powers under the SEA', *Boston College International and Comparative Law
    Review* 14 (1991), 249

Case notes
Barnard, C., Note on Case C-300/89, *Commission* v. *Council* [1991] ECR I-2,867,
    European Law Review 17 (1993), 127
de Sadeleer, N., Note on Case C-155/91, *Commission* v. *Council* [1993] ECR I-939,
    Journal of Environmental Law 5 (1993), 293
Geradin, D., Note on Case C-2/90, *Commission* v. *Belgium* [1992] ECR I-4,431,
    European Law Review 18 (1993), 145
    Note on Case C-155/91, *Commission* v. *Council* [1993] ECR I-939 *European Law
    Review* 18 (1993), 418
Hancher, L. and Sevenster, H., Note on Case C-2/90, *Commission* v. *Belgium* [1992]
    ECR I-4,431, *Common Market Law Review* 30 (1993), 351
Kramer, L., Note on Case C-300/89, *Commission* v. *Council* [1991] ECR I-2,867 in
    European Environmental Law Casebook (London: Sweet & Maxwell, 1994), 21
    Note on Case C-302/86, *Commission* v. *Denmark* [1988] ECR 4,602 in *European
    Environmental Law Casebook* (London: Sweet & Maxwell, 1994), 91
Kromarek, P., Note on Case C-302/86, *Commission* v. *Denmark* [1988] ECR 4,602,
    Journal of Environmental Law 5 (1990), 89
Robinson, J., Note on Case C-300/89, *Commission* v. *Council* [1991] ECR I-2,867,
    Journal of Environmental Law 4 (1993), 112
Somsen, H., Note on Case C-300/89, *Commission* v. *Council* [1991] ECR I-2,867,
    Common Market Law Review 29 (1992), 149
    Note on Case C-41/93, *France* v. *Commission* [1994] ECR I-1,829 *European
    Environmental Law Review* (1994), 238
Wachsmann, A., Note on Case C-155/91, *Commission* v. *Council* [1993] ECR I-939
    Common Market Law Review 30 (1993), 1,051
Wheeler, M., Note on Case C-2/90, *Commission* v. *Belgium* [1992] ECR I-4,431,
    Journal of Environmental Law 5 (1993), 133

UNITED STATES LAW

Books
Ackerman, B. and Hassler, W., *Clean Coal/Dirty Air or How the Clean Air Act Became
    a Multi-Billion Dollar Bail for High-Sulfur Coal Producers and What Should be Done
    About It* (New Haven: Yale University Press, 1981)
Aman, F., *Administrative Law in a Global Era* (Ithaca, NY: Cornell University Press,
    1992)

Anderson, F., Mandelker, D. and Tarlock, D., *Environmental Protection – Law and Policy* (Boston: Little Brown, 1990)

Barron, J. and Dienes, T., *Constitutional Law in a Nutshell* (St Paul, Minn.: West Publishing Co., 1991)

Breyer, S. and Stewart, R., *Administrative Law and Regulatory Policy* (Boston: Little Brown, 2nd edn, 1985)

Crandall, R. *et al.*, *Regulating the Automobile* (Washington, DC: Brookings Institution, 1986)

Findley, R. and Farber, D., *Environmental Law in a Nutshell* (St Paul, Minn.: West Publishing Co., 1992)

Grad, F. *et al.*, *The Automobile and the Regulation of its Impact on the Environment* (Springfield, Va.: National Technical Information Service, 1975)

Krier, J. and Ursin, E., *Pollution and Policy: A Case Essay on California and Federal Experience with Motor Vehicle Air Pollution, 1940–1975* (Berkeley: University of California Press, 1977)

Melnick, S., *Regulation and the Courts – The Case of the Clean Air Act* (Washington, DC: Brookings Institution, 1983)

Pashigian, P., *The Political Economy of the Clean Air Act: Regional Self-Interest in Environmental Legislation* (Center for the Study of American Business, 1982)

Percival, R. *et al.*, *Environmental Regulation – Law, Science and Policy* (Boston: Little Brown, 1992)

Plater, Z. *et al.*, *Environmental Law and Policy: Nature, Law, and Policy* (St Paul, Minn.: West Publishing Co., 1992)

Russel, L., Harrington, W. and Vaughan, W., *Enforcing Pollution Control Laws* (Washington, DC: Resources for the Future, 1986)

Sunstein, C., *After the Rights Revolution – Reconceiving the Regulatory State* (Cambridge, Mass.: Harvard University Press, 1990)

Tribe, L., *American Constitutional Law* (Minolea, NY: Foundation Press, 2nd edn, 1988)

Vig, N. and Kraft, M. (eds.), *Environmental Policy in the 1990s* (Washington, DC: CQ Press, 1990)

Articles

Ackerman, B. and Hassler, W., 'Beyond the New Deal: Coal and the Clean Air Act', *Yale Law Journal* 89 (1980), 1,466

Ackerman, B. and Stewart, R., 'Reforming Environmental Law', *Stanford Law Review* 37 (1985), 1,333

Adams, N., 'Title VI of the 1990 Clean Air Act Amendments and State and Local Initiatives to Reverse the Stratospheric Ozone Crisis: An Analysis of Preemption', *Boston College Environmental Affairs Law Review* 173 (1991)

Andreen, W., 'Defining the "Not in my Backyard Syndrome"': An Approach to Federal Preemption of State and Local Impediments to the Siting of PCB Disposal Facilities', *North Carolina Law Review* 63 (1985), 811

Annotation, 'Validity and Construction of Statute or Ordinance Requiring Return Deposits on Soft Drink or Similar Containers', ALR 3d 73

Baker, R., 'C&A Carbone v. Clarckstown: A Wake-Up Call for the Dormant Commerce Clause', *Duke Environmental Law and Policy Forum* 5 (1995), 67

Barber, S., '*National League of Cities* v. *Usery*: New Meaning for the Tenth Amendment?' *Supreme Court Review* (1976), 161

Been, V., '"Exit" as a Constraint on Land Use Exactions: Rethinking the Unconditional Conditions Doctrine', *Columbia Law Review* 91 (1991), 473
    'What's Fairness Got to Do with It?: Environmental Equity and the Siting of Locally Undesirable Land Uses', *Cornell Law Review* 78 (1993), 1,001

Blasi, V., 'Constitutional Limitations on the Power of States to Regulate the Movement of Goods in Interstate Commerce' in Sandalow and Stein (eds.), *Courts and Free Markets* (Oxford University Press, 1982), 174

Brietzke, S., 'Hazardous Waste in Interstate Commerce: Minimizing the Problem after *City of Philadelphia* v. *New Jersey*', *Valparaiso University Law Review* 24 (1989), 77

Burtraw, D. and Portney, P., 'Environmental Policy in the United States' in Helm (ed.), *Economic Policy Towards the Environment* (Oxford: Blackwell, 1993)

Cary, W., 'Federalism and Corporate Law: Reflections upon *Delaware*', *Yale Law Journal* 83 (1974), 633

Choper, J., 'The Scope of National Power *vis-à-vis* the States: The Dispensability of Judicial Review', *Yale Law Journal* 86 (1977), 1,552

Coenen, D., 'Untangling the Market-Participant Exemption in the Dormant Commerce Clause', *Michigan Law Review* 88 (1989), 395

Cohen, W., 'Congressional Power to Define State Power to Regulate Commerce: Consent and Preemption' in Sandalow and Stein (eds.), *Courts and Free Markets* (Oxford University Press, 1982), 523

Comment, 'Environmental Law: A Reevaluation of Federal Preemption and the Commerce Clause', *Fordham Urban Law Journal* 7 (1979), 649

Comment, 'Preemption Doctrine in the Environmental Context: A Unified Method of Analysis', *University of Pennsylvania Law Review* 127 (1978), 197

Conference Report, 'Federal versus State Environmental Protection Standards: Can a National Policy Be Implemented Locally?' *Environmental Law Reporter* 22 (1992), 10,009

Conrad, J., 'Glowing their Own Way: State Embargoes and Exclusive Waste-Disposal Sites under the Low-Level Radioactive Waste Policy Act of 1980', *George Washington Law Review* 53 (1985), 654

Cox, S., 'What May States Do about Out-of-State Waste in Light of Recent Supreme Court Decisions Applying the Dormant Commerce Clause? Kentucky as Case Study in the Waste Wars', *Kentucky Law Journal* (1995), 551

Culp Davis, K., 'Judicial, Legislative, and Administrative Lawmaking: A Proposed Research Service for the Supreme Court', *Minnesota Law Review* 71 (1986), 1

Currie, D., 'Motor Vehicle Air Pollution: State Authority and Federal Preemption', *Michigan Law Review* 68 (1970), 1,083
    'The Mobile-Source Provisions of the Clean Air Act', *University of Chicago Law Review* 46 (1979), 811

Danzig, A., 'The Commerce Clause and Interstate Waste Disposal: New Jersey's Options after the *Philadelphia* Decision', *Rutgers–Camden Law Journal* 11 (1979), 31

Delogu, O., '"NIMBY" is a National Environmental Problem', *South Dakota Law Review* 35 (1990), 198

Dister, R. and Schlesinger, J., 'State Waste Embargoes Violate the Commerce Clause: *City of Philadelphia* v. *New Jersey*', *Ecology Law Quarterly* 8 (1979), 371

Ditlow, C., 'Federal Regulation of Motor Vehicle Emissions under the Clean Air Act Amendments of 1970', *Ecology Law Quarterly* 4 (1975), 495

Dowling, N., 'Interstate Commerce and State Power', *Virginia Law Review* 27 (1940), 1

Duffy, C., 'State Hazardous Waste Facility Siting: Easing the Process through Local Cooperation and Preemption', *Boston College Environmental Affairs Law Review* 11 (1984), 755

Dwyer, J., 'The Commerce Clause and the Limits of Congressional Authority to Regulate the Environment', *Environmental Law Reporter* 25 (1995)

The Practice of Federalism under the Clean Air Act', *Maryland Law Review* 54 (1995), 1,183

Edelman, S., 'Federal Air and Water Control: The Application of the Commerce Power to Abate Interstate and Intrastate Pollution', *George Washington Law Review* 23 (1965), 1,067

Edgcomb, J., 'Cooperative Federalism and Environmental Protection: The Surface Mining Control Act of 1977', *Tulane Law Review* 58 (1983), 299

Elliott, D. *et al.*, 'Toward a Theory of Statutory Evolution: The Federalization of Environmental Law', *Journal of Law, Economics and Organization* 1 (1985), 313

Engel, K., 'Reconsidering the National Market in Solid Waste: Trade-Offs in Equity, Efficiency, Environmental Protection, and State Autonomy', *North Carolina Law Review* 73 (1995), 1,483

Eskeridge, W. and Ferejohn, J., 'The Elastic Commerce Clause: A Political Theory of American Federalism', *Vanderbilt Law Review* 47 (1994), 1,355

Eule, J., 'Laying the Dormant Commerce Clause to Rest', *Yale Law Journal* 91 (1982), 425

Farber, D., 'State Regulation and the Dormant Commerce Clause', *Constitutional Commentary* 3 (1986), 395

Fernandez, J., 'The Purpose Test: Shielding Environmental Statutes from the Sword of Preemption', *Syracuse Law Journal* 41 (1990), 1,201

Field, M., '*Garcia* v. *San Antonio Metropolitan Authority*: The Demise of a Misguided Doctrine', *Harvard Law Review* 99 (1985), 84

Fitzgerald, E., 'The Waste War: *Fort Gratiot Landfill Inc.* v. *Michigan Department of Natural Resources* and *Chemical Waste Management Inc.* v. *Hunt*', *Stanford Environmental Law Journal* 13 (1994), 78

'The Waste War: *Oregon Waste Systems Inc.* v. *Department of Environmental Quality*', *Boston College Environmental Affairs Law Review* 23 (1995), 43

Fixl, C., 'Hazardous Waste and Partial Import Bans: An Environmentally Sound

Exception to the Commerce Clause', *Villanova Environmental Law Journal* 3 (1992), 149

Florini, K., 'Issues of Federalism in Hazardous Waste Control: Cooperation or Confusion?' *Harvard Environmental Law Review* 6 (1983), 307

Florio, J., 'Federalism Issues Related to the Probable Emergence of the Toxic Substances Control Act', *Maryland Law Review* 54 (1995), 1,354

Foote, S., 'Beyond the Politics of Federalism: An Alternative Model', *Yale Journal on Regulation* 1 (1984), 217

'Administrative Preemption: An Experiment in Regulatory Federalism', *Virginia Law Review* 70 (1984), 1,429

Frank, J., 'Le Congrès' in Orban (ed.), *Le Système Politique des Etats-Unis* (Montréal: Presses Universitaires de Montréal, 1987), 153

Freund, P., 'Umpiring the Federal System', *Columbia Law Review* 54 (1954), 561

Gardbaum, S., 'The Nature of Preemption', *Cornell Law Review* 79 (1994), 767

Gerrard, M., 'The Victims of NIMBY?' *Fordham Urban Law Journal* 21 (1994), 495

Gold, M., 'Solid Waste Management and the Constitution's Commerce Clause', *Urban Lawyer* 25 (1993), 21

Gray, B., 'Regulation and Federalism', *Yale Journal on Regulation* 1 (1984), 93

Gudger, C. and Walters, K., 'Beverage Container Regulation: Economic Implications and Suggestions for Model Legislation', *Ecology Law Quarterly* 5 (1976), 265

Hahn, R. and Stavins, R., 'Incentive-Based Environmental Regulation: A New Era from an Old Idea?' *Ecology Law Quarterly* 18 (1991), 1

Harpring, M., 'Out Like Yesterday's Garbage: Municipal Solid Waste and the Need for Congressional Action', *Catholic University Law Review* 40 (1991), 851

Healy, M., 'The Preemption of State Hazardous and Solid Waste Regulations: The Dormant Commerce Clause Awakens Once More', *Washington Journal of Urban and Contemporary Law* 43 (1993), 177

Heller, T., 'Legal Theory and Political Economy of American Federalism' in Cappelletti *et al.* (eds.), *Integration through Law* (Walter de Gruyter, 1985), vol. I, 255

Henshaw, J., 'The Dormant Commerce Clause After *Garcia*: An Application to Interstate Commerce of Sanitary Landfill Space', *Indiana Law Journal* 67 (1992), 511

Hill, R., 'An Overview of RCRA: The "Mind Numbing" Provisions of the Most Complicated Environmental Statute', *Environmental Law Reporter* 21 (1991), 10,254

Hodas, D., 'Enforcement of Environmental Law in a Triangular Federal System: Can Three not be a Crowd when Enforcement Authority is Shared between the United States, the States and their Citizens?', *Maryland Law Review* 54 (1995), 1,552

Hoke, C., 'Preemption Pathologies and Civil Republican Values', *Boston University Law Review* 71 (1991), 685

Hosansky, D., 'Backers May Push Garbage Bill in Session after Election', *Congressional Quarterly* (15 October 1994), 2,949

Howard, D., '*Garcia* and the Values of Federalism: On the Need for a Recurrence to Fundamental Principles', *Georgia Law Review* 19 (1985), 789

Johnson, S., 'Beyond *City of Philadelphia* v. *New Jersey*', *Dickinson Law Review* 95 (1990), 131

Kennedy, H. and Weekes, M., 'Control of Automobile Emissions – California Experience and the Federal Legislation', *Law and Contemporary Problems* 33 (1968), 297

Kilbourn, S., 'Environmental Control: Higher State Standards and the Question of Preemption', *Cornell Law Review* 55 (1970), 846

Kraft, M. and Vig, N., 'Environmental Policy from the Seventies to the Nineties: Continuity and Change' in Vig and Kraft (eds.), *Environmental Policy in the 1990s* (Washington, DC: CQ Press, 1990), 11

Kramer, L., 'Understanding Federalism', *Vanderbilt Law Review* 47 (1994), 1,485

Krier, J., 'The Irrational National Air Quality Standards: Macro- and Micro-Mistakes', *UCLA Law Review* 22 (1974), 323

'On the Topology of Uniform Environmental Standards in a Federal System – And Why it Matters', *Maryland Law Review* 54 (1995), 1,226

La Pierre, B., 'Political Accountability in the National Political Process – The Alternative to Judicial Review of Federalism Issues', *Northwestern University Law Review* 80 (1985), 577

Latin, H., 'Ideal Versus Real Regulatory Efficiency: Implementation of Uniform Standards and "Fine-Tuning" Regulatory Reforms', *Stanford Law Review* 37 (1985), 1,267

Lefton, I., 'Constitutional Law – Commerce Clause: Local Discrimination in Environmental Protection Regulation', *North Carolina Law Review* 55 (1977), 461

Lessig, L., 'Translating Federalism: *United States* v. *Lopez*', *Supreme Court Review* (1995), 125

Lester, J., 'A New Federalism? Environmental Policy in the States' in Kraft and Vig (eds.), *Environmental Policy in the 1990s* (Washington, DC: CQ Press, 1990), 39

Levmore, S., 'Interstate Exploitation and Judicial Intervention', *Virginia Law Review* 69 (1983), 563

Levy, R., 'Federalism and the Environment: *National Solid Waste Management* v. *Alabama Department of Environmental Management*', *Whittier Law Review* 12 (1991), 635

Levy, R. and Glicksman, R., 'Judicial Activism and Restraint in the Supreme Court's Environmental Law Decisions', *Vanderbilt Law Review* 42 (1989), 343

Maltz, E., 'How Much Regulation is Too Much – An Examination of Commerce Clause Jurisprudence', *George Washington Law Review* 50 (1981), 47

Manley, R., 'Federalism and Management of the Environment', *Urban Lawyer* 19 (1987), 661

Mazmanian, D. and Morell, D., 'The "NIMBY" Syndrome: Facility Siting and the Failure of Democratic Discourse' in Vig and Kraft (eds.), *Environmental Policy in the 1990s* (Washington, DC.: CQ Press, 1990)

McMiller, M., 'Environmental Law – Federal Preemption of Local PCB Ordinance under Toxic Substances Control Act – *Rollins Environmental Services (FS) Inc.* v. *Parish of St James*', *Kansas Law Review* 35 (1987), 461

Merrit, D., 'The Guarantee Clause and State Autonomy: Federalism for a Third Century', *Columbia Law Review* 88 (1988), 1

Mesnikoff, A., 'Disposing of the Dormant Commerce Clause Barrier: Keeping Waste at Home', *Minnesota Law Review* 76 (1992), 1,219

Meyers, J., 'Confronting the Garbage Crisis: Increased Federal Involvement as a Means of Addressing Municipal Solid Waste Disposal', *Georgetown Law Journal* 79 (1991), 567

Michelman, F., 'States' Rights and States' Roles: Permutations of "Sovereignty" in *National League of Cities* v. *Usery*', *Yale Law Journal* 86 (1977), 1,165

Mintz, J., 'Economic Reform of Environmental Protection: A Brief Comment on a Recent Debate', *Harvard Environmental Law Review* 15 (1991), 149

Moos, C., '*American Can*: Judicial Response to Oregon's Non-Returnable Container Legislation', *Ecology Law Quarterly* 4 (1974), 145

Newman, J., 'A Consideration of Federal Preemption in the Context of State and Local Environmental Regulation', *UCLA Journal of Environmental Law and Policy* 9 (1990), 97

Note, 'Preemption as a Preferential Ground: A New Canon of Construction', *Stanford Law Review* 12 (1959), 208

Note, 'State Environmental Protection Legislation and the Commerce Clause', *Harvard Law Review* 87 (1974), 1,762

Note, 'Use of the Commerce Clause to Invalidate Anti-Phosphate Legislation: Will It Wash?' *University of Colorado Law Review* 45 (1974), 487

Note, 'The Oregon Bottle Bill', *Oregon Law Review* 34 (1975), 175

Note, 'The Preemption Doctrine: Shifting Perspectives on Federalism and the Burger Court', *Columbia Law Review* 75 (1975), 623

Note, 'Waste Embargoes Held a Violation of Commerce Clause: *Philadelphia* v. *New Jersey*', *Connecticut Law Review* 11 (1979), 292

Note, 'Technology-Based Emission and Effluent Standards and the Achievement of Ambient Environmental Objectives', *Yale Law Journal* 91 (1982), 792

Note, 'Constitutionally Mandated Southern Hospitality', *North Carolina Law Review* 69 (1991), 1,001

Note, '*National Solid Waste Management Association* v. *Alabama Department of Environmental Management*: Environmental Protection and the Commerce Clause – Is Environmental Protection a Legitimate Local Concern?' *Loyola Law Review* 37 (1991), 189

Note, '*Hunt* v. *Waste Management Inc.*: Alabama Attempts to Spread the Nation's Hazardous Waste Disposal Burden by Imposing a Higher Tax on Out-of-State Hazardous Waste', *Notre Dame Law Review* 67 (1992), 1,215

O'Connor, J., 'The Automobile Controversy – Federal Control of Vehicle Emissions', *Ecology Law Quarterly* 4 (1975), 661

Olson, 'The Quiet Shift of Power: Office of Management and Budget Supervision of Environmental Protection Agency Rulemaking under Executive Order 12,291', *Virginia Journal of Natural Resources* 4 (1984), 1

Oren, C., 'Prevention of Significant Deterioration: Control-Compelling versus Site-Shifting', *Iowa Law Review* 74 (1988), 1

Organ, J., 'Limitations on State Agency Authority to Adopt Environmental Standards More Stringent than Federal Standards: Policy Considerations and Interpretative Problems', *Maryland Law Review* 54 (1995), 1,373

Pancoast, J. and Payne, L., 'Hazardous Waste in Interstate Commerce: The Triumph of Law over Logic', *Ecology Law Quarterly* 20 (1993), 817

Pashigian, P., 'Environmental Regulation: Whose Self-Interests Are Being Protected?' *Economic Inquiry* 23 (1985), 551

Pedersen, W., 'Turning the Tide on Water Quality', *Ecology Law Quarterly* 15 (1988), 69

Peltzman, S., 'Toward a More General Theory of Regulation', *Journal of Law and Economics* 19 (1976), 211

Percival, R., 'Environmental Federalism: Historical Roots and Contemporary Models', *Maryland Law Review* 54 (1995), 1,141

Petersen, E. and Abramovitz, D., 'Municipal Solid Waste Flow Control in the Post-*Carbone* World', *Fordham Urban Law Journal* 22 (1995), 363

Pierce, R., 'Regulation, Deregulation, Federalism, and Administrative Law: Agency Power to Preempt State Regulation', *University of Pittsburgh Law Review* 46 (1985), 607

Pomper, D., 'Recycling *Philadelphia* v. *New Jersey:* The Dormant Commerce Clause, Postindustrial Natural Resources, and the Solid Waste Crisis', *University of Pennsylvania Law Review* 137 (1989), 1,309

Preston, J., 'The Environmental Shell Game in the Green Mountains: Is Vermont's CFC Law Hidden under Federal Preemption, the Commerce Clause or Vermont's Police Powers?' *Syracuse Law Journal* 41 (1990), 1,251

Project, 'The Role of Preemption in Administrative Law', *Administrative Law Review* 45 (1993), 107

Rapaczynski, A., 'From Sovereignty to Process: The Jurisprudence of Federalism after *Garcia*', *Supreme Court Review* (1985), 341

Redish, M. and Nugent, S., 'The Dormant Commerce Clause and the Constitutional Balance of Federalism', *Duke Law Journal* (1987), 569

Regan, D., 'The Supreme Court and State Protectionism: Making Sense of the Dormant Commerce Clause', *Michigan Law Review* 84 (1986), 1,091
'How to Think about the Federal Commerce Power and Incidentally Rewrite *United States* v. *Lopez*', *Michigan Law Review* 94 (1995), 554

Revesz, R., 'Rehabilitating Interstate Competition: Rethinking the "Race-To-The-Bottom" Rationale for Federal Environmental Regulation', *New York University Law Review* 67 (1992), 1,210

Roddewig, R. and Sechen, G., 'Recent Developments with RCRA Subtitle D and Commerce Clause Cases after *Hunt* and *Fort Gratiot* Decisions', *Urban Lawyer* 35 (1993), 797

Rose-Ackerman, S., 'Environmental Policy and Federal Structure: A Comparison of the United States and Germany', *Vanderbilt Law Review* 47 (1994), 1,587

Rosenthal, A., 'The Federal Power to Protect the Environment: Available Devices to Compel or Induce Desired Conduct', *Southern California Law Review* 45 (1982), 397

Rosso Grossman, M., 'Environmental Federalism in Agriculture: The Case of Pesticide Regulation in the United States' in Braden, Folmer and Ulen (eds.), *Environmental Policy with Political and Economic Integration* (Cheltenham, UK, Brookfield, US: Edward Elgar, 1996)

Sandalow, T., 'The Expansion of Federal Legislative Authority' in Sandalow and Stein (eds.), *Courts and Free Markets* (Oxford University Press, 1982), 49

Satterfield, J., 'A Tale of Sound and Fury: The Environmental Record of the 102d Congress', *Environmental Law Reporter* 23 (1993), 10,015

'High Hopes and Failed Expectations: The Environmental Record of the 103d Congress', *Environmental Law Reporter* 25 (1995), 10,089

Shapiro, H., '*C&A Carbone Inc.* v. *Clarckstown*: Supreme Court Uses Commerce Clause to Nix a Local Trash Flow-Control Ordinance', *Natural Resources and Environment Journal* (1994), 20

Slade, E., Wilson, D. and Wilson, J., 'State and Local Regulation of Nonreturnable Containers', *Wisconsin Law Review* (1972), 536

Smith, M., 'State Discrimination and Interstate Commerce', *California Law Review* 74 (1986), 1,203

Stewart, R., 'The Reformation of Administrative Law', *Harvard Law Review* 88 (1975), 1,667

'Pyramids of Sacrifice? Problems of Federalism in Mandating State Implementation of National Environmental Policy', *Yale Law Journal* 86 (1977), 1,196

'Quasi-Constitutional Law in Judicial Review of Environmental Decisionmaking: Lessons from the Clean Air Act', *Iowa Law Review* 62 (1977), 713

'Controlling Environmental Risks through Economic Incentives', *Columbia Journal of Environmental Law* 17 (1988), 1

'Interstate Commerce, Environmental Protection and US Federal Law' in Cameron, Demaret and Geradin (eds.), *Trade and the Environment – The Search for Balance* (London: Cameron & May, 1994), 342

Stigler, G., 'The Theory of Economic Regulation', *Bell Journal of Economics and Management Science* 2 (1971), 3

Stone, J., 'Supremacy and Commerce Clause Issues Regarding State Hazardous Waste Bans', *Columbia Journal of Environmental Law* 15 (1990), 1

Strohbehn, E., 'The Bases for Federal/State Relationships in Environmental Law', *Environmental Law Reporter* 12 (1982), 15,074

Sunstein, C., 'Protectionism, the American Supreme Court, and Integrated Markets' in Bieber *et al.* (eds.), *1992: One European Market* (Baden-Baden: Nomos, 1988), 127

Tarlock, D., 'Anywhere But Here: An Introduction to State Control of Hazardous Waste Facility Location', *UCLA Journal of Environmental Law and Policy* 2 (1981), 1

Tribe, L., 'Unraveling *National League of Cities:* The New Federalism and
   Affirmative Rights to Essential Governmental Services', *Harvard Law Review*
   90 (1977), 1,065
   'California Decline the Nuclear Gamble: Is Such a State Choice Preempted?'
   Ecology Law Quarterly 7 (1979), 679
Tushnet, M., 'Rethinking the Dormant Commerce Clause', *Wisconsin Law Review*
   (1979), 125
Vago, J., 'The Uncertain Future of Flow Control Ordinances: The Last Trash of
   Clarckstown?' Northern Kentucky Law Review 22 (1995), 1,481
Vig, N., 'Presidential Leadership: From the Reagan to the Bush Administration'
   in Kraft and Vig (eds.), *Environmental Policy in the 1990s* (Washington, DC: CQ
   Press, 1990), 33
Walston, R., 'State Control of Federal Pollution: Taking the Stick Away from the
   States', *Ecology Law Quarterly* 6 (1977), 429
Wasserman, U., 'United States: Environmental Deregulation', *Journal of World
   Trade Law* 17 (1983), 365
Welsch, D., 'Environmental Marketing and Federal Preemption of State Law:
   Eliminating the "Grey" Behind the "Green"', *California Law Review* 81
   (1993), 991
Weschler, H., 'The Political Safeguards of Federalism: The Role of States in the
   Composition and Selection of the National Government', *Columbia Law
   Review* 54 (1954), 543
Wirth, D., 'A Matchmaker's Challenge: Marrying International Law and
   American Environmental Law', *Virginia Journal of International Law* 32 (1992),
   379
Young, J., 'Expanding State Initiation and Enforcement under Superfund',
   University of Chicago Law Review 57 (1990), 1985
Ziebarth, A., 'Environmental Law: Solid Waste Transport and Disposal Across
   State Lines – The Commerce Clause versus Garbage Crisis', *Annual Survey of
   American Law* (1990), 365

COMPARATIVE LAW

Books

Braden, J., Folmer, H. and Ulen, T. (eds.), *Environmental Policy with Political and
   Economic Integration* (Cheltenham, UK, Brookfield/US: Edward Elgar, 1996)
Lenaerts, K., *Le Juge et la Constitution aux Etats-Unis d'Amérique et dans l'Ordre
   Juridique Européen* (Brussels: Bruylant, 1988)
Sandalow, T. and Stein, E. (eds.), *Courts and Free Markets* (Oxford University Press,
   1982)
Smith, T. and Kromarek, P. (eds.), *Understanding US and European Environmental
   Law* (London: Graham & Trotman, Martinus Nijhoff, 1989)
Vogel, D., *National Styles of Regulation: Environmental Policy in Great Britain and in
   the United States* (Ithaca: Cornell University Press, 1986)

Articles

Aman, A., 'A Global Perspective on Current Regulatory Reform: Rejection, Relocation, or Reinvention?' *Indiana Journal of Global and Legal Studies* 2 (1995), 429

Bermann, G., 'Taking Subsidiarity Seriously: Federalism in the European Community and the United States', *Columbia Law Review* 94 (1994), 331

Cappelletti, M. and Golay, D., 'The Judicial Branch in the Federal and Transnational Union: Its Impact on Integration' in Cappelletti *et al.* (eds.), *Integration through Law* (Walter de Gruyter, 1985), vol. I, 318

Cappelletti, M., Seccombe, M. and Weiler, J., 'Integration through Law: Europe and the American Federal Experience: A General Introduction' in Cappelletti *et al.* (eds.), *Integration through Law* (Walter de Gruyter, 1985), vol. I, 3

Charny, D., 'Competition among Jurisdictions in Formulating Corporate Rules: An American Perspective on the "Race to the Bottom" in the European Communities', *Harvard International Law Journal* 32 (1991), 423

Comment, 'Small Automobiles Causing Large Air Pollution Problems on a Global Basis: The European Economic Community Can Learn and Live from United States Legislation', *Dickinson Journal of International Law* 8 (1990), 313

Fischer, F., '"Federalism" in the European Community and the United States: A Rose by Any Other Name', *Fordham International Law Journal* 17 (1994), 390

Geradin, D., 'Free Trade and Environmental Protection in an Integrated Market: A Survey of the Case Law of the United States Supreme Court and the European Court of Justice', *Florida State University Journal of Transnational Law and Policy* 2 (1993), 141

Heller, T. and Pelkmans, J., 'The Federal Economy: Law and Economic Integration and the Positive State – The USA and Europe Compared in an Economic Perspective' in Cappelletti, Seccombe and Weiler (eds.), *Integration through Law* (Walter de Gruyter, 1985), vol. I, 245

Jacobs, F. and Karst, K., 'The "Federal" Legal Order: The USA and Europe Compared – A Juridical Perspective' in Cappelletti *et al.* (eds.), *Integration through Law* (Walter de Gruyter, 1985), vol. I

Kimber, F., 'A Comparison of Environmental Federalism in the United States and the European Union', *Maryland Law Review* 54 (1995), 1,658

Kommers, D. and Waelbroeck, M., 'Legal Integration and the Free Movement of Goods: The American and European Experience' in Cappelletti *et al.* (eds.), *Integration through Law* (Walter de Gruyter, 1985), vol. I

Kramer, L., 'The European Economic Community' in Smith and Kromarek (eds.), *Understanding US and European Environmental Law* (London: Graham & Trotman, 1989), 4

Lenaerts, K., 'Constitutionalism and the Many Faces of Federalism', *American Journal of Comparative Law* 38 (1990), 205

Mackenzie, Lord Stuart, 'Problems of the European Community – Transatlantic Parallels', *International and Comparative Law Quarterly* 36 (1987), 183

Majone, G., 'Controlling Regulatory Bureaucracies: Lessons from the American Experience', European University Institute Working Paper SPS No. 92/3

McGrory, D., 'Air Pollution Legislation in the United States and the Community', *European Law Review* (1990), 298

Mott, R., 'Federal–State Relations in US Environmental Law: Implications for the European Community', European University Institute Working Paper EPU No. 90/2

Pfander, J., 'Environmental Federalism in Europe and the United States: A Comparative Assessment of Regulation through the Agency of Member States' in Braden, Folmer and Ulen (eds.), *Environmental Policy with Political and Economic Integration* (Cheltenham, UK, Brookfield, US: Edward Elgar, 1996)

Rehbinder, E. and Stewart, R., 'Environmental Protection Policy' in Cappelletti *et al.* (eds.), *Integration through Law* (Walter de Gruyter, 1985), vol. I, 287

Smith, J. T., 'The Challenge of Environmentally Sound and Efficient Regulation of Waste – The Need for Enhanced International Understanding', *Journal of Environmental Law* 5 (1993), 91

Smith, J. T. and Sarnoff, J., 'Free Commerce and Sound Waste Management: Some International Comparative Perspectives', *International Environmental Reporter*, 8 April 1992, 207

Stein, E., 'On Divided-Power Systems: Adventures in Comparative Law', *Legal Issues of European Integration* (1983/1), 27

Stein, E. and Sandalow T., 'On the Two Systems: An Overview' in Sandalow and Stein (eds.), *Courts and Free Markets* (Oxford University Press, 1982), 1

Stewart, R., 'Environmental Law in the United States and the European Community: Spillovers, Cooperation, Rivalry, Institutions', *University of Chicago Legal Forum* (1992), 39

    'International Trade and Environment: Lessons from the Federal Experience', *Washington and Lee Law Review* 49 (1992) 1,329

    'Antidotes for the "American Disease"', *Ecology Law Quarterly* 20 (1993), 85

Vause, G., 'The Subsidiarity in European Union Law – American Federalism Compared', *Case Western Reserve Journal of International Law* 27 (1995), 61

INTERNATIONAL LAW

Books

Cameron, J., Demaret, P. and Geradin, D. (eds.), *Trade and the Environment – The Search for Balance* (London: Cameron & May, 1994)

Esty, D., *Greening the GATT – Trade, Environment and the Future* (Washington, DC: Institute for International Economics, 1994)

Hilz, C., *The International Toxic Waste Trade* (New York: van Nostrand Reinhold, 1992)

K. Kummer, *International Management of Hazardous Wastes: The Basel Convention and Related Legal Rules* (Oxford: Oxford University Press, 1995)

Runge, F., *Freer Trade, Protected Environment: Balancing Trade Liberalization and Environmental Interests* (New York: Council on Foreign Relations, 1994)

Vallette, J. and Spalding, H., *The International Trade in Waste – A Greenpeace Inventory* (Washington, DC: Greenpeace USA, 5th edn, 1990)

Walker, S., *Environmental Protection and Trade Liberalization: Finding the Balance* (Brussels: Facultés Universitaires St Louis Press, 1993)

Zaelke, D., Orbuch, P. and Housman, R. (eds.), *Trade and the Environment – Law, Economics and Policy* (Washington, DC: Island Press, 1993)

Articles

Barcello III, J., 'Product Standards to Protect the Local Environment – The GATT and the Uruguay Round Sanitary and Phytosanitary Agreement', *Cornell International Law Journal* 27 (1994), 755

Cameron, J. and Ward, A., 'The Uruguay Round's Technical Barriers to Trade Agreement' (WWF Research Report, 1993)

Charnovitz, S., 'Trade and the Environment – Examining the Issues', *International Environmental Affairs* (1992), 203

'Environmental Harmonization and Trade Policy' in Zaelke *et al.* (eds.), *Trade and the Environment – Law, Economics and Policy* (Washington, DC: Island Press, 1993), 267

'Dolphins and Tuna: An Analysis of the Second Panel Report', *Environmental Law Reporter* 24 (1994), 10,567

Dillon, 'The World Trade Organization: A New Legal Order for World Trade', *Michigan Journal of International Law* 16 (1995), 349

Dunoff, J., 'Reconciling International Trade with Preservation of the Global Commons: Can We Prosper and Protect?' *Washington and Lee Law Review* 49 (1992), 1,407

Goldman, P., 'The Legal Effects of Trade Agreements on Domestic Health and Environmental Regulation', *Journal of Environmental Law and Litigation* 7 (1992), 11

'Resolving the Trade and Environment Debate: In Search of a Neutral Forum and Neutral Principles', *Washington and Lee Law Review* 49 (1992), 1,279

Housman, R., 'A Kantian Approach to Trade and the Environment', *Washington and Lee Law Review* 49 (1992), 1,373

Housman, R. and Zaelke, D., 'The Collision of Environment and Trade: The GATT/Dolphin Decision', *Environmental Law Reporter* 22 (1992), 10,268

Huntoon, B., 'Emerging Controls on Transfers of Waste to Developing Countries', *Law and Policy of International Business* 21 (1989), 247

Jackson, J., 'World Trade and Environmental Policies: Congruence or Conflict?' *Washington and Lee Law Review* 49 (1992), 1,227

Petersmann, E. U., 'International Trade and International Environmental Law', *Journal of World Trade* 16 (1993), 43

'Trade and Environmental Protection: The Practice of GATT and the European Community Compared' in Cameron, Demaret and Geradin (eds.), *Trade and the Environment – The Search for Balance* (London: Cameron & May, 1994), 147

Putnam, R., 'Diplomacy and Domestic Politics: The Logic of Two-Level Games', *International Organization* 42 (1988), 427

Stewart, R., 'Environmental Regulation and International Competitiveness', *Yale Law Journal* 102 (1993), 2,039

Thomas, C. and Tereposky, G., 'The Evolving Relationship between Trade and Environmental Regulation', *Journal of World Trade* 27 (1993), 35

Trachtman, J., 'International Regulatory Competition, Externalization and Jurisdiction', *Harvard International Law Journal* 34 (1992), 48

Index

Books in the series

Trade and the environment is a penetrating analysis of the relationship between trade and environmental-protection policies in the European Community and the United States. It argues that the various tensions that may arise between such policies can be resolved by the combined intervention of the judiciary, which can invalidate state environmental standards impeding trade, and the legislature, which can set common standards for all states. The interaction between the judiciary and the legislature, writes Dr Geradin, shapes the balance between trade and environmental objectives in the EC and US systems. More generally, such interaction defines the progress of environmental protection in these systems.